New Castle County Delaware

Land Records

1673-1710

Carol Bryant

HERITAGE BOOKS
2008

HERITAGE BOOKS
AN IMPRINT OF HERITAGE BOOKS, INC.

Books, Cds, and more—Worldwide

For our listing of thousands of titles see our website at
www.HeritageBooks.com

Published 2008 by
HERITAGE BOOKS, INC.
Publishing Division
100 Railroad Ave. #104
Westminster, Maryland 21157

Copyright © 1999 Carol Bryant

Other books by the author:

Abstracts of Chester County, Pennsylvania Land Records: Volume 1: 1681-1730

Abstracts of Chester County, Pennsylvania Land Records: Volume 2: 1729-1745

Abstracts of Chester County, Pennsylvania Land Records: Volume 3: 1745-1753

Abstracts of Chester County, Pennsylvania Land Records: Volume 4: 1753-1758

Abstracts of Chester County, Pennsylvania Land Records: Volume 5: 1758-1765

New Castle County, Delaware Land Records, 1673-1710

New Castle County, Delaware Land Records, 1715-1728

All rights reserved. No part of this book may be reproduced or transmitted in any form or by any means, electronic or mechanical, including photocopying, recording or by any information storage and retrieval system without written permission from the author, except for the inclusion of brief quotations in a review.

International Standard Book Number: 978-1-58549-068-4

Table of Contents

Introduction . . . . v.

Liber A 1

Liber B 56

Liber C 138

Index 161

INTRODUCTION

Few records of the Swedish Colony (1638-16550 have survived. From 1655 to 1664 and from 1673 to 1674, the Dutch West India Company and the city of Amsterdam were proprietors of the land which became Delaware (ignoring claims by the Calverts of Maryland). the surviving records are held by the Archives of New York at Albany. For an excellent treatment of many of the Swedish families, see Peter Stebbins Craig, *The 1693 Census of the Swedes on the Delaware*. For a list of the Swedes who took the oath of allegiance in 1683 to the new English government in 1683 under William Penn, see *History of Delaware, 1609-1888*, by J. Thomas Scharf, p. 612.

The Duke of York was proprietor from 1664 to 1673 and from 1674 to 1682. These land records are held at Albany. *Original Land Titles in Delaware, commonly known as the Duke of York Record, 1646-1679*, was printed by order of the General Assembly of the State of Delaware (1899), reprinted by Family Line Publications in 1989.

The patent which granted William Penn territory, soon to be called Pennsylvania, was signed by King Charles in 1681. Delaware, as a part of Pennsylvania was referred to as the Lower Three Counties upon Delaware.

The Hall of Records at Dover holds copies of the deeds of New Castle County beginning in 1673. There are many gaps for which the records have been lost. This volume containing abstracts of all the records of Libers A, B, and C, covering the period (date of recordation), 1673 through 1710 with several pages missing throughout. Volum D is missing along with the first 58 pages of Liber E, leaving a gap, 1710-1715. The records covering the period, 1715 - 1728 were published in 1998 except for Liber F (1719-1722) which is missing. Work is progressing on completing the abstracts for the period, 1728-1749. The period, 1749-1752 was published in 1998. Missing are the records for the period 1752-1755, Liber R. The subsequent period, 1755-1762 was published earlier this year (1999) and contains the records found in Liber S and T.

F. Edward Wright
Westminster, Maryland
1999

NEWCASTLE, DE, BOOK A

Henry Toules & Robberd Monney of Maryland, planters. Lewis Johnson granted to Henry Toules & Robert Monney a tract on the western side of Delaware River & the south side of Appoquinimink Creek containing 400 acres opposite the land of Barrent Henrickson, land of Cornilius Buyo & Company & a proportion of marsh land below Drawyers Creek as by patent Henry Paulson. Signed Lewis Johnson. Delivered in the presence of Robberd Flacke & Thomas Snell. Recorded 30 Jan 1673. (A1:1).

Deed. On 21 Nov 1674 Know all ye men that come, I Henry Toules of the County of Cecil in Maryland, planter, assigned all the above said land to Robberd Monney. Signed Henry Toules. Delivered in presence of John Faucet & [the other name is unreadable]. (A1:1).

Dutch Patent Translated. Alexander D. Henyossia, in behalf of the right of Lord Burgermiester of the City of Amersterdam, governor of Delaware River has granted to Gerrit Van Swerigen a piece of land on the south side of Fort Amstill containing 1600 rods by 2000 rods conditioned on that within the 6 months of this date the same land to be improved or shall make a forfeiture of said land & a fine of 25 gilders. Dated 3 July 1664. Signed Alexander Henyossia. (A1:2).

Mortgage. Joseph Chew, late of Delaware, for valuable consideration granted to Johannes De Haes of New Castle in Delaware, merchant, a parcel of land being near the Appoquinimink Creek joining land formerly taken up by Jacob [unreadable] containing 400 acres as by patent [unreadable] Lewis Johnson. Joseph Chew to pay Johannes De Haes, 2000 pounds of good & merchantable tobacco & cash on 10 Mar now next & this conveyance will be void. Signed at Bohemia in Maryland this 22 June 1776. Signed Joseph Chew. Delivered in the presence of Augustine Herman, Ephraim Herman & George Oldfield. This is a copy of the original acknowledged by Joseph Chew on 7 Nov 1676. (A1:2)

Deed. On 28 May 1673 Whereas there is a patent in the Secretaries office at New York for 400 acres of land in the names of Edward Sapp & Timothy Love, the said land lying south east side of Sassafras Creek near the head of Appoquinimink Creek. Edward Sapp for valuable consideration granted to Timothy Love my whole right & title to the said patent & land. Signed Edward Sapp. Delivered in the presence of Walter Wharton & Garret Otta. (A1:3).

Deed. On 2 Aug 1676 Timothy Love & Mary his wife for valuable consideration granted to John Walker all right & title to land mentioned. Signed Timothy Love & Mary Love. Delivered in the presence of Morris Daniels &

John Browning. Recorded by Ephraim Herman, 1676. (A1:4).

Patent. On -- Feb 1671 Francis Lovelace, Esq. gentleman, governor General under his James, Duke of York, & Albany in the territories in America, has granted to Jacob Fianna a parcel of land being 188 acres being on the west side of the Delaware River, on the northwest side of Appoquinimink Creek being the land above the land of John Bradbarne & land of Abraham Coffin & a piece of marsh south of Drawyers Creek. Jacob Fianna to pay 1 1/2 bushels of winter wheat to the office or officers as shall be established in Delaware River. At Fort James in New York, Signed Francis Lovelace. Recorded by order of the governor on the date above by Matthew Nicolls. (A1:4).

Deed. On 26 Feb 1671/2 Jacob Fianna now living in Appoquinimink Creek granted to Morris Daniels & Timothy Love, planters of Maryland the land lying on Appoquinimink Creek. Signed Jacob Fianna. Delivered in the presence of Abraham Clement Petit & Claus C [the signature is unreadable]. (A1:5).

Deed. On 30 May 1673 Timothy Love for valuable consideration set over his share of said 188 acres to Morris Daniels. Signed Timothy Love. Delivered in the presence of Abraham Clement Petit & Thomas Rile (A1:5).

On 11 Nov 1676 George Moore of New Castle on Delaware for valuable consideration granted to James Crafford of St. George's Creek, all interest in a patent for 200 acres on the south side of St. George Creek opposite to Mr. Jacob Young's plantation being the boundaries mentioned on Patent from Governor Edmund Andros dated 5 Nov 1675. Signed George Moore. Delivered in the presence of Johannus De Haes & Ephraim Herman. (A1:6).

On 2 Jan 1676 Edmund Cantwell, Peter Allrichs & Johannes De Haes of New Castle on Delaware, executors of the will of Dirick Albertson, dec. for valuable consideration sold to Hendrick Williams of New Castle a patent with of lot of land bounded on the east by the river, land of Robert Derrick & land of Jacob Vandervere containing 35 yards in breadth & 100 yards in length as by the patent dated 11 Aug 1675 from Governor Francis Lovelace granted to Dirick Albertson. Signed Edmund Cantwell & Johanes De Haes. Delivered in the presence of Capt. John Collier & Justice John Moll. (A1:6).

Deed. On 2 Jan 1676 Reyneir Vander Coilen having married the daughter & sole heir of Barrent Egge, dec., whereas there is a plantation at the west side of the Delaware River being bounded on the west side of the land belonging to Peter Dewitt, east with the marsh that runs to the horse land, & land of Janvier Janson commonly called the Laymakers Hook containing 100 rods along the river & 100 rods into the woods, said plantation belonged to Barrent Egge by patent from Governor Francis Lovelace, Esq. dated 28 May 1669. Barrent Egge on 4 June 1674 made over to Cornelius Janson one half of the said land & patent & now the remaining half is granted to Peter Dewitt, Jan Barretson & Cornelius Jansen. Signed Reyneir Vander Coilen. Delivered in the presence of Edmund Cantwell, Johannes De Haes & Ephraim Herman. (A1:6).

Deed. On 20 Dec 1765 William Currier of Delaware River, planter to John Moll, inhabitant of New Castle. William Currier granted to John Moll a parcel of land lying on St. George's Creek which is surveyed by order of Capt. Edmund Cantwell by Henry Parker for William Goldsmith & William Currier for 600 acres & have made a clearing & log house by us, which half or moiety, I the same voluntarily surrender to John Moll. Signed William Currier. Delivered in the presence of Joseph Cookson, John Fisher & John Clark. (A1:7).

Deed. On 29 Jun 1676 Jacob Vandevere granted to Hendrick Williams of the town of New Castle, a parcel granted to Jacob Vandevere by Francis Lovelace by patent dated 1 May 1671 containing a lot of land in the town of New Castle next to Martin Roman containing 35 steps in breadth 100 steps in length. Signed Jacob Vandevere. Delivered in the presence of Edmond Cantwell & Johannes DeHaes. Acknowledged in court 7 Feb 1676/7. (A1:8).

Deed. On 8 Nov 1677 William Tom for 5000 pounds of tobacco, 3000 pounds in the year 1677 & the remainder in the year 1678 granted to Luke Watson a certain patent granted by Edmond Andros dated 15 Jan 1675 with a tract of land contained in the said patent lying on the Whore Kill on Delaware Bay bounded by Pagan Creek & land of Alexander Molisteynes containing 132 acres. Signed William Tom. Delivered in the presence of Edmund Cantwell & Ephraim Herman. (A1:8).

Deed. On 30 Nov 1677 John Edmundson of Talbot County in the province of Maryland & Sarah his wife to John Yeo of the County of Calvert in the province of Maryland. John Edmundson & Sarah his wife for _ thousand pounds of tobacco granted to John Yeo a tract of land called Mussell Cripp being on White Clay Kill near Christianna Kill as appears by patent dated 15 Jan 1675 granted to John Edmundson being 800 acres. Signed John Edmunds & Sarah Edmunds. Delivered in the presence of Thomas Have & John Standly. (A1:8).

Deed. On 5 Mar 1677/8 George Moore the son & heir of Anna Whale, late of the town of New Castle, dec. for a certain sum of money granted to John Ogle of Christianna Creek a patent from the right honorable Mayor Edmond Andrew Governor General, granted to Anne Whate, Dec by date 5 May 1675, whereas as there is a tract of land called Chelsey lying on the west side of Delaware River laid out to Anne Whale, the land on the south side of St. George's Creek the 1st neck of firm land with the creek & bounded by land of Peter Allrichs, Doctors Swamp, land surveyed for Thomas Spry & the Creek to the river containing 300 acres. Signed George Moore. Delivered in the presence of Thomas Spry & Ephraim Herman. Acknowledged in court 6 Mar 1677/8. (A1:9).

Deed. On 6 Mar 1677/8 John Test, late of London but now of Delaware, merchant for a certain sum of money granted to Marmaduke Rendall, of London, merchant all that land & patent made over to John Test on 6th instant by John Ogle of Christianna & Elizabeth his wife the contents of patent. Signed John Test. Delivered in the presence of John Yeo & Robberd Hutchison. Acknowledged in court 6 Mar 1677/8. (A1:10)

Deed. On 5 Nov 1678 Gerret Otto & Gurtie his wife, late widow of Cornelius Jorrigison, late of the town of New Castle, dec. Whereas Cornelius Jorrigison did possess a house & lot of land in the town of New Castle toward the strand between the houses & lots of Johannes & William Mauritts confirmed by the Governor Richard Nicholls dated 8 Jan 1667, which said house & lot was by the said Cornelius Jorrigison for the payment of his debts in his lifetime sold to Dick Smith of New York, who after the dec. of Cornelius Jorrigison failing his bargain, the said Gurtie, the late widow, Gerret Otto her present husband granted the said house & land to Jan Harmonson for the said debts. Signed Gerret Otto & Gurteen Otto. Delivered in the presence of John Pearson & Hendrick Forrest. (A1:11).

Deed. On 8 Jan 1667 Richard Nicholls, Esq. principal commissioner of his majesty in New England, Governor General under his royal highness James Duke of York & Albany & all the territories in the Americas & commander in Chief of all the forces employed by his majesty to reduce the Dutch nation & all their usurped lands & plantations. Whereas Jacob Allrichs had by virtue of a grant & purchase was in actual possession of a house & lot of land in the town of New Castle between the lots of Johannes & William Mauritts now Hendrick Jansen have since bought the house & lot. Richard Nicholls at Fort James in New York on the island of Manhattan confirm said lot to Hendrick Jansen. Signed Richard Nicholls. Recorded by Mathias Nicholls. (A1:11)

Deed. On 3 June 1678 John Ogle of Christianna Creek, planter & Elizabeth his wife to John Darby of Chester River in the province of Maryland, planter. John Ogle for 14,000 pounds of merchanable tobacco granted to John Darby a island or parcel of land lying on the south side of Christianna Creek commonly called Swarte Newton Island with one other parcel of land without the island. John

Ogle & Elizabeth Ogle. Delivered in the presence of Edmund Cantwell, Ephraim Herman & Thomas Woollaston. (A1:12).

A copy of a survey made by Walter Wharton to the County of New Castle on 3 Dec 1678. Laid out for Hendrich Walraven a tract of land on the north side of Appoquinimink Creek bounded on the south east by land of Derrick Williamson & Derrick Swenson, a branch called Derricks Beaver Dam, land of John Aronson called Bakers Delight & Derricks Creek containing 200 acres & 25 acres of marsh, surveyed Apr 1676, Signed Walter Wharton, surveyor. (A1:13).

A copy of survey made by Walter Wharton to the County of New Castle on 3 Dec 1678, by the virtue of a warrant dated Oct 1677. Laid out to John Anderson, alias Stalcop, a tract of land called Southern Land being on the west side of the Delaware River, east of a branch of Christianna Creek called Red Clay Kill bounded by the land of Thomas Jacobson & Company, a branch of Little Falls Kill containing 600 acres. Signed Walter Wharton. (A1:14).

Patent. On 25 Mar 1676 Edmond Andros, Esq. Lieut. Governor General under his royal highness James Duke of York & Albany & all the territories in the Americas send greetings. Whereas there is a tract of land on the west side of the Delaware River nigh unto the upper end of Bread & Cheese Island on the north side of White Clay Creek which divides this from the land of John Edmondson, which by virtue of a warrant has been laid out for Walraven Johnson Deffox & Charles Ramsey containing 570 acres. Now confirmed unto Walraven Johnson Deffox & Charles Ramsey, they making improvements & paying 5 bushels of good winter wheat to such officer or officers in authority. Signed Edmond Andros. Examined by Mathias Nicholls. (A1:14).

Patent. On 25 Mar 1676 Edmond Andros, Esq. Lieut. Governor General under his royal highness James Duke of York & Albany & all the territories in the Americas send greetings. Whereas there is a tract of land on the west side of the Delaware River on both sides of a branch of Christianna Creek called White Clay Halls, which by virtue of a warrant was laid for John Norner bounded by land of Walraven Johnson Deffox & Charles Ramsey, a small island in the creek & land of John Edmonson containing 340 acres. Now confirmed unto John Norner, making improvements & paying 3 bushels & 1 peck of good winter wheat to such officer or officers in authority. Signed Edmond Andros. Examined by Mathias Nicholls. (A1:15).

Patent. On 7 Apr 1673 Francis Lovelace, Esq. one of the gentlemen of his majesty, Honorable Privy Chamber & Governor General under his royal highness James, Duke of York & Albany & his territories in the Americas send greetings. Whereas there is a tract of land on the west side of the Delaware River on the south west side of Honde or Dog Creek on the northeast side of Naamons Creek containing 100 acres which lying unmanaged & belonging to no particular person, a grant has been desired by Capt. Edmond Cantwell & Johnannes DeHaes. Now confirmed unto Capt. Edmond Cantwell & Johannes DeHaes, making improvements & paying 1 bushel of good winter wheat to such officer or officers in authority. Signed Francis Lovelace. Examined by Mathias Nicholls. (A1:16).

Patent. On 25 Mar 1676 Edmond Andros, Esq. Lieut. Governor General under his royal highness James Duke of York & Albany & all the territories in the Americas send greetings. Whereas there is a tract of land on the west side of the Delaware River to the head of Appoquinimink Creek being a neck of land lying triangular between the two main branches of the Creek bounded on the north by the main branch of the creek, land of Abraham Coffin, the other branch called Sassafras Branch containing 800 acres returned by the surveyor general, 400 acres the 1/2 being granted by patent dated 17 June 1671 unto William Sinclar of New Castle, & by him forfeited, & granted by his majesty to Capt. Edmund Cantwell & the other 1/2 being 400 acres laid out to Cantwell. Now confirmed unto Capt. Edmond Cantwell making improvements & paying 8 bushels of good winter wheat to such officer or officers in authority. Signed Edmund Andros. Examined by Mathias Nicholls. (A1:17).

Patent. On 1 May 1671 Francis Lovelace, Esq. one of the gentlemen of his majesty, Honorable Privy Chamber & Governor General under his royal highness James, Duke of York & Albany & his territories in the Americas send greetings. Whereas there is a tract of land on the west side of the Delaware River, now in the occupation of Jean Paul Jacquet as his proper right being a corner lot in the market place toward the river, next to Harmon Reynerson & before & behind the brewer Peter Conwen being 30 foot in breadth & 130 foot in length. Now confirmed unto Jean Paul Jacquet making improvements & paying 1 bushel of good winter wheat to such officer or officers in authority. Signed Francis Lovelace. Examined by Mathias Nicholls. (A1:17).

Patent. On 25 Mar 1676 Edmond Andros, Esq. Lieut. Governor General under his royal highness James Duke of York & Albany & all the territories in the Americas send greetings. Whereas there is a tract of land on the west side of the Delaware River & on the northeast side of St. Augustine Creek which by virtue of a warrant has been laid out to Casparus Harmon the said land bounded by land of George [unreadable] & St. Augustine Creek containing 330 acres. Now confirmed unto Casparus Harmon making improvements & paying 3 bushels of good winter wheat to such officer or officers in authority. Signed Edmund

Andros. Examined by Mathias Nicholls. (A1:18).

Patent. On 3 May 1671 Francis Lovelace, Esq. one of the gentlemen of his majesty, Honorable Privy Chamber & Governor General under his royal highness James, Duke of York & Albany & his territories in the Americas send greetings. Whereas there is a tract of land on the west side of the Delaware River, now in occupation of Tynam Stidham bounded by the fall of Brandywine Kill, Rattle Snake Kill, the Black Kath Kill & Christianna Kill. Now confirmed unto Tynam Stidham making improvements & paying 1 bushel of good winter wheat when demanded. Signed Francis Lovelace. Examined by Mathias Nicholls. (A1:18).

Patent. On 15 Jan 1675 Edmund Andros, Esq. Lieut. Governor General under his royal highness James Duke of York & Albany & all the territories in the Americas send greetings. Whereas there is a tract of land on the west side of the Delaware River by virtue of a warrant has been laid out to Olle Fransen, Marchus Lawernceson & Neil Neilson lying about 2 miles above the Virtiridge Hook in a place called Bought bounded by Dogg Creek, land of Charles Peterson, Stoney Creek, a branch of Bought Creek called Poplar Branch containing 700 acres. The return of the survey by Capt. Edmund Cantwell it appears 300 acres were formerly laid out to Olle Franson, Peter Mounson & Neils Neilson by patent dated 16 Apr 1673, since which time Marchus Lawrenson is invested in by the right of Peter Mounson & the other 400 acres being new. Now confirmed unto Olle Fransen, Marchus Lawernceson & Neil Neilson where they have erected a mill & paying 7 bushels of good winter wheat to such officer or officers in authority. Signed Edmund Andros. Examined by Mathias Nicholls. (A1:19).

Patent. On 25 Mar 1676 Edmond Andros, Esq. Lieut. Governor General under his royal highness James Duke of York & Albany & all the territories in the Americas send greetings. Whereas there is a tract of land on Appoquinimink Creek bounded by Hook & Sassafras Creek containing 900 acres, which by virtue of a patent dated 7 June 1671 to Edmund Cantwell. Now confirmed unto Edmund Cantwell having made improvements & paying 9 bushels of good winter wheat to such officer or officers in authority. Signed Edmund Andros. Examined by Mathias Nicholls. (A1:20).

Patent. On 26 Mar 1669 Francis Lovelace, Esq. one of the gentlemen of his majesty, Honorable Privy Chamber & Governor General under his royal highness James, Duke of York & Albany & his territories in the Americas send greetings. Whereas there is a tract of land on the west side of the Delaware River, now in occupation of Jan Sibransen being near the horn neck commonly called Ride Hook being in breadth 150 rods to the land of Arent Jansen & 600 rods in length. Now confirmed unto Jan Sibransen making improvements & paying 1 bushel of good winter wheat when demanded. Signed Francis Lovelace. Examined by Mathias Nicholls. (A1:21).

Patent. On 28 May 1669 Francis Lovelace, Esq. one of the gentlemen of his majesty, Honorable Privy Chamber & Governor General under his royal highness James, Duke of York & Albany & his territories in the Americas send greetings. Whereas there is a tract of land on the west side of the Delaware River, now in the tenure of Olle Towson containing in breadth by the river 25 rods the length of the woods being 300 rods to the land of Garrett Sanders. Now confirmed unto Olle Towson making improvements & paying 1 bushel of good winter wheat when demanded. Signed Francis Lovelace. Examined by Mathias Nicholls. (A1:21).

Patent. On 23 Aug 1668 Richard Nicholls, Esq. Principal Commissioner from his Majesty unto all the colonies of New England, Governor General under his royal Highness James, Duke of York & Albany & of all his territories of America & commander in chief of all the forces employed by his majesty to reduce the Dutch nation & all their usurped lands & plantations to his majesties obedience, send greetings. Whereas there is a tract of land granted by Alexander De Hinyosa, late Governor at Delaware to Mathias Eckelson next to the land of Jurian Jansen containing along the river side 25 rods from there to the woods 600 rods. Now confirmed unto Mathy Eckelson making improvements & paying 1 bushel of good winter wheat when demanded. Signed Richard Nicholls. Examined by Mathias Nicholls. (A1:22).

Patent. On 20 Feb 1671 Francis Lovelace, Esq. one of the gentlemen of his majesty, Honorable Privy Chamber & Governor General under his royal highness James, Duke of York & Albany & his territories in the Americas send greetings. Whereas the Officers at Delaware granted to Roeloffe Anderson a tract of land containing 200 acres lying on the west side of the Delaware River, the north side of Appoquinimink Creek bounded by land of John Sherricks, land of Adam Peterson & Drawyers Creek with a portion of marsh land below the Drawyers Creek. Now confirmed unto Roeloffe Anderson making improvements & paying 2 bushels of good winter wheat when demanded. Signed Francis Lovelace. Examined by Mathias Nicholls. (A1:23).

Patent. On 20 Feb 1671 Francis Lovelace, Esq. one of the gentlemen of his majesty, Honorable Privy Chamber & Governor General under his royal highness James, Duke of York & Albany & his territories in the Americas send greetings. Whereas the Officers at Delaware granted to Garrett Otto a tract of land containing 180 acres lying on the west side of the Delaware River, the northwest side of Appoquinimink Creek bounded by the said creek, land of Hans Hanson (als Miller), Drawyers Creek & land of John Sherricks with a portion of marsh land below the Drawyers Creek. Now confirmed unto Garrett Otto making improvements & paying 1 bushel of good winter wheat when demanded. Signed Francis Lovelace. (A1:24).

Patent. On 5 Nov 1675 Edmond Andros, Esq. Lieut. Governor General under his royal highness James Duke of York & Albany & all the territories in the Americas send greetings. Whereas there is a tract of land which by virtue a warrant has been laid out for Henry Ward called Reedin Point bounded by the Beaver Dam, Krickett Swamp, Dragon Swamp, St. George's Creek & the river containing 446 1/2 acres with the marshes adjoining. Now confirmed unto Henry Ward having made improvements & paying 4 bushels of good winter wheat to such officer or officers in authority. Signed Edmund Andros. Examined by Mathias Nicholls. Surveyed on 17 Apr 1667 for 272 acres. (A1:24).

Survey. On 21 Jan 1678 Laid out for Richard Huddow a tract of land called New Ulrick lying on the west side of the Delaware River, the north side of the southwest branch of Drawyers Creek bounded by the Creek & land of Thomas Sadlers containing 200 acres. Laid out by William Taylor by order & appointment of Walter Wharton, Surveyor. Recorded 25 July 1678. (A1:26).

Patent. On 26 Feb 1671 Francis Lovelace, Esq. one of the gentlemen of his majesty, Honorable Privy Chamber & Governor General under his royal highness James, Duke of York & Albany & his territories in the Americas send greetings. Whereas the Officers at Delaware granted to Hans Hanson, alias Miller, a tract of land containing 180 acres lying on the west side of the Delaware River, the northwest side of Appoquinimink Creek bounded by the said creek, land of John Arenson & Jacob Anderson & land of Garrett Otto with a portion of marsh land below the Drawyers Creek. Now confirmed unto Hans Hanson, als Miller, making improvements & paying 1 bushel of good winter wheat when demanded. Signed Francis Lovelace. (A1:26).

Patent. On 14 Aug 1671 Francis Lovelace, Esq. one of the gentlemen of his majesty, Honorable Privy Chamber & Governor General under his royal highness James, Duke of York & Albany & his territories in the Americas send greetings. Whereas the Officers at Delaware granted to John Sherricks a tract of land lying on the west side of the Delaware River, the northwest side of Appoquinimink Creek bounded by the land of Garrett Otto & land of Roeloffe Anderson containing 200 acres. Now confirmed unto John Sherricks making improvements & paying 2 bushels of good winter wheat when demanded. Signed Francis Lovelace. (A1:2

Patent. On 14 Aug 1671 Francis Lovelace, Esq. one of the gentlemen of his majesty, Honorable Privy Chamber & Governor General under his royal highness James, Duke of York & Albany & his territories in the Americas send greetings. Whereas the Officers at Delaware granted to Barrrent Hendrickson a tract of land containing 280 acres lying on the west side of the Delaware River, the northwest side of Appoquinimink Creek bounded by the said creek, land of Adam Peterson, land of John Bradborne with 100 acres of marsh land below the Drawyers Creek. Now confirmed unto Barrent Hendrickson making improvements & paying 3 bushels of good winter wheat when demanded. Signed Francis Lovelace. (A1:28).

Patent. On 15 Jan 1675 Edmond Andros, Esq. Lieut. Governor General under his royal highness James Duke of York & Albany & all the territories in the Americas send greetings. Whereas there was a patent granted by Gov. Richard Nicholls, to Thomas Wollaston, John Ogle, John Hendricks & Harman Johnson for a tract of land lying on White Clay Creek near Christianna Creek on the Delaware River bounded by land of Hans Boon, land of James Craford, a creek at the head of Cheese Island containing 800 acres & also a piece of meadow known by the name of Marsh Cripple running up the creek about 1/2 mile, patent dated 1 Aug 1668. Whereas John Edmundson has made a purchase of the above land. Now confirmed unto John Edmundson Ward having made improvements & paying 8 bushels of good winter wheat to such officer or officers in authority. Signed Edmund Andros. Examined by Mathias Nicholls. (A1:29)

On the back side of the above said confirmation was written. John Edmundson does sign over all right to above said land to John Yeo. Signed John Edmundson. Delivered in the presence of Thomas Howe & John Hanly. (A1:30).

Deed. On 30 Apr 1678 John Yeo, of the town of New Castle to John Smith of New Castle. John Yeo for 16,000 pounds of good tobacco casked, granted to John Smith a tract of land called Mussell Cripple lying on White Clay Creek nigh unto Christianna Creek which John Yoe bought or John Edmundson of the County of Talbott of the province of Maryland as appears by the deed dated 30 Nov 1677. Signed John Yeo. Delivered in the presence of Samuel Land & John Hayles. (A1:30).

Patent. On 14 Aug 1671, Francis Lovelace, Esq. one of the gentlemen of his majesty, Honorable Privy Chamber & Governor General under his royal highness James, Duke of York & Albany & his territories in the Americas send greetings. Whereas there is a tract of land in the occupation of Garret Sanderson, bounded on the southwest side by land of Hans Blacqs & land of Olle Sversons & another piece of land lying next to the first piece bounded by land of John Hulkes & land of Arent Jansen, which is now confirmed to Garret Sanderson yielding & paying 2 bushels of wheat when demanded by persons in authority. Signed Francis Lovelace. Examined by Mathias Nicholls. (A1:30).

On the back of above patent. Whereas in this patent are included 2 parcels of land therefore Garret Sanderson assigns & makes over the plantation which lies between Jans Hulk, Arent Jansen now in the occupation of Peter Derritt unto Jan Barrentson for to have & to hold the same as his & Garret Sanderson did acknowledge to be paid for the same the first penny with the last. Delivered in the presence of Hans Blocqs, Hendrick Jansen & Gisbert Dirksen in New Castle on 3 Feb 1674. (A1:31).

Deed. On 25 Mar 1669. Francis Lovelace, Esq. one of the gentlemen of his majesty, Honorable Privy Chamber & Governor General under his royal Highness James, Duke of York & Albany & his territories in the Americas, send greetings. Whereas there is a tract of land in the occupation of Andries Mattsen, called the Indians or the Wilde Hook, bounded by land of Hans Peterson & Skill Potes Kill, which is now confirmed to Andries Mattsen, yielding & paying 1 bushel of wheat when demanded by persons of authority. Signed Francis Lovelace. Examined by Mathias Nichols. (A1:31).

On the back of above patent was written the following 2 assignments. Margrieta Andries, daughter, widow of Andries Mateysen, Dec who made of one half of the said land unto Paul Mounsen. Signed 2 Sep 1674 by Margrieta Andries, daughter. Delivered in the presence of H. Block & Mounse Paulson. (A1:32). Paul Mounsen made over to Hans Peterson, one half of the land. Signed 2 Sep 1674 Paul Mouse. Delivered in the presence of H. Block & Mounse Paulson. (A1:32).

Deed. On 25 Mar 1669, Francis Lovelace, Esq. one of the gentlemen of his majesty, Honorable Privy Chamber & Governor General under his royal Highness James, Duke of York & Albany & his territories in the Americas, sends greetings. Whereas there is a tract of land in the occupation of Hendrick Jansen & Bartle Euchelson a tract of land called Ames Land bounded by the kill, land of Jan Cornelius, Mattys Mattson, Martin Martinson, Hendrick Thackens containing 400 acres, which is now confirmed to Hendrick Jansen & Bartle Euchelson yielding & paying 4 bushels of wheat when demanded by persons of authority. Signed Francis Lovelace. Examined by Mathias Nichols. (A1:32).

Patent. On 16 June 1671, Francis Lovelace, Esq. one of the gentlemen of his majesty, Honorable Privy Chamber & Governor General under his royal Highness James, Duke of York & Albany & his territories in the Americas, sends greetings. Whereas there is a tract of land in the occupation of Roberd Morton containing 500 acres bounded by Appoquinimink Creek, land of John Hartop, Henry Hartop, Senica Brewer which is called Hangmans Hook, which is now confirmed unto Roberd Morton yielding & paying 5 bushels of wheat when demanded by persons of authority. Signed Francis Lovelace. Examined by Mathias Nicholls. (A1:33).

Deed. On 9 Dec 1676. Roberd Morton of Appoquinimink Creek to Gustavus Anderson of New Castle. Roberd Morton granted to Gustavus Anderson a tract of land containing 250 acres being one half of the 500 acres granted to him. Signed Rob. Morton. Delivered in the presence of Walter Wharton & John Strate. (A1:34).

Deed. On 1 Apr 1679. Whereas Justa Andries did on 24 Nov 1674 granted to me the said Hans Peterson, the one half of the land of Senica Brewer situated on Christianna Creek bounded by land granted unto Senica Brewer & company with Walraven Jansen, Andries Vinn by patent from Governor Lovelace. Now Hans Peterson granted to Andries Uriansen all the same half of the land which did belong to Senica Brewer excepting the said 66 foot of land next to the street towards Andries Uriansen also half of the wood land which is behind Andries' garden [note: "Andries the fins land"] which pieces of land Hans Peterson sold unto Mathias Mattyasen Smith so that the lands sold unto Andries Uriansen was one half of the land of Senica Brewer, excepting that parcel sold to Mathias Mattysen Smith & his successor Brewer Senicka having married his the said Andries Uriansen widow, the said Andries being dec. Hans Peterson make over to Brewer Senica all the said land. Signed Hans Peterson. Delivered in the presence of Hendrick Simmons & Eph. Harman. (A1:34).

Patent. On 6 Dec 1675. Edmund Andros, Esq. Lieut. Governor General under his royal highness James Duke of York & Albany & all the territories in the Americas send greetings. Whereas there is a tract of land on the west side of the Delaware River called St. Augustine's lying on the north side of Appoquinimink Creek opposite to the lower end of Reeden Island which by virtue of a warrant has been laid out to M. Augustine Herman, the said land bounded by the river on the east on the south with Appoquinimink Creek, land of Derrick Williamson & land of Derrick Lawrenson & also land of Claus Kirton on the north by a small creek called St. Augustine's Creek dividing this from a tract of land granted to M. Peter Allrichs & on the west with the main woods containing 400 acres belonging to as be the return of the survey by Capt. Edmund Cantwell, the said Augustine Herman transferred his rights to said land to his 2 sons, Ephraim & Casperus Harmon. Now confirmed unto Ephraim Harmon & Casparus Harmon making improvements & paying 4 bushels of winter where to such officers in authority. Signed Edmund Andrew. Examined by Mathias Nicholls. (A1:35).

Patent. On 25 Mar 1676. Edmund Andros, Esq. Lieut. Governor General under his royal highness James Duke of York & Albany & all the territories in the Americas send greetings. Whereas there is a tract of land called Calton lying on the west side of the Delaware River & on the north side of a branch of Blackbird Creek that divides this land from the land laid out to John Barker bounded by land of John Hartop containing 220 acres. Now confirmed to John Barker, making improvements & paying 2 bushels of wheat to such officers in authority. Signed Edmund Andros. Examined by Mathias Nicholls. (A1:36).

Patent. On 15 Jan 1675. Edmund Andros, Esq. Lieut. Governor General under his royal highness James Duke of York & Albany & all the territories in the Americas send greetings. Whereas there is a tract of land on the west side of Delaware River & the northwest side of Blackbird Creek by virtue of a warrant has been laid out for Persifill Wosterdell, John Barker, John [this was blank], James Williams & Edward Williams bounded by the creek containing 1200 acres. Now confirmed unto Persifill Wosterdell, John Barker, John _____, James Williams & Edward Williams, making improvements & paying 12 bushels of wheat to such officers in authority. Signed Edmund Andros. Examined by Mathias Nicholls. (A1:36).

Patent. On 1 May 1671. Francis Lovelace, Esq. one of the gentlemen of his majesty, Honorable Privy Chamber & Governor General under his royal highness James Duke of York & Albany & his territories in the Americas, send greetings. Whereas there is a lot of land at New Castle, now in the possession of Harmon Reyners being 190 foot by 82 foot lying between Jan Heady & Hans Banssens & Beaker Street. Now confirmed to Harmen Reyners, making improvements & paying quit rent. Signed Francis Lovelace. Mathias Nicholls. (A1:38).

Be it known that Harmen Reyners the before mentioned, for valuable consideration granted the rights to the above patent to Justus Anderson. Signed 2 July 1674.

Deed. On 8 May 1678. Know all men by these presents, I, Claus Daniels _____ of New Castle by virtue of a letter of attorney for my mother Jamethia Jaspers, who is proved to be the widow & sole heir of Harmon Reyners, dec., for valuable consideration to my mothers use granted to John Ogle the house & lot in the within mentioned patent & all right & interest of Harman Reyners & Jamethia Veddette to the said John Ogle. Signed Claus Daniels. Delivered in the presence of John Moll & Jean Paul Jacquitt. (A1:38).

Deed. On 10 Apr 1676. George Oldfield & Paternella his wife, executrix of the will of Capt. John Carr, dec. to John Moll. Whereas Capt. John Carr by his letter of attorney dated 10 Apr 1675 did give to his wife Paternella all his right & title to all his real & personal estate lying & being on the Delaware River provided his debts in New York & Delaware were paid & the over to be the heirs. Whereas Paternella by her letter of attorney dated 2 June 1675 empowered Thomas Spry of New Castle, Chirurgeon to sell & dispose of said estate. Said estate was purchased by John Moll, being a lot with houses belonging to Garrett Sweringen being in the town of New Castle bounded by the street called Harte Street, a lot belonging to Edmund Cantwell, Johannes DeHaes & 2 other lots of ground being in the town of New Castle bounded by Harte Street, Land Street & Susquehanna Street. George Oldfield & Paternella his wife for 3300 guilders granted to John Moll the said lots. Signed George Oldfield & Paternella Oldfield. Delivered in the presence of John Coseyns & John Mathews. (A1:39).

On 6 Mar 1677/8. John Ogle of Christianna & Elizabeth his wife for certain sum of money transported to John Test of this River of Delaware, merchant, all the said land patent & premises made over to him the said Ogle on 5 Mar this instant by George Moore, the son & heir of Anne Whale, dec. the contents which said patent stands recorded in Folio O & O. The above said deed was signed by John Ogle & Elizabeth his wife in the presence of John Leo & Robert Hutchison & was acknowledged in court. (A1:40).

Deed. On 3 mar 1677/8. Hans Hanson (Alias, Miller) of Appoquinimink Creek, planter to Benjamin Gumby of Appoquinimink Creek, planter. Hans Hanson granted to Benjamin Gumby a tract of land bounded by Appoquinimink Creek, land of Jam Arenson, James Andrison, Drawyers Creek & land of Garret Otto containing 200 acres being the land Francis Lovelace confirmed by patent dated 26 Feb 1671 to Hans Hanson. Signed Hans Hanson (alias, Miller) Delivered in the presence of Ephraim Harmon & Ebenezer Taylor. (A1:40).

Deed. On 3 June 1679. Benjamin Gumby of Appoquinimink Creek, planter to John Peterson of Appoquinimink Creek. Benjamin Gumby for certain consideration granted to John Peterson all the plantation as the within mentioned transport from Hans Hanson to Benjamin Gumby. Signed Benjamin Gumby. Delivered in the presence of Ephraim Harmon & Ebenezer Taylor. (A1:41).

Deed. On 14 May 1679. Justa Andries of Christiana Kill to Ralph Hutchison of New Castle, ordinary keeper. Justa Anderson for 3000 gilders granted to Ralph Hutchison a dwelling house in New Castle. Signed Justa Andries & Alicte Andries. Delivered in the presence of John Yeo & Tymen Stidham. (A1:42).

Deed. On 4 June 1679 Ralph Hutchison of the town of New Castle, inn holder to John Darby of the same town, inn holder. Ralph Hutchison granted to John Darby a dwelling house & other buildings lying in the City of New Castle bounded on the east by the river, the south by the house of Jane Hendrichson Drayer & to the north by the house & lot of Isaac Hayne lying with its fences Signed Ralph Hutchison. Delivered in the presence of John Moll & Peter Allrichs. (A1:43).

Deed. On 17 Apr 1678. Justa Andries of Christiana Creek, planter & Alicte his wife, to John Williams of the town of New Castle, merchant. Whereas Justa Andries by right of patent dated 29 Sep 1677 & for 2400 gilders granted unto the said John Williams a house & lot of land in the town of New Castle towards the riverside near the old fort between the lots belonging to Reyes Mill & Claus Peterson Smith containing in breadth 62 foot & in length 100 foot. Signed Justa Andries & Alicte Andries. Delivered in the presence of Edmund Cantwell & Eph. Herman. (A1:43)

Deed. On 3 June 1678. Jan Andersen of Christiana Creek, husbandman to Oele Poulsen alias Clocka Ode of Christiana Creek, husbandman. Jan Andersen granted to Oele Poulsen all right & title to one share of Bread & Cheese Island which is one full 6th part, which said land was sold to Jan Andersen by Oele Rawson & Neils Larsen. Signed Jan Andresen. Delivered in the presence of Samuel Land & Eph. Herman. (A1:44).

Patent. On 26 Feb 1671. Francis Lovelace, Esq. one of the gentlemen of his majesty, Honorable Privy Chamber & Governor General under his royal Highness James, Duke of York & Albany & his territories in the Americas send greetings. Whereas there is a tract of land containing 157 acres granted to John Aronson & Jacob Anderson being on the westward side of the Delaware River & on the northwest side of Appoquinimink Creek bounded on the south by with the reek land of Garret Sanders & Van Tuil, on the north with Drawyers Creek, land of Hans Hanson alias Miller. Now confirmed unto John Aronson & Jacob Anderson & they paying 1 1/2 bushels of winter wheat to such officers in authority. Signed Francis Lovelace. Recorded by Mathias Nicols. (A1:45)

Deed. On 3 June 1679. Jacob Anderson as the only heir & executor of John Aronson, dec. for consideration granted to Jan Peterson of Appoquinimink Creek, planter all that tract of land as described in the patent from Francis Lovelace to John Aronson & myself, Jacob Anderson. Signed Jacob Anderson. Delivered in the presence of Eph. Herman & Ebenezer Taylor. (A1:46).

Deed. On 2 Dec 1679 Harmon Janson Tybrants of Christiana Creek, planter & Belica his wife to William Rambo of Christiana Creek, planter. Harmon Janson granted to William Rambo a plantation with a tract of land lying between a littler creek & the land of Walraven Janson Devos, being part of the land granted to George Whale & George Moore by patent from Richard Nichols, governor, dated 1 Jan 1667 & known by the name of Mineques Plantation. Signed Harmon Janson & Belica Janson. Delivered in the presence of Samuel Land & Ebenezer Taylor. (A1:47).

Deed. On 2 Dec 1679. Hans Hanson alias Miller of Appoquinimink Creek, planter to Hendrick Williams of the town of New Castle, merchant. Hans Hanson for 400 gilders granted to Hendrich Williams a tract of land containing 400 acres being on the south side of Appoquinimink Creek, called Knolbushauer & bounded by the creek & land of Bobbin Morton being the land granted by patent by Francis Loveland, governor by patent dated 26 Feb 1671 to William Warner & Warner made over said land to John Johnson & said Johnson to Hans Hanson. Signed Hans Hanson alias Miller. Delivered in the presence of Eph. Herman & Benjamin Gumby. (A1:47).

Patent. On 5 Nov 1674 Edmund Andros, Esq. Lieut. Governor General of his royal highness James, Duke of York & Albany & all the territories in the Americas, send greetings. Whereas there is a tract of land on the west side of the Delaware River called Hampton which by virtue of a warrant was laid out to John Ogle, said land lying on the south side of St. George's Creek bounded by the creek, land of George Moore & land of Bernard Egburts containing 300 acres. Now confirmed unto John Ogle & him paying 3 bushels of winter wheat to officers of authority. Signed Edmund Andros. Recorded by Mathias Nicols. (A1:47).

On the back side of the above patent was the following deed.

Deed. On 30 Dec 1679. John Ogle of Christiana Creek, planter & Elizabeth his wife to Augustine Dixon of St. George's Creek, planter. John Ogle for consideration granted to Augustine Dixon all the land in the above patent. Signed John Ogle & Elizabeth Ogle. Delivered in the presence of Eph. Herman & Samuel Land. (A1:48).

Patent. On 20 June 1665. Richard Nicols, Esq. principal commissioner from his majesty unto New England, Governor General under his royal highness, James, Duke of York & Albany & all his territories in the Americas & commander in chief of the forces employed by his majesty to reduce the dutch nation & all their usurped land, for the good services performed by Mr. William Tom at Delaware, confirm & grant unto William Tom an island & plantation heretofore belonging to Peter Allrichs being 7 miles below New Castle, on account the said Peter Allrichs, who was in hostility against his majesty at the reducing of the Fort at Delaware & also granted to William Tom a tract of land lying at the mouth of the Delaware River between Christiana Creek & Vandrichts Hook containing 500 acres, also a small parcel of land in the town of New Castle containing 1/2 acre bounded by the mill & the strand. Said William Tom is to pay 8 bushels of winter wheat when demanded by persons of authority. Signed Richard Nicols. Written by Mathias Nicols. (A1:49).

Deed. On 2 Feb 1679/80. Thomas Spry of new Castle, chirurgeon to Jacob Young of St. George's Creek, planter. Thomas Spry for valuable consideration granted to Jacob Young a tract of land containing 160 acres called Doctors Commons on the south side of St. George's Creek bounded by land of Mrs. Anne Whale & Doctors Swamp. Signed Thomas Spry. Delivered in the presence of George Moore & Samuel Land. (A1:50).

Deed. On 4 Feb 1679/80. Oele Poulson of Christiana Creek, husbandman to Abraham Man of Christiana Creek, merchant. Oele Poulson for consideration granted to Abraham Man all right & share in 2 equal sixth parts of a small island in Christaina Creek called Bread & Cheese Island granted by patent from Governor Nicols to Oele Poulson in company with Thomas Jacobs & Thomas Snelling dated 3 Aug 1668, & all right & 1/3 part of 248 acres confirmed unto Oele Poulson, Thomas Jacobs & Arent Jansen by patent from Gov. Edmund Andros dated 17 Nov 1679. Signed Oele Poulson. Delivered in the presence of John Moll, Peter Allrichs, J.D. Hais & Will Simpill. (A1:50).

Patent. On 15 Jan 1675. Edmund Andros, Esq. Lieut. Governor General under his royal highness, James, Duke of York & Albany & the territories in the Americas send greetings. Whereas there is a lot in the town of New Castle which was laid out for James Wallen bounded by the river & the common being 60 foot by 300 foot allowing a pathway from the town dike that leads into the town. Now confirmed unto James Wallen & he paying 1 bushel of winter wheat to persons of authority. Signed Edmund Andros. Examined by Mathias Nicols. (A1:51).

The following deed was on the back of the above patent.

Deed. On 25 Feb 1679/80. James Wallen of the town of New Castle, hatter to Ephraim Herman of the town of New Castle. James Wallen for valuable consideration granted to Ephraim Herman the lot of land mentioned in the above patent. Signed James Wallen. Delivered in the presence of Will Simpill & F. D. Ring. (A1:52).

Patent. On 25 Mar 1676. Edmund Andros, Esq. Lieut. Governor General under his royal highness, James, Duke of York & Albany & the territories in the Americas send greetings. Whereas there is a tract of land called Good Neighborhood laid out by warrant to Casparus Herman bounded by the swamp, land of George Axton & St. Augustine's Creek containing 330 acres. Now confirmed unto Casperus Herman & he paying 3 bushels of winter wheat to persons of authority. Signed Edmund Andros. Examined by Mathias Nicols. (A1:54).

The following deed was on the back of the above patent.

Deed. On 1 Mar 1679/80. Casperus Herman of Delaware to Jean Biscuss, Martin Garritson & Mathias Mathison. Casperus Herman for consideration granted to Jean Biscuss, Martin Garritson & Mathias Mathison all the land described in the within patent. Signed Casperus Herman. Delivered in the presence of Eph. Herman & Machiel Bacon. (A1:54).

Patent. On 8 Jan 1667. Richard Nicolls, principal commissioner from his Maj. in New England Governor General under his royal highness, James, Duke of York & Albany & all his territories in the Americas & commander in chief of all the forces employed by his Maj. to reduce the Dutch Nation & all their usurped lands, sends greetings. Whereas there was granted on 5 Mar 1663 to Oele Ollason, Niels Nielson, Sr., Hendrick Neilson, Matthys Nielson & Niels Nielson, Jr. a plantation being at the Trinity Hook & for them to build houses near one another & on 15 June 1664 said land was confirmed unto the persons named. Now have confirmed said land to Oele Ollason, Niels Nielson, Sr., Hendrick Nielson, Mattys Nielson & Niel Nielson, Jr. & they to pay 5 bushels of winter wheat for his Majesty's use unto persons of authority. Signed Richard Nicolls. Recorded by Mathias Nicolls. (A1:55).

Patent. On 16 May 1670. Francis Lovelace, Esq. one of the gentlemen of his majesty, Honorable Privy Chamber & Governor General under his royal Highness James, Duke of York & Albany & his territories in the Americas send greetings. Whereas my predecessor, Col. Richard Nicolls on 8 Jan 1667 gave his patent to John Hindrickson, Neils Neilson Sr., Hendrich Neilson, Matty Neilson & Neil Neilson Jr. a tract of land lying on the Trinity Hook, which was confirmed unto them on 15 June 1664 since which time Oele Ollason being vested in the right & interest of John Hinderson & all them have requested my confirmation. Now confirmed unto Oele Ollason, Neil Neilson Sr., Hendrick Neilson, Matty Neilson & Neil Neilson Jr. them paying 5 bushels of wheat to persons of authority. Signed Francis Lovelace. Recorded by Mathias Nicolls. (A1:56).

Order. On 16 May 1670. Upon petition of Olle Ollason, Neils Neilson Sr. & others concerned in the patent granted by my predecessor, Col. Richard Nicolls for each of them to have a plantation with proportion of meadow ground for hay for their cattle on Trinity Hook, for which they had a grant before those parts were reduced. Mr. William Tom having by misinformation obtained a patent for all the meadow ground, whereon they had their proportions & hat by order of the court forbade them to cut hay or make bridges for their cattle to go into the marsh without his leave which with out relief will prove much to their prejudice. Having taken the same unto consideration I do think fit to order that the said Olle Ollason & Neil Neilson & the rest in the said patent expressed, shall enjoy the benefit of what is granted there in to them. Signed Francis Lovelace. A1:57)

Order. At a special court held by the Governor at New Castle in Delaware River the 13th & 14th of May 1675. In the case of the inhabitants of Verdridges Hook in the River, complaining that Mr. William Tom doth molest them in the enjoyment of the meadow ground next to their plantations & Mr. Tom making claims there unto by virtue of a patent obtained by him from Col. Richard Nicolls, the necessity of the _____ for this meadow or a sufficient proportion of ill Mr. Tom allegations being discourse of & taken into consideration as also Mr. Tom proposals is to say that those of Verdridges Hook should by consent enjoy the said meadow in question provided that he the said Mr. Tom might have liberty to admit the inhabitants of some other neighbors plantations who stood in need thereof to have equal benefit, like wise some of the meadow next to them being sufficient for them all & that the said Mr. Tom should likewise reserve freedom of the common age therefor himself the said proposal was allowed & the same ordered accordingly. Signed Mathias Nicolls. (A1:57).

Patent. On 25 Mar 1676. Edmund Andros, Esq. Lieut. Governor General under his royal highness, James, Duke of York & Albany & the territories in the Americas send greetings. Whereas there is a tract of land called Canaan laid out for William Sharpe, the said land on the north side of Duck Creek bounded by land of William Ford containing 500 acres. Now confirmed to William Sharpe & he paying 5 bushels of winter wheat to persons of authority. Signed Edmund Andros. Examined by Mathias Nicolls. (A1:57).

On the back side of the above patent.

Deed. On 2 Aug 1679. William of the County of Talbot in Maryland do sell all my right to the piece of land called Canann being 500 acres unto Christopher Ellett. Signed William Sharpe & Elizabit Sharpe. Delivered in the presence of John Phoker & Margret Canmill. (A1:58).

Deed. On 25 July 1678. Benjamin Nettleship of the county of Talbot in Maryland, the only heir of all the estate of Vissimus Nettleship, late of New Castle to Robert Hutchison of the town of New Castle. Benjamin Nettleship for 4000 pounds of merchandise & cash granted to Robert Hutchison a parcel of land called Ashelborne lying in New West Jersey on the south side of Cohansey Creek opposite the indian town containing 540 acres & all belongings of my brother Vissimus Nettleship of Sophia Jurians & Charles Rumsey. Signed Benjamin Nellisship. Delivered in the presence of Edmund Cantwell & Eph. Herman. (A1:58).

Release. On 22 Feb 1675/6. I, Charles Rumsey do hereby have given possession & deliver a tract of land called Ashelborne lying in Cohansey Creek containing 540 acres sold by my self & Sophia Jurianson, relict of Andries Jurianson & by virtue of a letter of attorney empowering me to make such delivery. Signed Charles Rumsey. Delivered in the presence of John Smith & Will. Hosur.

Certification. On 14 June 1675. These may certify whom it may concern, that we William Tom & Jno. Edmundson by virtue of a commission to us directed by Major John Fenwicke of London, merchant for settlement of the same, Mew Casaria being the eastern side of the Delaware Bay & River of which he is proprietor. Now know ye that William Tom & John Edmundson reposing our trust & confidence in William Taylor, Walter Wharton & Henry Parker for the surveying & laying out of the said land for any that shall require them there unto in order to settle, just as in Maryland. Signed John Edmundson & William Tom. (A1:59).

Deed. On 20 Feb 1675. Charles Rumsey & Sophia Jurianson, the relict of Andrew Jurianson of Delaware River to Vissimus Nettleship of Delaware River. Charles Rumsey & Sophia Jurianson granted to Vissimus Nettleship all their right to a tract of land called Ashelborne lying in New Cesaria or New Jersey on the eastern side of the Delaware River & the south side of Cohansey Creek opposite the indian town containing 540 acres. Signed Charles Rumsey & Sophia Jurianson. Delivered in the presence of Henry Parker & William Maker. (A1:60).

Survey. On 5 June 1675 Andrew Jurianson & Jno. Dunn, 540 acres of land called Ashelborne situated in New Cesaria, alias New Jersey on the east side of Delaware Bay, the south side of Cohansey & now called Fenwick River lying opposite to the tract of land laid out for a town called Bingfield. Signed Walter Wharton, by appointment of John Edmundson. (A1:61).

I do grant unto the persons within mentioned the within specified tract of land provided they settle the same with a year & make good their rights according to the law. In witness whereof I have hereunto set my hand this 8th of June 1675. John Edmundson. (A1:61).

Release. On 20 Feb 167_. I, Sophia Jurianson, the relict of Andrew Jurianson with specified do assign all my right to the interest of the said land mentioned in the certificate form my, my heirs & assignees to Vissimus Nettleship forever. Signed Sophia Jurianson. Delivered in the presence of Henry Parker & Will. Maker. (A1:61).

Patent. On 9 Dec 1675. Edmund Andros, Esq. Lieut. Governor General under his royal highness, James, Duke of York & Albany & the territories in the Americas send greetings. Whereas there is a tract of land called Bombeys Hook lying on the west side of the Delaware Bay, which by virtue of a warrant was laid out for Peter Byard, the said land lying on the mouth of Duck Creek bounded by the creek & the bay containing 600 acres. Now confirmed to Peter Byard & he paying 6 bushels of winter wheat to persons of authority. Signed Edmund Andros. Recorded by Mathias Nicolls. This above is a true copy of the original patent recorded & examined by me. Eph. Herman. 1687. (A1:1).

Deed. On 4 May 1679. Mechacksitt, Chief Sachama of Cohasink & Indian owner & proprietor of all that tract of land commonly called by the Christians Bonpies Hook & by the Indians Newsink for the consideration of 1 gun, 4 hands full of powder, 3 matscoats, one anchor of liquor & 1 kettle granted to Peter Byard of New York all that tract of land called Bompies Hook lying on the west side of the Delaware River beginning at the great pond being the upper most land stretching down along the river to Duck Creek. Signed by a mark, Mechacksitt & the mark of Maisapplnackin, the son of Mechacksitt. Delivered in the presence of J. Haes (as interpreter), John Adams, William Naringly & Eph. Herman. (A1:62).

Patent. On 1 May 1671. Francis Lovelace, Esq. one of the gentlemen of his majesty, Honorable Privy Chamber & Governor General under his royal Highness James, Duke of York & Albany & his territories in the Americas send greetings. Whereas there is a house & 2 lots of land at New Castle now in the occupation of Isaac Jayne as his right by purchase, bounded by the river, land of Cornelius George & land of Bernard Ekins. Now confirmed to Isaac Jayne, he paying 1 bushel of winter wheat to persons of authority. Signed Francis Lovelace. Examined by Mathias Micolls. (A1:63)

On the back of the above patent.

Deed. On 28 Dec 1680. Isaac Jayne for & in consideration of another house & lot exchanged lying in New Castle & a certain sum of money granted to Ephraim Herman all right to house & lots as described in the patent. Signed Isaac Jayne. Delivered in the presence of John Adams & Sybrant Valsk. (A1:64).

Patent. On 26 Feb 1671. Francis Lovelace, Esq. one of the gentlemen of his majesty, Honorable Privy Chamber & Governor General under his royal Highness James, Duke of York & Albany & his territories in the Americas send greetings. Whereas there is a tract of land granted by the officers of Delaware to Abraham Coffin a tract of land lying on the north side of Appoquinimink Creek bounded by the creek & land of Jacob Fiena containing 400 acres & a reasonable part of marsh land below Drawyers Creek for hay ground. Now confirmed to Abraham Coffin & he paying 4 bushel of winter wheat to persons of authority. Signed Francis Lovelace. Examined by Mathias Nicolls. (A1:64).

Deed. On 10 Sep 1680, the [above patent] standing patent of Governor Lovelace granted to Abraham Coffin 400 acres as mentioned was sold by Coffin to Lewis John who has it in possession some time afterward run away in debt to Joseph Chew the sum of 18188 lb. of tobacco & £19.10 & the said Joseph Chew obtained a judgment at the court held in New Castle the 6 Apr 1675 against Lewis Johnson for the sum mentioned & obtained an order to appraise the estate of Lewis Johnson & the above land in Appoquinimink since which Joseph Chew remained in possession there of until he made it over to Johannes DeHaes as his deed recorded in folio 3 dated 22 June 1676 & was acknowledged 8 Nov 1676 as recorded in Liber A. (A1:65).

Patent. On 1 Oct 1672. Francis Lovelace, Esq. one of the gentlemen of his majesty, Honorable Privy Chamber & Governor General under his royal Highness James, Duke of York & Albany & his territories in the Americas send greetings. Whereas Reyner Vande Cooly obtained patents from Col. Richard Nicolls for 2 tracts of land, one which he had purchased a lot of ground in New Castle from Harmon Reynderson Bruyn bounded by a lot then of Gov. Jacob Allrichs & land of Cornelius Wynharts & the other lot purchased of Hendrick Kipp lying at Beaver Street bounded by and of Herman Rynderson & Hart

Street. Whereas Reyner Vande Cooly sold the same unto Peter Wolferson, who have likewise made a purchase of a piece of meadow form Capt. John Carr containing 2 acres in the town bounded by land of John Webber & since conveyed to Hupbert Hendrickson. Now for confirmed to Hupbert Hendrickson & he paying 2 bushels of winter wheat to persons of authority. Signed Francis Lovelace. Examined by Mathias Nicolls. (A1:65).

Patent. On 1 Oct 1669. Francis Lovelace, Esq. one of the gentlemen of his majesty, Honorable Privy Chamber & Governor General under his royal Highness James, Duke of York & Albany & his territories in the Americas send greetings. Whereas there is a tract of land at New Castle lying behind Peter Cowenhoven's lot containing 2 or 3 morgans or 5 or 6 acres. Now confirmed to Peter Cowenhoven & he paying 1 bushel of winter wheat to persons of authority. Signed Francis Lovelace. Examined by Mathias Nicolls. (A1:66).

Patent. On 16 Feb 1674. Anthony Colve in the behalf of the high & mighty Lords the States General of the United Netherlands & his serene highness the Lord Price of Orange, etc. Governor General send greetings. Whereas the late commander John Carr in Delaware River granted unto Casperus Herman a tract of land below New Amstell on the south side of Appoquinimink Creek which said grant has since 5 Feb instant, renewed by commander Peter Allrichs. By the request of Ephraim & Casparus Herman I granted to Ephraim & Casparus the tract of land mentioned bounded by Drick Creek, St. Augustine Creek or Arins Creek containing 250 morgan more of less with express conditions that Ephraim Herman & Casparus Herman or whoever purchases their interest shall acknowledge the mighty lords the State General of the United Netherlands & his serene highness the Lord Prince of Orange to be the lawful proprietor. Signed in the Fort of William Hendrick in New Netherland. A. Colve. N. Bayard. (A1:67).

Patent. On 21 Mar 1676. Edmund Andros, Esq. Lieut. Governor General under his royal highness, James, Duke of York & Albany & the territories in the Americas send greetings. Whereas there is a tract of land on a branch of Christiana Creek called White Clay Creek above the falls on the upper side of land of John Nommers, which by virtue of a warrant was laid for Peter Thomason containing 220 acres. Now confirmed to Peter Thomason & he paying 2 bushels of wheat to persons of authority. Signed E. Andros. Examined by Mathias Nicolls. (A1:68).

On the back of the patent.

Deed. On 4 Dec 1680. Oele Thomason, brother & only heir of Peter Thomason, dec. for consideration granted to Peter Oilson (alias Tecco) one equal half part of the said described land. Signed Oele Thomason. Delivered in the presence of Hendrick Limmons, Charles Rumsey & Eph. Herman. (A1:69).

Survey. On 26 July 1678. Walter Wharton, surveyor, surveyed for Roeloff Andreson a tract of land called High Hook on the north side of Appoquinimink Creek bounded by Drawyers Creek, land of Claus Kirston, land of Casparus Herman & land of John Arinson containing 280 acres. Signed Walter Wharton. (A1:70).

Patent. On 21 Mar 1676. Edmund Andros, Esq. Lieut. Governor General under his royal highness, James, Duke of York & Albany & the territories in the Americas send greetings. Whereas there is a lot in the town of New Castle which by virtue of a warrant was laid out to Henry Vander Burch, bounded by the river, the common, a lot of James Wallems. Now confirmed to Henry Vander Burch & he paying 1 bushel of winter wheat to persons of authority. Signed Edmund Andros. Examined by Mathias Nicolls. The above patent was recorded at the request of Engelbirt Lot, shoemaker, who owns the above lot. (A1:70).

By virtue of a warrant from the court of New Castle dated 8 Nov 1678. Laid out for Engelbirt Lot, 2 lots in the town of New Castle, 1 which lot being the same whereon the old Fort stood, the other being a lot formerly laid out for Hendrick Vander Burch & the said Lot shall leave a sufficient street at the water side laid out 24 May 1679. Signed E. Cantwell. (A1:71)

Deed. On 19 Aug 1684 Arnoldus Delagrange of the county of New Castle to Robert Robinson of Christiana Creek. Arnoldus Delagrange for £40 granted to Robert Robins a tract of land bounded by land of Lucas Stidham, other land of Arnoldus Delagrange, land of John Stalcop containing 200 acres. Signed Arnoldus Delagrange. Delivered in the presence of John White, George Moore & Hans Peterson. Recorded 16 Sep 1684. (A1:72).

Declaration. On 16 Sep 1684. Whereas I, Gabriel Rappe of St. Martin in France have bought of John Moll of New Castle his plantation called the Exchange lying in Reeten Point Neck containing 1000 acres, ratified & confirmed on 3 Dec last & recorded 5 Dec last & recorded in the following day by William Welsh. Now I, Gabriel Rappe do declare that although I have bought the said plantation in my own name, that never the less, it was bought for Mr. Daniel Duthy of London, merchant, provided that Mr. Duthy shall pay for the said land. Upon request of Gabriel Rappe, I, John Moll be fully satisfied when I receive £285 & shall convey said land to Mr. Daniel Duthy of London. Signed G.Rappe & Jno. Moll. Delivered in the presence of John Cann, John Williams Neering,

James William & Lunder William Neering. Recorded 16 Sep 1684. (A1:73).

Deed. On 9 Apr 1681 Lucas Peterson of Delaware River to Henrick Franson of Swanwick. Lucas Peterson for a certain sum of money paid to my son Jonas Schargin granted to Hendrick Franson a tract of land lying at Swanwick between the farms of Peter Duvill & Jan Barrettson being in breadth 40 rods & in length 400 rods. Signed Lucas Peterson & Jonas Schargin. Delivered in the presence of Peter Allrichs & William Temple. (A1:74).

Deed. On 20 Aug 1684. Hendrick Franson, late of Swanwick to Ambrose Baker of the town of New Castle. Hendrick Franson granted to Ambrose Baker all the above described tract. Signed Hendrick Franson. Delivered in the presence of Ed. Cantwell, Mathias Diring & William Cruse. Recorded 20 Aug 1684. (A1:74).

Survey. On 15 Aug 1684 Ep. Herman, surveyor laid out to George Moore a tract of land called Putney lying on the west side of the Delaware River, south of the southern most branch of Christiana Creek bounded by land of Samuel Land & land of Gils Barrett containing 185 acres. Signed Ep. Herman. (A1:75)

Deed. I, George Moore of New Castle do assign all might right to said tract to Job Nettleship & Edward Boulton. Signed George Moore. Recorded Aug 1684. (A1:75).

Patent. On 5 Aug 1684. William Penn by the Kings authority, proprietary & Governor of the province of Pennsylvania, New Castle & other territories, send greetings. Whereas there is a tract of land called Brussells lying about 6 miles below the town of New Castle, back in the woods between Maryland & Appoquinimink Roads bounded by land of John Williams, the Maryland Road, a run called Mr. Tom's Run, land which was formerly Olla Poulson & since bought by Hendrick Limmons, land laid out to Hans Corderus & Red Lyon Run containing 420 acres which 220 acres thereof is the land Hendrick Limmon bought of Olla Poulson & the other 200 acres is the land laid out for Hendrick Limmons & also 25 acres of meadow land lying south of Red Lyon Creek bounded by land of John William & the creek, which said meadow & 220 acres tract was by virtue of a warrant surveyed for Olle Poulson on 2 Oct 1682. Now confirmed to Hendrick Limmons & he paying 1 bushel of winter wheat per 100 acres. Signed William Penn. (A1:75).

Patent. On 26 Mar 1684. William Penn by the Kings authority, proprietary & Governor of the province of Pennsylvania, New Castle & other territories, send greetings. Whereas there is a tract of land in the county of New Castle called

Westminster on the south side of White Clay Creek bounded by the creek containing 140 acres granted by the Governor Penn by a warrant dated 1 Sep 1683 & laid out to Peter Classon, who assigned it over to Jonas Arskin. Now confirmed to Jonas Arskin & he paying 1 bushel of winter wheat per 100 acres. Signed William Penn. (A1:76).

Patent. On 26 Mar 1684. William Penn by the Kings authority, proprietary & Governor of the province of Pennsylvania, New Castle & other territories, send greetings. Whereas there is a tract of land called Barren Point on the north side of the main branch of Christiana Creek bounded by Muddy branch containing 200 acres granted to Jonas Arskins. Now confirmed to Jonas Arskins & he paying 1 bushel of winter wheat per 100 acres. Signed William Penn. (A1:77).

Patent. On 26 Mar 1684. William Penn by the Kings authority, proprietary & Governor of the province of Pennsylvania, New Castle & other territories, send greetings. Whereas there is on the north side of White Clay Creek called the Hopyard bounded by the creek containing 430 acres granted by a warrant from me, William Penn dated 18 Oct & part by a warrant dated 5 July 1683 to John Ogle. Now confirmed to John Ogle & he paying 1 bushel of wheat per 100 acres. Signed William Penn. (A1:78).

Deed. On 4 Jan 1683. Justa Anderson of the town of New Castle, planter & Elke his wife to Magnus White, late of Boston, now of New Castle. Justa Anderson & Elke his wife for £100 granted to Magnus White a tract of land called Abrahams Delight, lately purchased of Abraham Inglos, lying on the north side of St. Augustine Creek bounded by land of Peter Allrichs containing 120 acres. Signed Justa Anderson & Elke Anderson. Delivered in the presence of John Mandy & J._ackewen. (A1:79).

Deed. On 19 Nov 1684 John Pearson of the county of New Castle, planter to Christopher Ellet of the County of New Castle. John Pearson for 2000 pounds of merchantable tobacco granted to Christopher Ellet a tract of land called Pearson's Lodge, bounded by Duck Creek, land of Morris Liston, land of Michael Offley containing 126 acres. Signed John Parsons. Delivered in the presence of Casp. Herman & John White. Recorded 19 Nov 1684. (A1:79).

Deed. On 1 Sep 1684. Engelly Barns, widow of Jan Barns late of Swanwick, dec. for consideration a security to be made & given for the due payment of the portion of Branch Barns, my daughter by my husband Barns, I have granted to the county of New Castle for the time being as a court of Orphans all that part of land called Barns Land lying at Swanwick near the town of New Castle bounded by the land of Barbara Marslander, land of John Hulks & lands of Aron

Johnsons, last in the possession of Jan Barns, my late husband & now in the possession of me, Engelly Barns. To hold the said court of Orphans of New Castle for the time being, provided that if the said Engelly Barns shall carefully bring up, Branch, her daughter, by her late husband Jan Barns & furnish her with meat, drick, apparel, lodging & all other necessaries at her own proper costs until the child reaches the age of 21 or the day of marriage & the said Engelly Barns shall pay to Branch, the sum of £32.10 being the 1/2 part of her father's estate. Signed Engelly Barns. Delivered in the presence of James William & John White. Recorded 16 Sep 1684. (A1:81).

Deed. On 1 Sep 1684 Engelly Barns of Swanwick, widow of Jan Barns, dec. to James Halliday of Swanwick, planter. Whereas there is a marriage intended, shortly to be had between the said James Halliday & the aforesaid Engelly Barns & the said Engelly Barns being willing & desirous to settle the inheritance of her the said Engelly Barns before marriage have granted to James Halliday the land called Barns Land in Swanwick near the town of New Castle bounded by land of Barbara Marslander, land of John Hulks & land of Arent Jansens provided that solemnization of the intended marriage & for the use of Engelly Barns during her natural life & after her decease to the use of James Halliday subject to the payment of the portion due to Branch the daughter of Engelly Barns by my late husband Jan Barns according to settlement made by deed at Orphans Court. Signed Engelly Barns & James Halliday. Delivered in the presence of James William & John White. Recorded 16 Sep 1684. (A1:82).

Deed. On 12 Aug 1684 Artman Haym of Swanwick & Matty his wife to Barbara Marslander of Swanwick. Artman Haym & Matty for £15 granted to Barbara Marslander a tract of land on the west side of the Delaware River bounded by land of Hans Black & Olle Toarson, which said land is in the possession of Barbara Marslander. Signed Artman Haym & Matty Haym. Delivered in the presence of Wm. Welsh, Jan White & Jan Land. Recorded 20 Aug 1684. (A1:82).

Patent. On 21 Mar 1676. Edmund Andros, Esq. Lieut. Governor General under his royal highness, James, Duke of York & Albany & the territories in the Americas send greetings. Whereas there is a tract of land called Good Neighborhood, lying on the northeast side of St. Augustine's Creek laid out by virtue of a warrant to Casparus Herman bounded by the swamp, land of George Axton & the creek containing 330 acres. Now confirmed to said Casparus Herman & he paying 3 bushels of wheat to persons of authority. Signed Ed. Andros. Examined by Mathias Nicolls. (A1:84).

Deed. On 1 Mar 1679. Casparus Herman for good reasons granted to Jan

Biscus, Martin Garrettson & Mathyasan Divos all right to said patent. Signed Casparus Herman. Delivered in the presence of Eph. Herman & Margell Baron. Recorded 1684. (A1:84).

Deed. On 19 Nov 1684. John Biscus, Roaloffe Anderson & Matthyas Divos granted all right & interest in said patent Hibert Laurenson. Signed Jan Biscus, Roaloffe Anderson & Mathyas Divos. Delivered in the presence of Isaac Stover & John White. Casparus Herman declared in court that Roaloffe Anderson had the right of Martin Garrettson. Recorded 19 Nov 1684. (A1:85).

Survey. On 6 Mar 1682/3. By virtue of a warrant from William Penn, Esq. dated 22 Feb 1682, laid out for Hans Corderus, cooper a lot of ground in the town of New Castle to the east of a lot laid out to Eldred Egbertson, smith, the south with Mineque Street or Susquehanna Street, the west a vacant lot & north Beaver Street containing in length 162 feet & 60 foot in breadth. Signed Ep. Herman, Surveyor. (A1:85).

Deed. On 20 Nov 1683. Hans Corderus, cooper to John Hermanson of the town of New Castle, carpenter. Hans Corderus for 1 young heifer & a calf granted to John Hermanson all the before mentioned lot. Signed Hans Corderus. Delivered in the presence of Arnoldus Delagrange & Eph. Herman. Recorded 18 Nov 1684. (A1:86).

Patent. On 5 Aug 1684. William Penn by the Kings authority, proprietary & Governor of the province of Pennsylvania, New Castle & other territories, send greetings. Whereas there is a tract of land called New Nybreght lying on the north side of the main branch of St. George's Creek above the bridge bounded by land of Robert Jones, land of Robert Loams, Dragon Swamp & land of Darby & Parker containing 1000 acres granted by warrant, 600 acres by warrant dated 1 Oct 1683 & 400 acres by warrant dated 21 Feb 1682 laid out & now confirmed to Henry Vandenburgh. Signed William Penn. (A1:86).

Patent. On 22 Jul 1684. William Penn by the Kings authority, proprietary & Governor of the province of Pennsylvania, New Castle & other territories, send greetings. Whereas there is a tract of land called Poplar Neck on the north side of Red Lyon branch bounded by land of Olle Poulson containing 200 acres granted by a warrant dated 27 Feb 1682 & laid out to Hans Corderus, who by deed dated 10 Jan 1683 granted to Hendrick Vandenburgh & now confirmed unto Henry Vandenburgh. Signed William Penn. (A1:87).

Patent. On 26 Mar 1684. William Penn by the Kings authority, proprietary & Governor of the province of Pennsylvania, New Castle & other territories, send greetings. Whereas there is a tract of land on the south side of White Clay Creek bounded by land of John Smith, the swamp, containing 98 acres including a small island containing 10 acres which by virtue of a warrant dated Sep 1682 & laid out for John Nomers & now confirmed to John Nomers. Signed William Penn. (A1:88).

Patent. On 5 Aug 1684. William Penn by the Kings authority, proprietary & Governor of the province of Pennsylvania, New Castle & other territories, send greetings. Whereas there is a tract of land called Four Brothers lying on the south side of the southern most branch of Christiana Creek bounded by Christiana Creek & Doctor Spry's land containing 316 acres granted by warrant & laid out by Ephraim Herman, the then surveyor on 12 Aug 1682 to Samuel Land of New Castle, planter & now confirmed unto Samuel Land. Signed William Penn. (A1:89).

Patent. On 5 Aug 1684. William Penn by the Kings authority, proprietary & Governor of the province of Pennsylvania, New Castle & other territories, send greetings. Whereas there is a tract of land Ommeland bounded by the river, Great Creek, the King's Road & the valley containing 1473 acres granted by warrant dated 23 Feb 1682 to Peter Allrichs & now confirmed to Peter Allrichs. Signed William Penn. (A1:90).

Power of Attorney. On 5 Oct 1682. Thomas Taylor of the City of Bristol, mariner for employers Charles Jones & Company, merchants of Bristol have appointed my loving friend, William Frampton of Philadelphia to be my lawful attorney for me & my employers to recover monies due. Signed Thomas Taylor. Delivered in the presence of John Moll & John White. (A1:90).

Survey. On 5 Oct 1682. By virtue of a warrant from Edmund Andros, Governor & confirmed by the court laidout for James Crawford a tract of land called Rowls Grats lying nearest Duck Creek bounded by land of James Beswicke, land of Michael Offly, land of William Sharke & Thomas Bell containing 400 acres. Signed Eph. Herman. (A1:91).

Deed. On 21 July 1685. Judith Crawford, widow & executrix of James Crawford, dec. to James Rowland, mariner. Judith Crawford granted to Samuel Rowland all the afore mentioned 400 acres. Signed Judith Crawford. Delivered in the presence of Eph. Herman & Jan Jacquet. Recorded 1 Aug 1685. (A1:91).

Deed. On 26 June 1685. Olle Poulson of the County of New Castle, to Henry Lemmon of the County of New Castle. Olle Poulson granted to Henry Lemmon a tract of land containing 220 acres & 25 acres of marsh called Poplar Neck bounded by land of John Williams. Signed Olle Poulson. Delivered in the presence of John Harmon, Arent Gannen & John White. Recorded 143 Aug 1685. (A1:92)

Deed. on 21 July 1685. Peter Abrink of Appoquinimink to Adam Peterson. Peter Abrink for £17.10 granted to Adam Peterson a tract of land on the north side of Appoquinimink Creek called Nustiel bounded by the cart road which goes to the head of Bohemia Landing near the house of Adam Peterson, land of Daniel Lindsey containing 1909 acres granted by virtue of a warrant dated 11 Oct 1682 to Peter Abrink. Signed Peter Abrink. Delivered in the presence of John Mandy & John White. Recorded 13 Aug 1684. (A1:93).

Deed. On 21 July 1685. Olla Toarson, son of Olla Toarson late of the county, dec. to Barbara Marslander of Swanwick. Olla Toarson for £75 granted to Barbara Marslander all his right & interest in a tract of land by patent granted to his father, Olla Toarson by patent & all the land his father purchased of Lucas Peterson being in Swanwick now in the tenure of Barbara Marslander by a contract dated 22 Dec 1679 agreed to with the said Olla Toarson, & Else Toarson, widow of Olla Toarson, to Peter Marslander, late husband of the said Barbara Marslander, now on payment of the last sum agreed upon Ola Toarson confirmed said land to Barbara Marslander. Signed Olla Toarson. Delivered in the presence of John Cann & John White. Recorded 14 Aug 1685. (A1:93).

Patent. On 22 Dec 1684. Thomas Lloyd, James Claypoole & Robert Turner, or any two of them being appointed commissioners by William Penn, Governor, send greetings. Whereas there is a tract of land called Burwick being on the south side of Christiana Creek bounded by land of Charles Rumsey, land of Englebrit Lots containing 436 acres by a warrant from the Governor dated 13 May 1684 & laid out to Hendrick Vandenburgh & now confirmed to Hendrick Vandenburgh. Signed James Claypoole & Robert Turner. Recorded 20 Aug 1685. (A1:94).

Patent. On 5 Aug 1684. William Penn by the Kings authority, proprietary & Governor of the province of Pennsylvania, New Castle & other territories, send greetings. Whereas there is a tract of land called Rockland lying on the north side of Swerrill Creek bounded by land of Jacob Hendrickson, Brandywine Creek, containing 400 acres granted by warrant dated 23 Feb 1682 to Mathyas Divos & confirmed to Mathyas Divos. Signed William Penn. (A1:97).

Letter of Attorney. On 10 July 1685. Isaac Kingsland of New Barbadoes of East New Jersey in the county of Essex, the lawful attorney for Nathaniel Kingsland of the Island of Barbados, Esq. by Power of Attorney remaining now in the

Secretaries Office of this Province have appointed Edward Gibben of the Province of Pennsylvania, merchant, the lawful attorney of Nathaniel Kingsland to receive of Peter Allridge on New Castle, several negroes both men, women & children & if the said Edward Gibbens shall peacefully deliver up the same the Edward Gibbens to give receipts or discharges as law requires & upon refusal shall prosecute. Signed Isaac Kingsland. Delivered in the presence of Ch. Gordon, George Willocks & Ja. Emmett. (A1:97).

Patent. On 5 Aug 1684. William Penn by the Kings authority, proprietary & Governor of the province of Pennsylvania, New Castle & other territories, send greetings. Whereas there is a tract of land on the north side of White Clay Creek bounded by Brewers Run & Mill Run containing 400 acres granted by warrant dated 15 Sep 1682 to John Smith & Joseph Cookson & Joseph Cookson by deed dated 8 Dec 1683 granted his part to John Cann & now confirmed to John Cann & John Smith. Signed William Penn. (A1:98)

Deed. On 13 Apr 1685. Christian Jurianson, the eldest son of Andries Jurianson, dec. an now of the full age of 21 years & upwards, whereas I do find the court of New Castle on 7 & 8 May 1678 for several good reasons & for the best benefit of myself & my other brothers now still in minority agree with my father in law, Brewer Sennexen that he the said Brewer Sennexen should bring up & maintain my other 4 brothers until they come of age at which time he is to pay unto us the said children the full sum of 2500 gilders to be distributed equally amongst us the said orphans or marriage in consideration whereof he the said Brewer Sennexen is to have the plantation & personal estate of my dec. father Andries Juriansen. And since I satisfied that what the court above said in our behalf was for our good & do hereby approve what the courts have done in mine & by brothers behalf & with our father in law, Brewer Sennexen, I hereby confess to have received 500 guilders which was my share of 2500 gilders. Signed Christian Juriansen. Delivered in the presence of Mathyas Vanderhden, Lyman Whitewill & Eph. Herman. (A1:99).

Memorandum. On 28 Jan 1684. John Barker of Blackbird Creek, tailor to Isaac Welden of Philadelphia, skinner. John Barker for £27 granted to Isaac Welden all right in my plantation where I now live in Blackbird Creek containing 200 acres. John Barker doth hereby promise to pay penalty sum of £50 to surrender & acknowledgment of the same land in court to maintain the title of the said land. Signed John Barker. Delivered in the presence of E. Priscot, Mary Barker, Daniel Smith & John Foster. (A1:100).

Deed. On 20 Apr 1685. Brewer Sennexen of Christiana Creek, husbandman to Humphry Best & Edward Green both of Philadelphia. Brewer Sennexen for £60 granted to Humphry Best & Edward Green a one full half part, being the lower section, of a tract of land by patent from Gov. Edmund Andros dated 5 Mar 1676 granted to Peter Thomason & since on 4 Dec 1682 by Olla Thomason the brother & only heir of Peter Thomason, dec. to Peter Oalson, alias Pecco, late of Christiana Creek, planter, who by deed dated 9 Dec 1682 granted the same land to Brewer Sennexson, the said land being White Clay Creek above the falls bounded by land of John Nommer containing 220 acres. Signed Brewer Sennexen. Delivered in the presence of Eph. Herman & Daniel Smith. Recorded 23 Apr 1685. (A1:101)

Deed. On 28 Mar 1685. Peter Andries Hallman of Verdred Hook in the county of New Castle, successor & administrator of the estate of Lasse Oalson, dec. of the same place to Hans Peterson of the county of New Castle. Peter Andries Hallman for £15.16 granted to Hans Peterson a tract of land on Verdred Hook bounded by land of Suker Oalson containing 50 acres. Signed Peter Andries Hallman. Delivered in the presence of Jer. Collett, Cornelius Empson & John White. Recorded 16 June 1685. (A1:102).

Bond. On 12 June 1685. I, Peter Allrichs of New Castle stand bound to Charles Jones of Bristol & Company, merchants in the sum of £82, with the sum of £41 to be paid to the said Charles Jones & Company on 12 Dec next. Signed Peter Allrichs. Delivered in the presence of William Hagen & Cornelius Purt. (A1:103).

Bond. On 16 June 1685. I, Edmund Cantwell of New Castle do justly stand indebted & bound to Charles Jones of Bristol & Company, merchants for the sum of £67.19 conditioned on payment of £33.19.6 in coin only, in the town of Philadelphia at or before 6 Dec next. Signed E. Cantwell. Delivered in the presence of William Hig, Hans Coderus & John Baker. Memorandum. On 16 June 1685, it is mutually agreed by & between Edmund Cantwell & Thomas Taylor, agent for Charles Jone & Company, that the said Edmund Cantwell shall pay the sum mentioned in the within bond in coin or in merchantable leaf tobacco. Signed Thomas Taylor, E. Cantwell. Delivered in the presence of William Haig & Hans Corderus. Mr. Hallawell, the successor of Edmund Cantwell produced a receipt in full from (the attorney of Charles Jones & Company) Andries Robins on 6 Dec 1687 for the above bond. (A1:104).

Bond. On 11 June 1685. William Guest & John Cann of the county of New Castle justly stand indebted & bound to Charles Jones of Bristol & Company, merchants for the sum of £48 conditioned on payment of £23.13.10 in coin only, in the town of Philadelphia at or before 10 Dec next. Signed Wm. Guest & John Cann. Delivered in the presence of William Haig, John Walker &

Wiborough Walker. (A1:105).

Deed. On 24 Nov 1677. John Edmundson of Talbot County in the province of Maryland to John Moll of the town of New Castle. John Edmundson granted to John Moll a house & lot of land, with the houses standing on & belonging to the same right & title which John Edmundson bought the house from Martin Rosamond, dec. in the town of New Castle bounded by the land of Peter Allrichs, the street & the house that Martin Rosamond went to live after said purchase. Signed at Treat Haven Creek in Maryland, John Edmundson. Delivered in the presence of John Stanley & John Morely. Acknowledged said bill of sale to be his voluntarily act & cede before us in New Castle 23 May 1685. Signed John Cann, James William & William Guest, Justices of the County. (A1:105).

Deed. On 2 June 1685. John Walker of New Castle to Andrew Peterson of Cecil County, Maryland. John Walker for £12 granted to Andrew Peterson a tract called New Saxony lying on Drawers Creek bounded by Saxon branch & Walker branch containing 150 acres confirmed by patent from Gov. Penn dated 26 Mar 1684. Signed John Walker. Delivered in the presence of Giles Barret, Mary White & John White. Recorded 29 June 1685. (A1:106).

Deed. On 2 June 1685. Mary Block & Barbara Marslander of Swanwick & Christian Stalcop of Christiana to Cornelius Empson of Skillpot Creek. Mary Block, Barbara Marslander & Christian Stalcop for 450 gilders granted to Cornelius Empson a tract of land near Mill Creek that falls into Skillpot Creek by a dutch patent dated 16 May 1663 . Signed Mary Block, Barbara Marslander & Christian Stalcop. Delivered in the presence of William Phillips, Edward Land & George Moore. Recorded 29 June 1685. (A1:107).

Affidavit. On 27 June 1685. Humphry Davenport saith that on 21 June 1685 did hear Elizabeth Ogle, widow of John Ogle say that as soon as she was able she would pay Capt. Minveil his debt that was contracted by her husband of John Coderus for she said that she was now not able to pay the bill of 11 beavers further saith not. Sworn before me 27 June 1685. James William. Registered 29 June 1685. (A1:108).

Affidavit. On 27 June 1685. Robert Hutchinson saith that on 21 June 1685 did hear Elizabeth Ogle, widow of John Ogle say that as soon as she was able she would pay Capt. Minveil his debt that was contracted by her husband of John Coderus for she said that she was now not able to pay the bill of 11 beavers further saith not. Sworn before me 27 June 1685. James William. Registered 29 June 1685. (A1:108).

Articles of Agreement. On 2 July 1685. John White of the town of New Castle to Susanna Welsh of the town of New Castle. John White for £150 to be paid sold his house in the town of New Castle to Susannah Welsh to be delivered to Susannah Welsh on 29 Sep next & on delivery Welsh shall pay £20, then £10 when convenient, £20 by the end of the year which will 29 Sep 1686 & £50 on 29 Sep 1687, £50 29 Sep 1688 & the said John White shall have use of the log house until 25 Mar next. Signed John White & Susannah Welsh. Delivered in the presence of Sarah Welsh & Sara Budd. (A1:108).

Deed. On 4 Apr 1685. Henry Vandenburgh of New Castle, merchant to William Hague of the province of East New Jersey, gentleman. Henry Vandenburgh for £45 granted to William Hague a tract of land called Bud-wick lying on the south side of Christiana Creek bounded by land of Charles Rumsey & land of Angle Bratt Lot containing 436 acres. Signed Henry Vandenburgh. Delivered in the presence of Samuel Land, John White & Richard Blackleach. Recorded 24 Apr 1685. (A1:109).

Bond. On 30 Apr 1685. William Tate of the county of New Castle is indebted to John Jacquet of Swanwick, administrator of the estate of Peter DeWit in the sum of £33 12 shillings which he shall pay £16 16 shillings 6 pence or merchantable corn shall be paid to John Jacquet. Signed William Shute. Delivered in the presence of Samuel Land & John White. Recorded 5 June 1685. (A1:111).

Deed. On 30 Mar 1685. Artman Haym of Swanwick to John Jacquet, Jr. Artman Haym for £25 granted to John Jacquet a tract of land bounded by the land of Catherine Johnson & Belchy the widow of Herman Johnson., excepted that Artman Haym shall reserve all the marsh lying on the south sid of the creek called Forkins Kill. Signed Artman Haym. Delivered in the presence of John Mandy & John White. Recorded 23 Apr 1685. (A1:112).

Deed. On 27 Mar 1685. Hans Peterson of the County of New Castle to Cornelius Empson of Skillpot Creek. Hans Peterson for £625 which £125 has already been paid & the £500 being secured, granted to Cornelius Empson all those tracts of land called Wilde Hook & Chestnut Hill bounded by Mattson's Run containing 103 acres & a tract bounded by Wilde Hook containing 133 acres as by survey dated 23 & 25 Oct 1680 by a warrant granted from the court of New Castle on 2 Mar 1677/8 & another tract at Wilde Hook bounded by Skillpot Kill containing 600 rod being land was by patent from Governor Lovelace confirmed to Andries Matson as the by patent dated 14 Nov 1668 & since made over to Hans Peterson & another tract on Skillpot Kill containing 157 acres confirmed by Governor Andros to Hans Peterson of 5 Nov 1675 as described in patent, all such lands being 600 acres of land more or less & is now in the tenure of Cornelius Empson with the exception that Cornelius Empson is to pay Hans Peterson £500 on 5 Feb 1686 either in the town of New Castle or in the City of London in England & if not paid Hans Peterson may repossess land as if this deed was never made. Signed Hans Peterson & Cornelius Empson. Delivered in the presence of Jer. Collet & John White. Recorded 16 June 1685. (A1:113).

Patent. On 25 Mar 1676. Edmund Andros, Esq. Lieut. Governor General under his royal highness, James, Duke of York & Albany & the territories in the Americas send greetings. Whereas there is a lot of land in the town of New Castle laid out to Samuel Land bounded by a lot of John Moll, the commons, Mingus Street. Now confirmed to Samuel Land & he to pay 1 bushel of winter wheat to persons of authority. Signed Edmund Andros. Examined by Mathias Nicolls. (A1:115).

Patent. On 9 Oct 1683. William Penn by the Kings authority, proprietary & Governor of the province of Pennsylvania, New Castle & other territories, send greetings. Whereas there is a lot of land in the town of New Castle on Land Street bounded by the lot of Hendrick Vandenburgh, a lot of William Crosse granted by warrant dated 18 Oct 1683 by myself to Girbert Derkson. Now confirmed to Girbert Derkson & he paying 1 bushel of wheat to persons of authority. Signed William Penn.

Deed. On 2 Apr 1685 John Moll of the town of New Castle, to William Rakestraw, late of Oxfordshire in England. Whereas Charles Rumsey by patent of confirmation from Gov. Edmund Andros dated 25 Mar 1676 granted to Charles Rumsey & Walraven Johnson Defox a tract of land on the upper half of Bread & Cheese Island bounded by White Clay Creek & land of John Edmunds containing 570 acres & Walraven Johnson Defox made over on 24 May 1675 all his right to said land to Charles Rumsey. Charles Rumsey by deed did dispose of said land as follows: to John Cann, which is now in the possession of Joseph Barns about 60 acres on the upper west end of the whole tract, John Watkins, the sawer & Samuel Barker, which now in the possession of John Cann 300 acres being on the lower end of the tract & the remainder 210 acres to me, John Moll. Now John Moll for £80 granted to William Rakestraw all right to the 210 acres. Signed John Moll. Delivered in the presence of Eph. Harman, Arnoldus Delagrange & William Backman. Note: On 20 Apr 1685 Christian Moll, wife of John Moll of the town of New Castle & John Moll, Jr. son of the said John Moll & Christian his wife, do hereby freely consent to the sale of the land to William Rakestraw. Signed Christian Moll & John Moll, Jr. Delivered in the presence of Eph. Herman [Harmon & Herman seem to be the same person but this is the way both were spelled in the document], Arnoldus Delegrange, William

Backman & John White. Recorded 21 Apr 1685. (A1:117).

Mortgage. On 21 Apr 1685. William Rakestraw, late of Oxfordshire in England but now of the county of New Castle to John Moll of New Castle. William Rakestraw for £87 10 shillings to be paid in 3 payments, granted to John Moll a tract of land situated on White Clay Creek bounded by land of John Cann in the possession of Joseph Barns, land of John Watkins & Samuel Barns containing 210 acres. Signed William Rakestraw. Delivered in the presence of Eph. Herman, Arnoldus Delagrange & William Backman. Recorded 26 May 1685. (A1:118).

Patent. On 5 Aug 1684. William Penn by the Kings authority, proprietary & Governor of the province of Pennsylvania, New Castle & other territories, send greetings. Whereas there is a tract on the west side of the town of New Castle called Stein Bakers at Brickmakers Point bounded by the marsh laid out for 12 acres & granted by warrant dated 18 Oct 1683 to John Williams Nearing. Now confirmed to John Williams Nearing & he paying 1 bushel of winter wheat to persons of authority. Signed William Penn. (A1:121).

Patent. On 20 Mar 1684. William Penn by the Kings authority, proprietary & Governor of the province of Pennsylvania, New Castle & other territories, send greetings. Whereas there is a tract of land on the north side of White Clay Creek bounded by Mill Run, land of Joseph Cookson, land of John Smith & land of Joseph Barns containing 400 acres which by warrant dated 15 Sep 1682 was granted to Richard Smith, who by deed dated 28 Dec last past granted the same to Samuel Land of New Castle, tailor. Now confirmed to Samuel Land & he paying 4 bushels of winter wheat to persons of authority. Signed William Penn. (A1:122).

Deed. On 16 Feb 1684. Samuel Land for consideration granted to John Cann of New Castle, all right to above patent. Signed Samuel Land. Delivered in the presence of Edward Green & Will Guest. Recorded 6 Mar 1684. (A1:123).

Patent. On 15 Nov 1684. Thomas Lloyd, James Claypoole & Robert Turner, or any two of them being appointed commissioners by William Penn, Governor, send greetings. Whereas there is a tract in the county of New Castle called Fishing Place on the Southeast side of the southern most branch of Christiana Creek bounded by the creek, Tillyps Run & Spry's Run & takes in 16 acres of marsh & in all contains 435 acres granted by warrant & laid out on 4 Oct 1680 to John Ogle. Now confirmed to John Ogle & he paying 1 bushel of winter wheat per 100 acres, to persons of authority. Signed James Claypoole & Robert Turner. (A1:123).

Deed. On 9 Jan 1684. Elizabeth Ogle of Christiana Creek, administrator of the estate of John Ogle, lately dec. to John White of New Castle. Elizabeth Ogle for £87 10 shillings granted to John White all my right to the within mentioned patent. Signed Elizabet Ogle. Delivered in the presence of Hen. DeBurgh, Tho. Wollaston & Robert Hutchison. Recorded 19 Jan 1684. (A1:124).

Patent. On 30 July 1684. William Penn by the Kings authority, proprietary & Governor of the province of Pennsylvania, New Castle & other territories, send greetings. Whereas there is a tract called Oake Holelyin on the north side of Duck Creek adjoining the land of Joseph Moore named Bristol bounded by Moore's land containing 200 acres granted by a warrant to Joseph Griffith, by him to William Grant, who since granted to Anthony Tomkins of New York, merchant & was laid out & surveyed by Richard Noble, deputy to the surveyor on 21 Nov 1681. Now confirmed to Anthony Tomkins & he paying 2 bushels of winter wheat to persons of authority. Signed William Penn. (A1:125).

Bond. On 21 May. This bill binds me, Griffith Jones of Philadelphia, merchant to pay or cause to be paid Casparus Herman the full sum of £106 13 shillings 6 pence, that is to say £50 in current money, £22 if he can in current money if not in merchantable goods on or before 21 May next. Signed Griffith Jones. Delivered in the presence of Daniel Smith & Tho. Wollaston. Recorded 21 Jan 1684/5. (A1:126).

Whereas sundry ____ have been depending betwixt Charles Pickering & Edward Green concerning the ship friends, adventurers & other ways it is then concluded by & between the said parties that upon the final concluding & ending of said accompts the said Charles Pickering shall may or cause to be paid to the said Edward Green the sum of £80 when demanded is being provided that all tobacco bills due in Snt. Joneses Appoquinimink be delivered up which is now performed & acknowledged except three hogsheads of tobacco received by said Green from Hans Manson als. Miller for which he hath paid the like quantity from Mr. John Hilyard als it is agreed that the said Green shall with all convenient expedition this following spring cause to be shipped by New England to Philadelphia 63,000 foot of pine boards for the use of Charles Pickering for which the said Charles Green shall receive £180 of like money or the value thereof as witness this day above. Signed Charles Pickering. Delivered in the presence of John Hilyard & Samuel Buckley. (A1:126).

Deed. On 9 Jan 1684. John Watkins of Christiana Creek to Charles Rumsey of Christiana Creek. John Watkins for £50 granted to Charles Rumsey all the plantation called Nonsuch lying on the south side of Christiana Creek bounded by a little creek called Nonsuch Creek & near the head of a run called Basil Run containing 640 acres which said 640 acres was taken up & bought by John Watkins & Charles Rumsey in partnership. Signed John Watkins. Delivered in the presence of James Williams, Tho. Wollaston & John White. Recorded 21 Feb 1684. (A1:126).

Bond. On 9 Nov 1684. Arnoldus Delagrange of Christiana Creek stands in debted to Hans Peters of Skillpots Creek in the sum of £80 & with £44 to be paid to Hans Peters on or before 1 May next & for better securing said debt Arnold Delagrange does hereby mortgage unto Hans Peters a bond & mortgage of Robert Robersons it being for the sum of £40 to be paid on or before 1 Mar next. Signed Arnoldus Delagrange. Delivered in the presence of Simon Stidham & Robert White. Recorded 20 Jan 1684. This bond was acknowledged to be satisfied at court 17 Mar 1685/6. (A1:127).

Deed of Gift. On 26 Jan 1684. John Taylor of Appoquinimink give & granted Peter Tonsogoe, my son in law all my right & title to 100 acres part of 250 acres lying on the head of second Drawers Creek called West Stone. Signed John Taylor. Delivered in the presence of Samuel Buckley & John Quarterman. The above writing was acknowledged in open court by the administrix of John Taylor's estate on 2 June 1685. (A1:128).

Deed. On 4 July 1682. Edmund Cantwell, administrator of the estate of William Tom of the town of New Castle, dec. to John Williams of the town of New Castle, merchant. Whereas on 4 Feb 1678/9, I the said Edmund Cantwell did expose to sale at public outcry within the town of New Castle a island & 200 acres of land lying below the town of New Castle by the river bounded by land of Mr. William Jones called Mr. Tom's Plantation & the island called Apin Island & it was granted by Gov. Lovelace to Will Tom. Now for the satisfying of creditors of Will Tom have for 1050 gilders granted to John Williams as remaining purchaser all the said lands. Signed Ed. Cantwell. Delivered in the presence of Jo. Haes & E. Herman. Recorded Sep 1685. (A1:128).

Contract. This contract made between us Isaac Tayne & Mary Hyberts before marriage that I, Isaac give all my whole estate to my wife if I die first so long as she keep her a widow but if she shall come to marry again then shall all whole the estate return to my friends. I, Mary Hyberts do give to my husband Isaac Tayne all my whole estate to his own proper use & behoof of Isaac Tayne. Signed Isaac Tayne. Delivered in the presence of George Moore, Jan Hendrickson & Jan Bicks. (A1:129).

Deed. On 4 Oct 1685. Paul Larson of Christiana Creek & Mary his wife to Justus Anderson of the town of New Castle. Paul Larson & Mary his wife for a certain parcel of land being on Elk River by a firm deed made over & confirmed to Justus Anderson unto the said Paul Larson & granted to Justus Anderson a tract of land being in Fire Hook of Christiana Creek which said land was granted to Paul Larson by Patent from Gov. Lovelace dated 24 Mar 1668/9 & another tract of land granted by patent from Gov. Lovelace to Jurian Jansen who sold said land to Lawrene Hendrickson who sold the land to Paul Larson & said land was surveyed in one tract to Paul Larson bounded by Christiana Creek containing 200 acres. Signed Paul Larson & Mary Larson. Delivered in the presence of Samuel Land, Charles Rumsey & John White. Recorded 20 Oct 1685. (A1:130).

Patent. On 30 July 1684. William Penn by the Kings authority, proprietary & Governor of the province of Pennsylvania, New Castle & other territories, send greetings. Whereas there is a lot of land in the town of New Castle bounded by a lot of Henry Vandenburgh, Land Street & Mingus Street being land laid out to Hendrick Vandenburgh, merchant by the surveyor Edmund Cantwell on 3 July 1679. Now confirmed to Henry Vandenburgh & paying 1 bushel of winter wheat to persons of authority. Signed William Penn. (A1:131).

Patent. On 30 July 1684. William Penn by the Kings authority, proprietary & Governor of the province of Pennsylvania, New Castle & other territories, send greetings. Whereas there is a tract of land called Pomtrel on the north side of Duck Creek bounded by the creek, the mouth of Elliots Branch containing 315 acres granted by warrant to William Grant, passed it to Anthony Tomkins of New York, merchant. Now confirmed to Anthony Tomkins & he paying 1 bushel of winter wheat per 100 acres to persons of authority. Signed William Penn. (A1:132).

Patent. On 26 Mar 1684. William Penn by the Kings authority, proprietary & Governor of the province of Pennsylvania, New Castle & other territories, send greetings. Whereas there is a tract of land called Two Brothers on the north side of White Clay Creek bounded by the said creek containing 300 acres being granted by warrant & laid out by surveyor on 11 Aug to Thomas & John Ogle. Now confirmed to Thomas & John Ogle & they paying 1 bushel of winter wheat per 100 acres to persons of authority. Signed William Penn. (A1:133).

Patent. On 30 July 1684. William Penn by the Kings authority, proprietary & Governor of the province of Pennsylvania, New Castle & other territories, send greetings. Whereas there is a tract of land called Oxford on the north side of White Clay Creek bounded by the land called Two Brothers containing 118 acres granted by warrant from William Penn dated 5 July 1683 & laid out to John Ogle. Now confirmed to John Ogle & he paying 1 bushel of winter wheat to persons of authority. Signed William Penn. (A1:133).

Patent. On 30 July 1684. William Penn by the Kings authority, proprietary & Governor of the province of Pennsylvania, New Castle & other territories, send greetings. Whereas there is a tract of land called Mill Point on the north side of Christiana Creek bounded by land called Chestnut Wood belonging to John & Andrew Stalcop & Samuel Peterson, near the mill run called Chestnut Run, Mill Creek & land of Lucas Stedham containing 300 acres which was by warrant from myself on 17 Jan last past to Samuel Peterson of Christiana Creek & was surveyed by Thomas Peterson deputy to Wim Welsh on 16 Feb last past. Now confirmed to Samuel Peterson & he paying 1 bushel of winter wheat per 100 acres to persons of authority. Signed William Penn. (A1:134).

Patent. On 5 Aug 1684. William Penn by the Kings authority, proprietary & Governor of the province of Pennsylvania, New Castle & other territories, send greetings. Whereas there is a tract of land called New Vien on the south side of Christiana Creek bounded by the creek & land of Robert Hutchison containing 400 acres granted by warrant from myself dated Dec 1683 to John Garrettson of the county, planter. Now confirmed to John Garrettson & he paying 4 bushels of winter wheat to persons of authority. Signed William Penn. (A1:135).

Patent. On 30 Dec 1680. Edmond Andros, Esq. Lieut. Governor General under his royal highness James Duke of York & Albany & all the territories in the Americas send greetings. Whereas Capt. Edmund Cantwell by virtue of a letter of Administration on the estate of William Tom of New Castle, dec., did expose to sell at public outcry an island & a plantation thereupon granted to the said William by Gov. Nicolls & John Williams being the high bidder made purchase of the same & requests a confirmation by me & also a piece of new land lying on the back side of the island laid out by virtue of a warrant of resurveyed for the said John Williams, the said island lying about 7 miles below the town of New Castle in the butt of the river containing 60 acres additional bounded by a creek commonly called Mr. Tom's Creek, land of Peter Allrichs, the highway that leads to Maryland, a branch of Ridly & the swamp of Red Lyon Creek containing 507 1/4 acres of dry land & 50 acres of marsh. Now confirmed to John Williams & he paying 5 1/2 bushels of winter wheat to persons of authority. Signed E. Andros. Past the office John West. (A1:136).

Patent. On 29 Se9 1677. Edmond Andros, Esq. Lieut. Governor General under his royal highness James Duke of York & Albany & all the territories in the Americas send greetings. Whereas there is a lot of land & house in New Castle being towards the riverside near the old fort between the lots belonging to Reyes Mill and Claise Peterson Smith, which said house & lot did belong to Capt. John

Carr as by patent from the late Gov. Lovelace dated 1 May 1671 & said house & land having been legally attached & condemned by the court of New Castle for debts proved in court to be due from the said Capt. Carr & the same was put to public sale & by virtue there of it is in the possession of Justus Andries. Now confirmed to Justus Andries & he paying 1 bushel winter wheat to persons of authority. Signed E. Andros. Examined by Mathias Nicolls. This patent was registered for the behoof of John Williams Neering according to deed in Ephraim Hermans late Book of Records folio 53 which said deed was made from Justus Andries to said Williams. (A1:137).

Deed. On 21 Oct 1685. Marcus Lauranson to Stoffell Myers of the county of New Castle. Marcus Lauranson for 1600 gilders granted to Stoffell Myers all his tract of land being abut 2 miles from Verdrydy's Hook in the place called The Bought bounded by Dog Creek, land of Charles Peterson, Stony Creek, a creek called Poplar Branch, & the main river laid out & containing 700 acres confirmed by patent from Gov. Andros dated 15 Jan 1685 to Olla Franson, Marcus Laurenson & Neils Neilson. Marcus Laurenson sells his share to Stoffell Myers. Signed Stoffell Myers. Delivered in the presence of Charles Pickering & John White. Recorded 21 Oct 1685. (A1:138).

Deed. On 21 Oct 1685. Stoffell Myers of the county of New Castle to Thomas Clifton. Stoffell Myers for £16 granted to Thomas Clifton all his interest in a tract of land being abut 2 miles from Verdrydy's Hook in the place called The Bought bounded to the south with the run, the east with land of Neils Neilson, west with land of Olla Franson & north the woods, being part of a tract laid out & containing 700 acres confirmed by patent from Gov. Andros dated 15 Jan 1685 to Olla Transon, Marcus Laurenson & Neils Neilson, which Marcus Laurenson did by deed this date granted his interest to Stoffell Myers containing 133 acres. Signed Stoffell Myers. Delivered in the presence of Charles Pickering & John White. Recorded 21 Oct 1685. (A1:139).

Deed. On 22 Oct 1685. Jane Taylor, widow of John Taylor, dec. of Drawers Creek to Edward Green of the county of New Castle, merchant. Whereas the late John Taylor did contract with Edward Green to sell to Edward Green all his plantation called Lackford Hall situated on Drawers Creek for £100 & since dying before completely finishing the deeds of the land, requiring Jane Taylor, relict & administrix of John Taylor for £100 granted to Edward Green all that tract of land bounded by Drawers Creek, Walker's Branch, Snoding's Branch & Second Drawers Creek containing 620 acres being confirmed by patent dated 26 Mar 1684 by Gov. Penn. Signed Jane Taylor. Delivered in the presence of Charles Pickering & John White. Recorded 22 Oct 1685. (A1:140).

Patent. On 29 Jan 1684. Thomas Lloyd, James Claypoole & Robert Turner, or any two of them being appointed commissioners by William Penn, Governor, send greetings. Whereas there is a tract being on the west end of the town of New Castle bounded by land of Peter Allrichs & land of Cornelius & Mathias Deering containing 300 foot in length & 480 in breadth, granted by a warrant dated 4 June 1679 by Gov. Andros to Peter Tavehamnaker. Now confirmed to Peter Tavehamnaker & he paying 1 bushel of winter wheat to persons of authority. Signed James Claypoole & Robert Turner. (A1:141).

Patent. On 26 Mar 1684. William Penn by the Kings authority, proprietary & Governor of the province of Pennsylvania, New Castle & other territories, send greetings. Whereas there is a tract of land called Lackford Hall being on the south side of Second Drawers Creek bounded by Walker's Branch, Snoding's Branch & Second Drawers Creek containing 620 acres granted by patent dated 3 Mar & laid out by survey 21 Oct 1681 to John Taylor. Now confirmed to John Taylor & he paying 1 bushel of winter wheat per 100 acres. Signed William Penn. (A1:141).

Patent. On 1 Dec 1684. Thomas Lloyd, James Claypoole & Robert Turner, or any two of them being appointed commissioners by William Penn, Governor, send greetings. Whereas there is a tract of land called Phillips Poit on the north side of Snoding Branch bounded by the said branch, land of Phillips containing 210 acres granted by a warrant & laid out 24 Oct 1681 to William Phillips. Now confirmed to William Phillips & he paying 1 bushel of winter wheat per 100 acres to persons of authority. Signed James Claypoole & Robert Turner. (A1:142).

Patent. On 26 Mar 1684. William Penn by the Kings authority, proprietary & Governor of the province of Pennsylvania, New Castle & other territories, send greetings. Whereas there is a tract of land on the north side of Second Drawers Creek bounded by a swamp & the creek containing 220 acres, granted by a warrant dated 3 Mar & laidout 24 Oct 1681 to John Taylor. Now confirmed to John Taylor & he paying 1 bushel of winter wheat per 100 acres to persons of authority. Signed William Penn. (A1:143).

Patent. On 1 Dec 1684. Thomas Lloyd, James Claypoole & Robert Turner, or any two of them being appointed commissioners by William Penn, Governor, send greetings. Whereas there is a tract of land called Rowles Sepuckre on the north side of Drawers Creek bounded by the creek containing 250 acres granted by warrant dated 26 Dec 1677 to Walter Rowles. Now confirmed to Walter Rowles & he paying 1 bushel of wheat per 100 acres. Signed James Claypoole

& Robert Turner. (A1:143).

Patent. On 29 July 1685. Thomas Lloyd, James Claypoole & Robert Turner, or any two of them being appointed commissioners by William Penn, Governor, send greetings. Whereas there is a tract of land lying on the north side of White Clay Creek bounded by the creek, land of Abraham Man & land of John Moll containing 500 acres of land granted by warrant from ourselves dated 1 Mar 1684 to John Cann. Now confirmed to John Cann & he paying 1 bushel of wheat per 100 acres to persons of authority. Signed James Claypoole & Robert Turner. (A1:144).

Patent. On 26 Mar 1684. William Penn by the Kings authority, proprietary & Governor of the province of Pennsylvania, New Castle & other territories, send greetings. Whereas there is a several islands & other parcels of fast land on the east side of the main branch of Duck Creek now called Pompies Hook hereafter called Byard's Plantation, Sassafras Island, Great Island, Poplar Island standing in the Bay & Duck Creek containing 825 acres granted by warrant from me & laid out 5 Apr to Peter Byard. Now confirmed to Peter Byard & he paying 1 bushel of winter wheat to persons of authority. Signed William Penn. (A1:145).

Patent. On 26 Mar 1684. William Penn by the Kings authority, proprietary & Governor of the province of Pennsylvania, New Castle & other territories, send greetings. Whereas there is a tract on the east side of Red Clay Creek bounded by the creek land of Thomas Jacobson & company containing 600 acres granted by warrant dated 22 Oct 1677 to John Anderson alias Stalcop. Now confirmed to John Anderson & he paying 1 bushel of wheat per 100 acres to persons of authority. Signed William Penn. (A1:146).

Note: Whereas there was a list of debts given by Ephraim Herman to Griffith Jones, who is to stand the rest & venter of getting the same & to pay the one just half part thereof as by his engagement doth appear the number off the said bills being 52, beginning at one bill of John Richardson for 2245 pounds of tobacco & ending at number 52 at an order to Edward Isake for £4. Whereas Ephraim Herman & Richard Noble have fully assigned & set over to me, Griffith Jones of Philadelphia for the standing 52 bills, bills, orders & accounts of persons, debtors unto the said Ephraim & Richard the which I hereby acknowledge to have received to satisfaction. Therefore know all men by these presents that the said Griffith Jones do hereby bind & oblige my self to pay or cause to be paid to them the said Ephraim Herman & Richard Noble or order the full & equal just half part of all & every of the above said sums mentioned in the 52 bills & at the prices therein mentioned to be by me paid & delivered in this town of New Castle clear of all charges at or before 24 Dec next, whether I shall receive all or part thereof the true performance whereof I bind my self firmly by these presents on 20 Mar 1684. Signed Griffith Jones. Delivered in the presence of Peter Byard & E. D. Ring. [written below: the above engagement is discharged]. (A1:147).

Deed. On 7 Dec 1685. John Darby of the county of New Castle to Robert Dyer & Edward Blake, late of London in the kingdom of England, citizens. John Darby for £235 granted to Robert Dyer & Edward Blake all that tract of land or island being on the south side of Christiana Creek commonly called Swarton Nutten Island or Darby's Island containing 300 acres bounded by the Creek, by land formerly of Serjant Ersking & a little creek as by the patent from Gov. Nicolls dated 1 Jan 1667 with other tracts of land lying on Swarten Nullen Island containing 100 acres commonly called Bishye by patent dated Gov. Lovelace dated 1 Sep 1668. Signed John Darby. Delivered in the presence of James Williams, Gerardus Wessell & John White. In open court 15 Dec 1685, Elizabeth Darby, wife of John Darby & John Darby acknowledged said deed. Delivered in the presence of John Cann & Will Stocdall. Recorded 15 Dec 1685. (A1:148).

Deed. On 26 Feb 1685. John Matson of Crane Hook, farmer to Hendrick Vandenburgh of the town of New Castle, merchant. John Matson granted to Hendrick Vanderburgh all right to all my land lying on Crane Hook for 200 acres of land which Hendrick Vandenburgh is to give the said John Matson & being on the main branch of St. George's Creek & he the said John Matson is have the first choice taking 200 acres out of 1000 acres called nin a tract & Hendrick Vandenburgh to make good the title & to deliver to John Matson one good horse & John Matson to have free use of the land for 2 years of the date hereof at Crane Hook to plow & sow with the liberty of the house & outhouses, whereof John Matson with the consent of his wife bind himself. Signed John Matson & Care Matson. Delivered in the presence of Samuel Land & Hind. Lemmens. (A1:149).

Judgment. On 29 Dec 1685. We whose names are here under written being this day requested by Capt. Gabriel Rappe & Mr. John Moll to endeavor to compose arbitrate & end the business between them the said John Moll & Rappe as well as purchase of the said John Moll's plantation & land by Rappe heretofore bought as of the judgment upon the protested bill of exchange of £115 this day by the said John Moll obtained against the said Gabriel Rappe do hereby return forward & definition as follows: Imprimis that the agreement & bargain made between John Moll & Capt. Rappe for the said plantation in Reeden Point Neck with all land belonging dated 3 Sep 1683 & confirmed 3 Dec 1683 shall hereby be void & that the same from this day forward return to John Moll, he to have &

enjoy all the improvements, cultivation & other amendments of the said Rapp upon the same & that Capt. Rappe from this day further have no claim or right. The said agreement to be void & canceled. 2nd Capt. Rappe is upon demand to divide back to John Moll all the cattle which he bought & received of him which is 22 head to be at least as good as he received also 3 sows big with pigs with the hand mill & materials, 2 log chains, 1 large iron pot & a pot hanger, 2 beds & boulsters, 2 hammocks, one plaw, 1 grind stone, some covering for bedding, sundry tools & household stuff, 1 plowcoulter to be delivered back to John Moll in condition as he delivered them to Rappe. 3rd. Capt. Rappe is to make over to John Moll a certain man servant named Lewis Boniot, a husbandman for the full time of his remaining servitude to serve the said John Moll from this date & also Capt. Rappe is to discharge John Moll of a bill of £15 being due from carpenter called Elye Lucosy & lastly Capt. Rappe is now to pay his bill to John Moll within the space of 6 months the sum of £6 & is to pay all charges of this last action all which being performed by Capt. Rappe, then John Moll is to cancel his last above mentioned judgment this day obtained for £115 with the other charges & damages & both parties after the above is performed shall give good & sufficient releases & discharges to each other. Signed John Cann, Cornett Empson, Eph. Herman & Abraham Man. We, John Moll & Gabriel Rappe do fully consent & agree to the above written award & do hereby promise to punctually perform the same. Signed John Moll & Rappe. (A1:150).

Release. On 14 Jan 1685/6. I, John Moll do hereby acknowledge to have this day received from Capt. Gabriel Rappe according to the award of the arbitrators the following particulars, 1st the plantation & 100 acres of land with all whit is belonging, 2nd 22 head of cattle with the tools, bedding & implements according to the award 3rd one man servant Lewis Bonyat for his fill time of servitude, 3 sow big with pigs. Signed John Moll. Delivered in the presence of Eph. Herman & John Healy. (A1:151).

Release. I, Ephraim Herman do hereby for myself, to all intents & purposes forever discharge Griffith Jones of Philadelphia, merchant for me & Richard Noble of a certain contract & engagement made between me & Richard Noble & Griffith Jones having received full satisfaction on 16 Mar 1685/6. Signed Eph. Herman. Delivered in the presence of Henry Jones & Reneer Vander Coolen. (A1:151).

Patent. On 5 Nov 1684. Thomas Lloyd, James Claypoole & Robert Turner, or any two of them being appointed commissioners by William Penn, Governor, send greetings. Whereas there is a tract of land lying on the south side of Christiana Creek bounded by Crane Hook Land, land of Jacob Clawsons, Christiana Creek containing 200 acres granted by warrant dated 5 Jan 1678 to

Henry Lemmens. Now confirmed to Henry Lemmens & he paying 1 bushel of wheat per 100 acres to persons of authority. Signed James Claypoole & Robert Turner. (A1:152).

Deed. On 21 Apr 1685. Humphrey Best & Edward Green of Philadelphia to Brewer Sennexen of Christiana Creek, husbandman. Humphrey Best & Edward Green granted to Brewer Sennexen a tract of land being the moiety or equal half part of a patent granted by Gov. Andros to Peter Thomason, dec. dated 5 Mar 1676 for 220 acres which said land was by Olla Thomason, the brother of Peter Thomasson on 4 Dec 1682 granted to Peter Oalson alias Puro who by deed dated 9 Dec 1682 granted to Brewer Sennexson above named & Brewer Sennexson on 20 Apr this instant made over the same land to us the said Humphrey Best & Edward Green. The said land lying on White Clay Creek adjoining the land of John Nommers to hold the said half conditioned that Humphrey Best & Edward Green shall make improvements on the above said land & keep said houses & fences in good repair for the term of 3 years with the expiration being Apr 1688 & make the payment of £60 to said Brewer Sennexson if not Brewer Sennexson to take full possession of said land without any hindrance. Signed Humphrey Best & Edward Green. Delivered in the presence of Eph. Herman & Daniel Smith. Recorded 23 Apr 1685. (A1:153).

Patent. On 7 Apr 1673 Francis Lovelace, Esq. one of the gentlemen of his majesty, Honorable Privy Chamber & Governor General under his royal highness James, Duke of York & Albany & his territories in the Americas send greetings. Whereas Mathys DeRing & Emelius DeRing stand possessed of a house & lot of land in New Castle between the church yard & the lot of George Wale, now confirmed to Mathyas DeRing & Emelius DeRing & they shall pay 1 bushel of wheat to persons of authority. Signed Francis Lovelace. Examined Mathias Nicolls. (A1:154).

Deed. On 17 Mar 1685/6. John Sybrance of Fort Hook to John Prestner in Swanwick. John Sybrance for £4 granted to John Prestner a tract of marsh land situated betwixt the land of James Hallyday, the marsh of Bilchye Johnson, the creek & the river being the land lately in the occupation of Adam Hay. Signed John Sybrance. Delivered in the presence of John Moll, John White & Sybrance Johnson. Recorded 17 Mar 1685/6. (A1:155).

Deed. On 4 Jan 1685/6. Reyner Vandercoolen of the town of New Castle, innholder to Gerardus Wessells of the town of New Castle, chyrurgion. Reyner Vandercoolen granted to Gerardus Wessells a lot of land in the town of New Castle bounded by the lot of Sarah Welsh, widow, which being a parcel of land that Reyner Vandercoolen purchased of Peter Allrichs. Signed Reyner

Vandercoolen & Margaret Vandercoolen. Delivered in the presence of Garrett Smith, Nicolass Daniel Price & John Mandy. Recorded 16 Mar 1685/6. (A1:155).

Notice. On 14 Jan 1685/6. I, Gabriel Rappe do hereby acknowledge to have this day delivered full possession of the plantation & 1000 acres of land called The Exchange with all house & other appurtenances, also the cattle, hogs, tools & implements with the man servant called Lewis Bonyart for his full time of service according to the award of Arbitration to John Moll. Signed Rappe. Delivered in the presence of Eph. Herman, John Healy, Lewis Bonyart & Ferninand Rauau. (A1:156).

Certificate. This may certify all whom it may concern that I, Thomas Allen, commander of his Majesties Ketch Quaker have passed Manuell D'Bados to serve his Majesty on board the Ketch from on board the sloop supply of New York, Mr. Joseph Troy & Martin Gevin under my hand on board his majesties Ketch Quaker the 2nd day of Mary 1686. Signed Thomas Allen. This above said certificate at the request of Francis Richardson, merchant at New York was the 7th day of May 1686 registered. (A1:156).

Patent. On 22 Dec 1684. Thomas Lloyd, James Claypoole & Robert Turner, or any two of them being appointed commissioners by William Penn, Governor, send greetings. Whereas there is a tract of land called Taylors Chance on the north side of Duck Creek bounded by the said creek, land of Ellits containing 215 acres granted by warrant & laidout on 22 Oct 1681 unto John Taylor. Now confirmed to John Taylor & he paying 2 bushels of wheat to persons of authority. Signed James Claypoole & Robert Turner. (A1:157).

Notice. I, Griffith Jones of Philadelphia, merchant do hereby for myself to all intents & purposes forever discharge Ephraim Herman, late of the town of New Castle & Richard Noble, both jointly of all manner of accounts & contracts whatsoever between us from the beginning of the world to this day, having received full satisfaction. Signed Griffith Jones. Delivered in the presence of Samuel Land, Henry Jones & Reyner Vandercoolen. (A1:157).

Notice. On 17 Mar 1685/6. I, Griffith Jones of Philadelphia, merchant do hereby for myself acknowledge to stand justly indebted to Eph. Herman, late of the town of New Castle the sum of £40 of which shall be paid in 3 months time as £26 shall be paid in tobacco at the rate of 10 shillings per 100 pounds & the remaining sum of £14 shall be paid in tobacco or merchants pay equivalent to tobacco. Signed Griffith Jones. Delivered in the presence of Samuel Land, Henry Jones & Reyner Vandercoolen. (A1:157).

Notice. On 17 Mar 1685/6. I, Griffith Jones of Philadelphia, merchant do hereby for myself acknowledge to stand justly indebted to Eph. Herman, late of the town of New Castle the sum of £20 on 1 Nov next, of which shall be paid in tobacco at the rate of 10 shillings per 100 pounds, pork at the rate of 2 pence per pound, indian corn shelled at the rate of 2 shillings, 6 pence per bushel. Signed Griffith Jones. Delivered in the presence of Samuel Land, Henry Jones & Reyner Vandercoolen. (A1:157).

Deed. On 10 May 1686. Edward Greene of the county of New Castle to Benjamin Blackleach. Edward Greene for £50 granted 200 acres with a clapboard house commonly called Bridge Neck which said land joins the bridge on Drawyers Creek which said land was bought from Bryan Omella, his right by a patent signed by Gov. Andros dated 15 Jan 1675 which called this land by the name Dixon, I do hereby defend him, the said Benjamin Blackleach from the executors of the said Bryan Omella & from all other persons whatsoever for a more firm security in case of mortality I do behind over 1000 acres of lands lately surveyed & all my other estates in New Castle County real or personal to indemnify & save harmless the said Benjamin Blackleach, & I also give a bond of this date for security. Signed Edw. Greene. Delivered in the presence of James Claypoole, Jr. & Amos Nicolls. (A1:159).

Deed. On 8 Mar 1685/6. Samuel Peterson & Justa Paulson & Arman Stidham, inhabitants of the county of New Castle Hans Peterson of the county of New Castle. Samuel Peterson, Justa Paulson & Arman Stidham granted all our rights to our patent belong to a tract of land & a water mill in a creek called Skillpot Creek joined by the land of Justa Peterson to Hans Peterson. Signed Samuel Peterson, Justa Paulson & Arman Stidham. Delivered in the presence of Thomas Wollaston & Charles Rumsey. Recorded 16 Mar 1685/6. (A1:159).

Deed. On 7 Mar 1681 John Walker & Wybergh his wife of Appoquinimink to Richard Noble of Appoquinimink. John Walker & Wybergh his wife for £25 granted to Richard Noble a tract of land commonly called High Hook lying on the north side of Appoquinimink Creek just below Drawyers Creek bounded by the land of Bryan Omella & Jacobus Andries containing 200 acres which said land was formerly granted to Roalofe Andries & since was sold to John Walker, also a tract of land on the southeast side of Drawyers Creek just before High Hook containing 100 acres granted by patent from Gov. Lovelace unto my predecessor, Jan Syericks, dec. dated 4 Aug 1671. Signed John Walker & Wybergh Walker. Delivered in the presence of Eph. Herman & [name unreadable]. Recorded 20 July 1686. (A1:160).

Deed. On 2 July 1686. Edward Greene of the province of Pennsylvania, merchant to Hendrick Vandenburgh of the town of New Castle, merchant. Edward Greene granted to Hendrich Vandenburgh a tract of land on the north side of Appoquinimink Creek bounded by Drawyers Creek & the swamp containing 400 acres excepting 200 acres Edward Greene sold to a French man. Said land was patented to Clais Kerson & Bernard Brand then sold to Bryan Omella & the executors of the said Bryan Omella sold to Edward Greene. Signed Edward Greene. Delivered in the presence of Wm. Dyer, Samuel Land, Wm Dyer, Jr., Thomas Wollaston & Edward Ewster. Recorded 22 July 1686. (A1:161).

Deed. On 20 July 1686. Neils Neilson, late of the county of New Castle to Peter Baynton of the county of New Castle, merchant. Neils Neilson for £32 10 shillings granted to Peter Baynton a tract of land near Verdreytys Hook bounded by the river Delaware, Bought Creek, land of Baynton formerly belonging to Marcus Lawrenson contained in patent granted by Gov. Andros to Olla Franson, Marcus Lawrenson & Neils Neilson dated 15 Jan 1675 containing 133 acres, formerly in the tenure of Neils Neilson. Signed Neils Neilson. Delivered in the presence of Hend. Lemmens, Olla Franson & John White. Recorded 20 July 1686. (A1:162).

Deed. On 24 May 1686. Thomas Clifton of the county of New Castle to Peter Baynton of the county of New Castle, merchant. Thomas Clifton for £60 granted to Peter Baynton a tract of land near Verdrytys Hook bounded by the river, land of Neils Neilson & land of Olla Franson containing 133 acres now in the tenure of Thomas Clifton being part of land contained in patent granted by Gov. Andros to Olla Franson, Marcus Lawrenson & Neils Neilson dated 15 Jan 1675, the said Marcus Lawrenson by deed dated 21 Oct 1685 sold the same to Stoffell Myers & Stoffell Myers by his deed dated 21 Oct 1685 sold the same to Thomas Clifton. Signed Thomas Clifton. Delivered in the presence of Abraham Man, Samuel Land & John White. Recorded 20 July 1686. (A1:164).

Deed. On 21 July 1686. Edward Greene of the county of New Castle, merchant to Benjamin Blackleach, late of the county. Edward Greene for £50 granted to Benjamin Blackleach a tract of land called Dyason containing 200 acres on the north side of Drawyers Creek bounded by land of Claus Carson being by the patent dated 15 Jan 1675 from Gov. Andros granted to Bryan Omella & since sold by the executors of Bryan Omella to Edward Greene. Signed Edward Greene. Delivered in the presence of Amos Nicolls & James Bowen. Recorded 22 July 1686. (A1:165).

Deed. On 22 July 1686. Benjamin Blackleach, late of the county of New Castle to John Peterson of the said county. Benjamin Blackleach for £50 granted to

John Peterson a tract of land called Dyason containing 200 acres of land on the north side of Drawyers Creek bounded by land of Claus Carson being the tract of land Benjamin Blackleach bought of Edward Greene. Signed James Claypoole as attorney for Benjamin Blackleach. Delivered in the presence of Amos Nicolls & James Bowen. Recorded 22 July 1686. (A1:166).

Deed. On 22 July 1686. Amos Nicolls of the county of New Castle to Edmund Percus of the county of New Castle. Whereas there was laid out 2 tracts of land for Amos Nicolls, one tract of land called Newton on the south side of Scott's Run bounded by the run, the Kings road containing 525 acres surveyed on 8 Aug 1684 by Henry Holisworth & one other tract on the east side of Scott's Run between the head of Cann branch the head of St. George's Creek bounded by Scott's Run crossing the King's Road, other land of Amos Nicolls containing 200 acres of land surveyed 1 Apr 1686 by James Claypoole, Jr. Now Amos Nicolls for £28 granted to Edmund Percus 200 acres of land being part of the tract of 525 acres & part of the tract of 200 acres with that house which the said Amos Nicolls procured to be built by Thomas Louis of the county & is now in the possession of Amons Nicolls. Signed Amos Nicolls. Delivered in the presence of Richard Noble & Robert Hutchison. Recorded 22 July 1686. (A1:167).

Deed. On 20 July 1686. Adam Stidham & Benedictus Stidham, both of Brandywine Creek, husbandmen to Erasmus Stidham of Brandywine Creek. Adam Stidham & Benedictus Stidham granted to Erasmus Stidham all our right to a tract of land on the south side of Brandywine Creek of Timothy Stidham our father of Brandywine Creek, late dec. with all our right & interest after the dec. of our mother in law Christian. Signed Adam Stidham & Benedictus Stidham. Delivered in the presence of Thomas Pierson, Andries Friend & Mat. Kellis. Recorded 20 July 1686. (A1:168).

Notice of Debt. On 25 Mar 1685. Henry Patrick of the City of London, mariner & Richard Noble of the county of New Castle, merchant do acknowledge ourselves to be justly indebted to our lord the King the full sum of £1000 to which payment will be made & bind ourselves with our estate real & personal jointly. The condition of this present obligation is such that whereas the ship Dispatch of London, Henry Patrick, commander is here permitted to load on board the commodities & productions of this river now if the above ship or vessell shall carry all the goods that shall be leaden on board in the said ship to some other of his majesties english plantations & there unloaded & put the same on shore, the danger of the seas excepted & the rates & duties according to law be first paid that then this obligation be void otherwise to remain & be in full force & strength & virtue. Signed Henry Patrick & Richard Noble. Delivered in the presence of John White & Samuel Land. (A1:169).

Memorandum. On 27 Apr 1686. It is hereby agreed between Thomas Lloyd of the City of New York, gentleman & myself that in case the bills of exchange for £200 drawn by me the 1st Oct last past on the commissioners of the customs in London return protested for nonpayment then the sum & charges on the said bills & protest shall be deducted out of the £510 due to me from the Thomas Lloyd & the remainder of Lloyd's bond & debt to be fully paid & completed with the space of 2 years from the date thereof but in case the bills of exchange are answered & paid in England then the sum of £510 shall be paid with the space of 3 years from the date of the said bond in equal payments yearly, that is to say £120 annually until the whole sum of £510 is paid according to bond & agreement. Signed in New York, Thomas Lloyd & Wm. Dyer. (A1:169).

Bond. On 1 Maay 1686. I, Thomas Lloyd of the City of New York, gentleman, am held firmly bound to William Dyer of the city of New York, gentleman for the penal sum of £1020 to be paid to William Dyer in New York. The condition of the obligation is such that if the above bound Thomas Lloyd shall pay to William Dyer the full sum of £510 the in the manner following, £260 before 1 May 1687 & £260 before 1 May 1688. Signed Tho. Lloyd. Delivered in the presence of James Graham, John White & John Robins. Memorandum. That merchantable flour in cask at money prices delivered at the bridge of New York shall be accepted as payment of any of the said sums mentioned in the condition. (A1:170).

Bond. On 22 June 1686. I, Hendrick Vandeburgh of the town of New Castle, merchant am held firmly bound to William Dyer of the province of Pennsylvania, gentleman for the penal sum of £120 to be paid to William Dyer. The condition of this obligation is such that Hendrick Vandeburgh shall pay William Dyer the just sum of £60 in the form following, £30 before 25 Mar next & £30 before 25 Mar 1688. Signed Hendrick Vandeburgh. Delivered in the presence of Peter Allrichs, William Dyer, Jr., Samuel Land & Edward Ewister. (A1:170).

Notice. This day received of Mr. Mathyas & Mr. Emilius DeRinge, 3 pieces of linen that which being a full balance of all out former dealings & do by these presents discharge the aforesaid Mathyas & Emiluis DeRinge from all debts either by bill or account. Signed Pot. Gronondicke. (A1:171).

Bond. On 27 Oct 1686. I, Samuel Curtis of Alloway Creek near Salem in West New Jersey, planter, am held firmly bound to Major William Dyer of the province of Pennsylvania for the penal sum of £10 to paid Major Dyer. The condition of this obligation is such that Samuel Curtis shall pay to Major William Dyer the sum of £5 before 25 Mar next. Signed Samuel Curtis. Delivered in the presence of John Walker, Edward Ewister & William Dyer, Jr. (A1:171).

Deed. On 22 June 1686. Henry Vandenburgh of New Castle, merchant to Major William Dyer of the province. Henry Vandenburgh granted to Major William Dyer the within specified tract of land butted & bounded as mentioned. Signed Henry Vandenburgh. Delivered in the presence of Peter Allrichs, Samuel Land, William Dyer, Jr. & Edw. Ewister. I, Anna Vandenburgh, spinster the now wife of Hen: Vandenburgh do also agree to the sale of the within mentioned lands. Signed Anna Vandenburgh. Delivered in the presence of Edw. Greene & Tho. Wollaston. Recorded 22 Oct 1686. The above deed was written on the back side of a patent registered in Folio 22 P. 23. (A1:172).

Deed. On 19 Oct 1686. Woola Toolson of the county of New Castle to Adam Theo (alias) Hay of Swanwick. Woola Toolson for £20 granted to Adam Theo (alias) Hay a tract of land at Porter Hook bounded on the south by land of Artman Haynes, on the north by land of Jacob Clason, on the east by the Delaware River & the west by the woods containing 25 rod broad & 600 rod length. Signed Woola Toolson. Delivered in the presence of Tho. Pierson & John White. Recorded 19 Oct 1686. (A1:172).

Deed. On 20 Oct 1686. Roalofe Anderson & Jacob Artson, both of the county of New Castle to Isaac Decon, Jacob Decon, Robert Ashton & Richard Darken of the county of New Castle, yeomen. Whereas there is a tract of land called Chelsy on the south side of St. George's Creek bounded by land formerly granted to Peter Allrichs, the swamp, Doctor's Swamp, land surveyed for Thomas Spry, the river containing 300 acres granted to Roalofe Anderson & Jacob Artson by patent from Gov. Andros dated 24 Sep 1680. Now Roalofe Anderson & Jacob Artson for £100 granted to Isaac Decon, Jacob Decon, Robert Ashton & Richard Darken all the 300 acres. Signed Roalofe Anderson & Jacob Artson. Delivered in the presence of William Alloway & Gerardus Wessells. Recorded 22 Oct 1686. (A1:173).

Deed. On 17 Oct 1686. Justa Anderson of the town of New Castle, to John Richardson of the county of New Castle. Justa Anderson for £100 granted to John Richardson a tract of land being on Fern Hook on Christiana Creek which said land was confirmed to Paul Laurenson by patent from Gov. Lovelace dated 24 Mar 1668/9 & also a tract of land being at Fern Hook on Christiana Creek granted by a patent from Jurian Janson by Gov. Lovelace as the above patent which said Jurian Janson sold the said land to Laurans Hendrickson & by

Laurans Hendrickson to Payl Laurenson by deed dated 11 Oct 1685, which said land was surveyed in one tract bounded by Christiana Creek containing 200 acres. Signed Justa Anderson. Delivered in the presence of Tho. Pierson & John White. Recorded 23 Oct 1686. (A1:175).

Deed. On 22 Dec 1686. Humphrey Best & Edward Greene both of the County of New Castle to John Grampton of the County of New Castle, planter. Humphrey Best & Edward Greene for £60 granted to John Grampton the one full moiety & half part of a tract of land by patent from Gov. Andros dated 5 Mar 1676 granted to Peter Thomason & sold by Olla Thomason, only brother & heir of Peter Thomason, dec. on 4 Dec 1682 to Peter Oalson, late of Christiana Creek, planter, who by deed dated 9 Dec 1682 sold the same to Brewer Sennexson & the said Sennexen by deed dated 20 Apr 1685 granted the land to Humphrey Best & Edward Greene. The said land on White Clay Creek above the falls within the county of New Castle on the upper side of land of John Nommers bounded by land of Nommers & the Great Run containing 220 acres & Humphrey Best & Edward Greene granted the lower most half part to John Grampton, excepting a mortgage to Brewer Sennexen for £60 which John Grampton has intended to pay. Signed Humphrey Best & Edward Greene. Delivered in the presence of Tho. Pierson, John White & Hugh Marsland. Recorded 22 Dec 1686. (A1:177).

Articles of Agreement. On 16 Mar 1686/7. Between Peter Allrichs of the town of New Castle, gentleman & John Harmonson of the town of New Castle, carpenter. It is hereby agreed that John Harmonson shall make & build a water mill on the Great Creek on the south west side of the town of New Castle on or before 30 Oct next being agreed that the said mill shall remain in partnership the one moiety & half part to John Harmonson & it is also agreed that every working day during the time affixed for building the said mill that the said John Harmonson & John Abraham, the son in law of said Harmonson shall work the days work shall is hereby valued at 6 shillings per day to be paid half by Peter Allrichs & half by John Harmonson & diet to be allowed. Also it is agreed that there is a wind mill now standing in the town of New Castle which of right belongs to Peter Allrichs which said Peter Allrichs sell one half moiety to John Harmonson in the condition it is now standing with all buildings, stones & iron works & the said John Harmonson to pay £25 to be paid by the discount of one moiety of the 6 shillings a day for the said work on the water mill & upon finishing the water mill, Peter Allrichs will give John Harmonson 1 gold guinea to the value of 27 shillings. Signed Peter Allrichs & John Harmonson. Delivered in the presence of John Cann, Henry Burgh & John White. (A1:179).

Deed. On 15 Feb 1686/7. Adam Hay (alias) Theo of Swanwick to John Priestner of Swanwick, smith. Adam Hay for £15 granted to John Priestner a tract of land being at Pert Hook bounded by land of Jacob Clawson, land of Artman Haym, a small creek containing 500 dutch rods in length & 25 rods in breadth. Signed Adam Hay (alias) Thee. Delivered in the presence of Richard Noble & John White. Recorded 15 Feb 1686/7. (A1:180).

Deed. On 17 Apr 1687. Arnoldus Delagrange to George Robins, Richard Mankin & John Firheld. Arnoldus Delagrange granted to George Robins, Richard Mankin & John Firheld a tract of land being 158 acres being the remainder of 558 acres by the resurveyed of 1684, the said land in on the north side of Christiana Creek bounded on the east with land of Robert Robins & the Mill Creek. Signed at the manor of Ephraim Herman in Bohemia. Signed Arnoldus Delagrange. Delivered in the presence of Pieter Deconink & John Moll. Recorded 21 Apr 1687. (A1:180).

Deed. On 20 Apr 1687. Justus Anderson of the town of New Castle to Derrick Vandenburgh, late inhabitant of New York, mason. Justus Anderson for £25 granted to Derrick Vandenburgh a tract of land in the town of New Castle bounded with the house & land of John Henrickson, the house & ground of Justus Anderson & Front Street being one moiety of the said Justa Anderson's lot. Signed Justus Anderson. Delivered in the presence of John Priestner & William Chambers. Recorded 20 Apr 1687. (A1:180).

Deed. On 20 Apr 1687. Francis Huckin of the county of New Castle, carpenter, the true & lawful attorney of Edmund Perkus of the county of New Castle. Whereas there are 2 tracts of land one called Newtown situated on the south side of Scot's Run containing 520 acres as by deed from Amos Nicolls to Edward Perkus dated 22 July 1686 & also one other tract of land bounded by the former containing 200 acres also granted by Amos Nicolls to Edmund Perkus on same deed. Now Francis Huckin in the capacity of Edmund Perkus granted to John Times of the county of New Castle, merchant, 200 acres being part of both parcels. Signed Francis Huckin. Delivered in the presence of William Burrows, John Smith & John Landriken. Recorded 20 Apr 1687. (A2:181).

Deed. On 15 Sep 1684. Arnoldus Delagrange of the county of New Castle to Olla Pawells of the county of New Castle. Arnoldus Delagrange granted to Olla Pawells a tract of land on the south side of Christiana Creek called the Ferne Hook bounded by the Pawell Larse land, the Creek, other land of Delagrange & the king's road containing 200 acres. Signed Arnoldus Delagrange. Delivered in the presence of Edmund Cantwell & John White. Recorded 16 Sep. (A1:182).

Patent. On 7 Apr 1673 Francis Lovelace, Esq. one of the gentlemen of his majesty, Honorable Privy Chamber & Governor General under his royal highness James, Duke of York & Albany & his territories in the Americas send greetings. Whereas William Tom of New Castle upon Delaware has obtained a patent from my predecessor for a tract of land formerly belonging to Peter Allrichs below the town of New Castle which is in his tenure & there lying below the said land is a piece of land having no particular owner, which said William Tom has requested of me for his further accommodation. I have confirmed & granted to William Tom the 200 acres lying below the ground afore mentioned & William Tom paying 2 bushels of wheat to persons of authority. Signed Francis Lovelace. Examined by Mathias Nicolls. (A1:183).

Deed. Know all men by these presents that I, Edmund Cantwell of the town of New Castle, gentleman, by virtue if a letter of Administration to me dated 10 Nov 1677 on the estate of William Tom, dec. by the right Honorable Sir Edmund Andros, the Governor of New York, I have by these presents make over to Hans Hanson Miller all my right & title to (N.B. The residue of this deed is torn away & defaced in the old record thereof). (A1:184).

Survey. A copy of the survey of Walts Wharton surveyor, made Dec, 3, 1672, Math 10 1676. Surveyed for Roaloffe Andries a tract of land called High Hook on the north side of Appoquinimink Creek bounded by the swamp on the lower side of Drawyers Creek, land of Clawes Kerston, land of Casparus Herman, the Great Branch & land of John Arenson containing 280 acres. Signed Walt. Wharton. (A1:184).

Survey. By virtue of a warrant from court of New Castle Oct 1677. Laid out for Andries Sennexson & Brewer Sennexson a tract of land called Claysburgh on the north side of White Clay Creek bounded by the creek & Mill Brook containing 600 acres. Signed Walt. Wharton, Surveyor. (A1:185).

Patent. On 23 July 1684. William Penn by the Kings authority, proprietary & Governor of the province of Pennsylvania, New Castle & other territories, send greetings. Whereas there is a lot of land in the town of New Castle bounded on the east side by the lot of Giles Barret, on the south with Susquehanna Street, the west with a vacant lot & the north by Beaver Street granted by an order from the court of New Castle dated 8 Sep 1682 to John Cann. Now confirmed to John Cann & he paying 1 bushel of wheat to persons of authority. Signed William Penn. (A1:185).

Lower Counties of Delaware. In pursuance of a resolve of the Honorable House of Assembly of the Lower Counties on Delaware appointing us a committee for causing the several records of transactions in the several courts with the county of New Castle, relating to the titles of lands, before the year 1700 and warrants, surveys, patents, deeds, wills signed, executed & recorded before the same year in the several public offices within the county aforesaid, to be transcribed by the officers respectively in whose custody they remain & compare them with the originals and make report to the house of our proceedings as in the premises we do now humbly report to the Honorable House that we have carefully caused such parts of the same records to be transcribed as related in anywise to the titles of lands within the said county and have diligently compared the same with the original and do certify that the foregoing Book marked (A) beginning with folio 1 on the 30 Jan 1673 and ending with folio 185 on the 23 July 1684 containing nothing but true and genuine proceedings faithfully & literally copied from the original records remaining in the recorders office for the said county of New Castle. Signed Evan Rice & Tho. McKean.

NEW CASTLE COUNTY DEED BOOK B.

Deed. On 11 Feb 1686/7. Henry Everson of Crane Hooke to Hendrick Vandenburgh of the town of New Castle. Henry Everson granted to Hendrich Vandenburgh an island on the southwest side of Crane Hooke bounded on the southwest side of a creek called Bathstone Creek, northeast by land of John Gramton & bounded by the river Delaware. Signed Hendrich Everson. Delivered in the presence of Hendrick Simmons, Hans Peterson & Mathias Janson. Recorded 15 Feb 1686/7. (B2:1).

Deed. On 15 Feb 1686/7. Anthony Bryant of the town of New Castle to Hendrick Vandenburgh of the town of New Castle. Anthony Bryant for a certain sum of money granted to Hendrick Vandenburgh a tract of land on the southwest side of the town of New Castle bounded on the Northeast with land of Anthony Bryant, on the northwest with land of John White, on the southwest with the street bounding the Dominy's land & on the southeast with the street to the river being 180' in breadth & 300 feet in length. Signed Anthony Bryant. Delivered in the presence of Hendrick Simmons, John Nomers & John Gramton. Recorded 15 Mar 1686/7. (B2:2).

Deed. On 15 Mar 1686/7. Elizabeth Ogle, widow & administratrix of John Ogle, dec. to Hendrick Vandenburgh of the town of New Castle. Elizabeth Ogle for £28 granted to Hendrick Vandenburgh a house & lot of land being in the town of New Castle bounded on the northeast by Brewers Street, the northwest with the street which runs from the river to Brewers Street, the southeast with the Market place & the southwest with the log house of George Moore being in breadth 120' & in length 190'. Signed Elizabeth Ogle. Delivered in the presence of Reynier Vander Coolsen & John White. Recorded 15 Mar 1686/7. (B2:3).

Deed. On 16 Feb 1686/7. Jacob Young, late of St. George's Creek to Hendrick Vandenburgh of the town of New Castle. Jacob Young for £30 granted to Hendrick Vandenburgh a tract of land called Doctors Commons on the south side of St. George's Creek bounded by the Creek, land of Mrs. Ann Whales & the swamp containing 160 acres which was formerly purchased by Jacob Young from Thomas Spry, of the town of New Castle, chirurgion by deed dated 2 Feb 1679/80. Signed Jacob Young. Delivered in the presence of Mary White, John Roe & John White. Recorded 15 Mar 1686/7. (B2:4).

Deed. On 11 Feb 1686/7. John Mattson, alias Sireek of Crane Hook to Hendrick Vandenburgh of the town of New Castle. John Mattson, alias Sireek for a certain sum of money granted to Hendrick Vandenburgh a tract of land in Crane Hooke bounded by the church, the Delaware River & land of John Gramton containing 2 lots. Signed John Mattson. Delivered in the presence of Hendrick Simmons, Hans Peterson, Hendrick Everson & Mathias Janson. Recorded 15 Feb 1686/7. (B2:5).

Patent. On 30 July 1684. William Penn, Governor of the Province of Pennsylvania, New Castle & other territories to John Harmonson of New Castle, carpenter. Whereas there is tract of land called Knotsenburgh, situated towards the upper part of Red Lyon Run bounded on the north by Red Lyon Run, below the Maryland path & a branch containing 440 acres, granted 300 acres of it by warrant from the court of New Castle & 140 acres by myself on 30 May 1683 to John Harmonson. Now confirmed to John Harmonson the 440 acres he paying 1 bushel of winter wheat per 100 acres to persons of authority. Signed William Penn. (B2:7).

Deed. On 15 Feb 1686. John Harmonson of the town of New Castle, carpenter to Hendrick Vandenburgh of the town of New Castle. John Harmonson for a certain sum of money granted to Hendrick Vandenburgh a tract of land called Knotsenburgh containing 440 acres. Signed Jan Harmonson. Delivered in the presence of John Williams Neering & Edward Gibbs. Recorded 15 Feb 1686/7. (B2:8).

Deed. On 14 Mar 1686/7. Oalla Toarson of the county of New Castle to Hendrick Vandenburgh of the town of New Castle. Oalla Toarson for £40 granted to Hendrick Vandenburgh a tract of land lying in the neck between St. George's Creek & the Creek called Arenty Creek bounded by land of George Astons, land of Abraham Enloff, a swamp, land of Whales, Doctor's Swamp, land of Mr. Whales & Mr. Peter Allrichs containing 200 acres being surveyed for Patrick Carr 9 July 1675 & by Patrick Carr sold to Oalla Toarson by deed dated 23 Mar 1679/80. Signed Oalla Toarson. Delivered in the presence of John Mandy & John White. Recorded 15 Mar 1686/7. (B2:9).

Deed. On 24 June 1687. Robert Turner of Philadelphia, merchant & Susannah his wife to Edward Blake of the County of New Castle. Whereas there is certain house & lot of land in the occupation of Sarah Welsh situated in the town of New Castle near the strand having on the west the lot of Peter Allrichs, the north land of A. Geranrdry Ceessells, the east with Thwart Street which leads from the strand to the market place & on the south by land of John Moll being 187' in length & 58' in breadth which said house & land was formerly sold to John Cann by Johannes Dehaes & Ephraim Herman, executors of the last will of Marten Rosemond, dec. as by deed dated 6 Sep 1682 & since by deed dated 19 June 1685 John Cann sold the same to John White of the town of New Castle. John White by deed dated 23 Oct 1685 sold the same to Susannah Welsh, the present wife of Robert Turner. Now Robert Turner & Susannah his wife for £200 granted to Edward Blake the said house & lot of land. Signed Robert Turner & Susannah Turner. Delivered in the presence of John White & John Mandy. Recorded 21 July 1687. (B2:11).

Mortgage. On 28 June 1687. Edward Blake of the town of New Castle to Sarah Welsh, widow of William Welsh, late of the town of New Castle. Whereas there is a house & lot of land which said Edward Blake purchased of Robert Turner & Susannah Welsh being in the town of New Castle dated 24 June 1687. Now, Edward Blake for £200 granted to Sarah Welsh the said lot & house, provided upon the condition that Edward Blake truly pay to Sarah Welsh in the town of Philadelphia the full sum of £200 silver or the like sum in winter wheat on or before 20 Sep next & £30 on or before 29 Oct yearly until the year 1693. Signed Edward Blake. Delivered in the presence of John Mandy & John White. Recorded 21 July 1687. (B2:13).

Deed. On 19 July 1687. Woola Franson, late of the county of New Castle to Peter Bainton of the county of New Castle, merchant. Woola Franson for £29 16 shillings granted to Peter Bainton a tract of land being near Verderybys Hook bounded on the south with the Delaware River, the east with Bainton's land, formerly belonging to Marcus Lauranson & west with Stoney Creek as contained in patent granted by Governor Andross to Woola Franson, Marcus Lauranson & Neils Neilson dated 15 Jan 1675 containing 134 acres being part of the land contained in the said patent & formerly in the occupation of Woola Franson. Signed Woola Franson. Delivered in the presence of Robert Robinson & John White. Recorded 19 July 1687. (B2:15).

Guarantee. On 21 Apr 1687. Oalla Franson of the county of Salem on the Delaware River stand firmly bound to Peter Bainton for the sum of £200, the condition being that Oalla Franson shall truly confirm the sale of a tract of land being near Verderybys Hook bounded on the south with the Delaware River, the east with Bainton's land, formerly belonging to Marcus Lauranson & west with Stoney Creek as contained in patent granted by Governor Andross to Woola Franson, Marcus Lauranson & Neils Neilson dated 15 Jan 1675 containing 134 acres being part of the land contained in the said patent now in the possession of Peter Bainton & after said confirmation said obligation to be void. Signed Woola Franson. Delivered in the presence of Peter Mouson, Hendrick Lawson & Joseph Hewitt. Recorded 19 July 1687. (B2:17).

Release. On 19 Sep 1687. Jurion Andries, the eldest son of Andries Jurionson, dec. to Brewer Sinnexen at Christiana Creek. Whereas Jurion Andrieson is now aged 21 years & upwards & whereas the Orphans Court did on 7 & 8 May 16_8 for several good & weighty reasons & for the best benefit of myself as well as my other brothers, now still in minority & agree with my father-in-law, Brewer Sinnexen that he the said Brewer should bring up & maintain me & my brothers until they come of age at which time he is to pay unto us the said children the full sum of 2500 guilders to be distributed equally amongst us the said orphans or to us that come of age or marry in consideration whereof the said Brewer Sinnexen is to have the house & the land & other personal estate of my said deceased father, Andries Jurionson which is in this county. I have received of my father-in-law, Brewer Sinnexen the full sum of 500 guilders which is share of said estate. Signed Jurion Andries. Delivered in the presence of Arnoldus DeLegrange, George Reed, Elizabeth Reed & Gisbert Wallraven. Recorded 20 Sep 1687. (B2:18).

Articles of Agreement. On 20 Apr 1683, between Arnoldus Delagrange, Brewer Sinnexen & Gisbert Wallraven [this name was also written as Gisbert Janson DeVoes], all of Christiana Creek touching the division of all their land at Christiana Creek according to the patent granted the by Gov. Lovelace. It is agreed that Arnoldus Delagrange shall have the land which shoots eastward from his dwelling house to the marsh bounded by the street between him & Brewer Sinnexen's home lot, the Great Creek & Mill Creek. Gisbert Janson is to have the land west of his home lot bounded by land of William Rainboes, Christiana Creek & land of Brewer Sinnexen. Brewer Sinnexen's land is bounded by the fence of Delagrange, Christiana Creek, land of Gisbert Wallraven, land of William Rainboe & land of Gisbert Johnson. Gisbert Janson DeVoes for him & his brother Jonas shall claim by way of inheritance by his father Wallraven Janson DeVoes, deceased, their share is bounded by the land of Brewer, the Great Creek, Christiana Creek, land of Gisbert Jansen &

associates Mill Creek (not passing over the 60 acres of land which Brewer Sinnexen took up last fall, 1682) reserving out of said land about 40 acres next to the water mill which parcel of land which is left in common to them all. Also whereas the meadow ground for hay lying on the east side of Mr. DeLagrange's home lot as far as Mill Creek was not exactly divided & shared between parties, Arnoldus DeLagrange's part of the marsh lyeth in 2 parcels, the first bounded by the Great Creek, east with his dwelling house, north to the marsh & the other bounded by Delagrange's home lot, a gully, land of Brewer Sinnexens, Mill Creek & land of Gisbert Wallravens sons marsh & land of Gisbert Jansen the acres being what it will. Brewer Sinnexen's fast land is bounded by his house, the Great Creek, Gisbert Jansen's line & land of Delagrange the acres be what it will. Gisbert Jansen DeVoes & associates share of the fast land is bounded by Delagrange's house, a little creek which runs through to the Mill Creek & land of Brewer Sinnexen. Signed Arnoldus DeLagrange, Brewer Sinnexen & Gisbert Jansen. Delivered in the presence of Eph. Herman & William Osbourn. Recorded 20 Sep 1687. (B2:19).

Mortgage. On 20 Sep 1687. John Richardson of Christiana Creek, merchant to Arnoldus DeLagrange of the county of New Castle, merchant. John Richardson stands bound to Arnoldus DeLagrange of £264 for & in consideration of a plantation parted in 3 tracts of land containing in all the 450 acres which land is lying on the north side of Christiana Creek & next Brewer Sinnexen's land. Said land is security for payment to be made, £32 on 1 Nov next & £100 to paid in to be paid in the town of Hull on 20 May next. Signed John Richardson. Delivered in the presence of John Cann, Peter Allrichs & Edward Blake. Recorded 21 Sep 1687. (B2:24)

Deed. On 15 Mar 1686/7. Thomas Gillet & Elizabeth Ogle, widow, both of the County of New Castle to James Claypoole of the City of Philadelphia, merchant. Thomas Gillet & Elizabeth Ogle for £55 granted to James Claypoole a tract of land being on both sides of White Clay Creek bounded by land of Brewer Sinnexen containing 150 acres. Signed Thomas Gillet & Elizabeth Ogle. Delivered in the presence of Thomas Peirson & Robert Hutchinson. Recorded 20 Apr 1687. (B2:25).

Deed. On 16 Sep 1687. Joseph Boll of Elke River in the County of Cecil in the province of Maryland to Arnoldus DeLagrange of Christiana Creek, merchant. Joseph Boll for a certain sum of money granted to Arnoldus DeLagrange a tract of land called Middle Way being between Christiana Creek & Elke River bounded by the swamp, the run called Back Run containing 300 acres, granted to Joseph Boll by warrant of the court of New Castle dated 20 Oct 1682. Signed Joseph Boll. Delivered in the presence of William Guest & John Gramton.

Recorded 18 Oct 1687. (B2:27).
Deed. On 21 Sep 1687. Arnoldus DeLagrange of Christiana Creek to John Richardson of the county of New Castle, yeoman. Arnoldus DeLagrange for £132 granted to John Richardson 2 tracts of land being on the north side of Christiana Creek, one being occupied by DeLagrange containing 4 parcels of land, the first bounded by Christiana Creek & land of Brewer Sinnexen containing 34 acres, the 2nd parcel bounded by land of Brewer Sinnexen, land of William Rainboes, Christiana Creek & land of Gisbert Wallraven containing 181 acres, the 3rd parcel bounded by the creek, & the 4th parcel bounded by land of Brewer Sinnexen & land of Gisbert Wallraven both parcels being 30 acres, & 1/3 part of 17 acres of land lying on Little Falls Creek laid out for a mill according to contract being 5 1/2 acres containing in all 250 1/2 acre & also another tract which is called Content bounded by Little Fall Creek, land of John Stalcops containing 194 acres which he purchased from Lucas Stedham. Signed Arnoldus DeLagrange. Delivered in the presence of John Cann, Peter Allrichs & Edward Blake. Recorded 21 Sep 1687. (B2:28).

Deed. On 19 Apr 1687. Charles Rumsey of the county of New Castle to John Richardson of the county of New Castle. Whereas there is a tract of land on the south side of Christiana Creek below Swart Nuton Island containing 500 acres granted to John Erskin & company by Patent from Governor Richard Nicolls dated 1 Jan 1667 & by Jonas Erskins, son & heir of said John Erskin, dec. & as lawful attorney for his mother, Jane Erskin, granted the same to John Wattkins & Charles Rumsey as by deed dated 1 Mar 1680/1. Which said land is bounded by Non Such Creek &, a run called Bessie containing 640 acres & called Non Such, as by survey dated 19 Sep 1682 & which John Watkins granted the whole to Charles Rumsey by deed dated 9 Jan 1684 & recorded in Book A Page 37. Now Charles Rumsey for £53 granted to John Richardson 300 acres of Non Such bounded by the run called Bessie. Signed Charles Rumsey. Delivered in the presence of Edward Blake & John White. Recorded 20 Apr 1687. (B2:31).

Deed. On 6 Dec 1687. John Sybrance, the son of John Sybrance late of the county of New Castle, dec. to Robert French. Whereas there is a tract of land being at Port Hooke in the county of New Castle containing 600 rod in length & 25 rod in breadth bounded to the northeast with the land of Herman Johnson, the northwest with woods, southwest with the land of John Priestner & a marsh of James Hallyday & on the southeast by a creek called Forksons Creek, which said land fell by division of the lands of John Sybrance, dec. to the said John Sybrance, his son as his share & has continued in peaceable possession & occupation of John Sybrance, Jr. Now John Sybrance for £20 granted to Robert French the said tract of land. Signed John Sybrance. Delivered in the presence of John Folk, Sybran Johnson & John White. Recorded 6 Dec 1687. (B2:34).

Deed. On 10 Mar 1685/6. Joseph Hallman (it is listed as both Hallman & Allman) & Margret Allman his wife living in the county of New Castle near a place called Thorough Fare, planters to George Taylor living at the N.W. branch of Duck Creek, carpenter. Joseph Allman with Margret his wife for £20 granted to George Taylor a parcel of land containing 200 acres lying in the county of New Castle bounded on the east side with the creek called the northwest branch on the south east with land of Morris Liston, on the southwest by land of Micall Offly & on the northwest by land of Andrew Love formerly taken up by Francis Hutchinson & James Boswick by situation of 400 acres, surveyed by Richard Hancock then surveyor, by order of Ephraim Herman, one half part whereas belonged to Andrew Love & the other half to Joseph Hallman. Signed Joseph Allman & Margret Allman. Delivered in the presence of John Taylor, Gabriel Wilkison & Joseph Holding. Recorded 15 Feb 1686/7. (B2:35).

Patent. On 25 Mar 1676. Edmund Andros, Esq., Governor under his Royal Highness, James, Duke of York & Albany & his territories of America to John Moll of the town of New Castle. Whereas there is a lot of land in the town of New Castle where the magazeen house stood bounded on the south east by the river, west the common, north east with the street next to the fort & on the southwest by land of Jacob Vanderveer containing in breadth 25 yards & in length 100 as by return of a survey brought by Capt. Edmund Cantwell, the surveyor. Now confirmed to John Moll & he paying one bushel of good winter wheat to persons in authority. Signed Edmund Andros. Examined by Mathias Nicolls. (B2:37).

Deed. On 6 Dec 1687. John Moll, late of the town of New Castle but now of Bohemia in Maryland, gentleman & Christian, his wife to James Claypoole of the town of New Castle, surveyor. John Moll & Christian his wife for £10 granted to James Claypoole all right to that lot of land as described in the before patent. Signed John Moll & Christian Moll. Delivered in the presence of James Walliam & Ephraim Herman. Recorded 8 Dec 1687. (B2:38).

Deed. On 6 Dec 1687. James Claypoole of the town of New Castle, surveyor to Elisabeth Courtrie of the town of New Castle, widow. James Claypoole for £12 granted to Elisabeth Courtrie the lot of land here before mentioned [in prior deed & patent]. Signed James Claypoole. Delivered in the presence of John Cann & Peter Allrichs. Recorded 7 Dec 1687. (B2:39).

Debt. Capt. Bridgman to Peter Allrichs, Cape Hinlopen on 17 Dec 1685. I acknowledge my self indebted to Peter Allrichs of New Castle the sum of £7 1 shilling to be paid in rum molasses & sugar, to witt, one half in rum & the remainder as above written. Signed Richard Bridgeman. Delivered in the presence of Jno Knight & Wm Wigand. Recorded 17 Dec 1687. (B2:40).

Patent. On 26 Mar 1684. William Penn, Governor of the province of Pennsylvania & territories. Whereas there is a tract of land called Hope situated on the west side of the Delaware River, the north side of White Clay Creek bounded by the Creek & a small run called Turkey Run containing 219 acres granted by warrant from Governor Penn dated 30 May 1683 to John Cann who assigned it over to Joseph Cookson & Joseph Cookson requesting me to confirm the same by patent. William Penn confirms the 219 acres to Joseph Cookson & Joseph Cookson paying 1 bushel of winter wheat per hundred acres to persons of authority. Signed William Penn. (B2:40).

Mortgage. On 20 Aug 1678. James Williams of Appoquinimink Creek, carpenter to Thomas Snelling of Appoquinimink Creek, planter. James Williams stands bound to Thomas Snelling in the full sum of 1800 pounds of good tobacco & cash containing the same to be paid at of before 10 Nov next. The condition of this obligation is such that if the above bound James Williams does make over to Thomas Snelling a good assurance of a tract of land lying on the west side of Black Bird Creek containing 240 acres. Signed James Williams. Delivered in the presence of Benjamin Gumley & Susanna Rowles. (B2:42).

Deed. On 15 Oct 1678. Thomas Snelling of Appoquinimink Creek, planter to Ann Westerndale of Appoquinimink Creek, widow. Thomas Snelling for valuable consideration make over unto Ann Westerndale all right & interest in the enclosed mortgage, with the power upon non performance thereof to arrest, imprison & recover from James Williams all or whatsoever damages as she shall or may sustain by non performance thereof. Signed Thomas Snelling. Delivered Susanna Rowels & Thomas Allen. (B2:42).

Deed. On 1 Mar 1688. Neils Neilson of the county of New Castle to Peter Bainton of the county of New Castle, merchant. Neils Neilson for £30 & a gun granted to Peter Bainton a tract of land in the bower near Werdesties Hook being part of a tract bounded to the south with the River Delaware, the east with Honey Creek & west with Dog Creek as contained in a patent granted to Neils Neilson, Wolla Transon & Peter (it was also said to be Paul) Mounsen, the whole tract containing 300 acres granted in the year 1673 & another tract adjoining the 300 acres comprising of 400 acres which was granted by Edmund Andros, Governor, to Miles Bilson, Wolla Transon & Marius Lawrensen by patent dated 15 Jan 1675. Whereas Neils Neilson confirms all his right & interest in said acres to Peter Bainton. Signed Neils Neilson. Delivered in the presence of John White & Mary White. Recorded 21 Mar 1688. (B2:43).

Deed. On 9 Feb 1686. Elizabeth Ogle, relict & executrix of John Ogle, late of the county of New Castle, dec. to Peter Yocombe of the county of Philadelphia. Elizabeth Ogle for £20 10 shillings granted to Peter Yocombe a certain farm situated in the county of New Castle containing 430 acres bound as expressed in patent granted to John Ogle, dec. dated 26 July 1684 by William Penn. Signed Elizabeth Ogle. Delivered in the presence of John White. Recorded 13 May 1688. (B2:44).

Deed. On 18 June 1688. John Garretson of the county of New Castle to Mary Mandy, widow & relict of John Mandy, late of the town of New Castle, dec. John Garretson for £30 granted to Mary Mandy, one house & lot in the town of New Castle, now in the tenure of Mary Mandy bounded on the northeast by the house of John Henrickson, the southeast with the strand or Front Street, southwest with the house & ground lately belonging to James Crawford & to the northwest with the market place or green. Signed John Garretson. Delivered in the presence of Edward Blake & John White. Recorded 19 June 1688. (B2:45).

Lease. On 20 Apr 1687. Ephraim Herman of Bohemia in Maryland, gentleman to Joseph Allman of Delaware River, planter. Ephraim Herman for rents, conditions & services to be well & truly performed by the said John Allman, has granted to John Allman all that tract of land commonly called Second Dennis Point being bounded on the south by Duck Creek, the west with a marsh, the north with the road that leads to the land of Christopher Ellits now Joseph Holdings plantation & to the east with the marsh that parts this from Dennis Point containing 200 acres, being part of a greater parcel of land belonging to Ephraim Herman called the Good Land, on the Delaware River which lease is to begin with the day of the date herewith & to continue for & during the natural lives of him the said Joseph Allman, & his wife Margret, his son Joseph & no longer upon terms & conditions that follow. Joseph Allman is obliged with the space of 3 years now next to actually live on said land & to clear & plant said land so as to improve & kept in good repair all the houses & structures during the term of this lease. Joseph Alman & other leasees are not to make any waste of any wood or timbert upon the said land except it be for the necessary use of the plantation unless it shall be of such wood as shall happen to be in the clear ground which said wastage be the sad leasors revenues to him. The leasees are obliged with the space of 5 years to plant an orchard upon the same land at least 100 apple trees & to keep the same always fenced & tended. The lease shall not be assigned unless with the full consent of the leasor. Joseph Allman, Margret his wife & Joseph his son are firmly bound & obliged to pay to Ephraim Herman, annually on 25 Mar the yearly rent of, for the first 3 years 2 fat capons, the next 7 years 4 shillings or the value in good winter wheat, the next 7 years 8 shillings, the next 7 years 12 shillings & after those 7 years 16 shillings forever after during the term of the lease. Signed Joseph Allman. Delivered in the presence of Casparus Tollier & Daniel Mackarty. (B2:46).

Memorandum. On 22 Dec 1687. It is agreed & concluded between the leasor, Eph. Herman & the leasee, Joseph Hallman, in case the leasee shall happen to die & leave his wife a widow & that then in case of her 2nd marriage or otherwise she should happen to remove to another place, shall then have the liberty if she thinks fit to assign this within lease over to any other good honest person for the term of her natural life & no longer & that if the son, Joseph being the 3rd person mentioned in this lease after he is of full age & by the dec. of his father & mother the leasee in his hands shall have the like liberty if he sees cause to assign the lease to any other good, honest person, always provided that the leasor shall have the first offer refusal & choice given him or them of such assignment & the leasor shall have it back in his hands at £5 cheaper than any other assignee. Signed Joseph Allman. Delivered in the presence of John Lannegan & Edmond. Green. (B2:48).

Patent. On 29 July 1685. Thomas Lloyd, James Claypoole & Robert Turner, or any two, being appointed commissioners of property under William Penn to Jacob Vanderveer. Whereas there is a tract of land on the north side of Brandywine Creek according to a former patent granted by Governor Francis Lovelace on 24 Mar 1668 bounded by Indian Run & Brandywine Creek containing 535 acres by a warrant dated 8 May 1684. Jacob Vanderveer now requests said land to be confirmed the same by patent. Now confirmed to Jacob Vanderveer & he paying one bushel of winter wheat per hundred acres to persons appointed for the purpose. Signed James Claypoole & Robert Turner. (B2:51).

Notice. On 6 Apr 1688. The difference between Lucas & Erasmus Stedham & Jacob Vanderveer about a tract of land lying on the north side of Brandywine Creek was this day heard before us the commissioners of property, who after well weighing said cause did unanimously declare that the said tract of land not being over plus land but a tract by it self though contiguous to the land the said Vanderveer now lives on & the said tract having had in quiet possession about 25 years is & ought to remain & is here decreed to be the right & property of the said Jacob Vanderveer. Signed William Markham, Sr. & John Goodson. (B2:52).

Notice. On 19 May 1688 in Philadelphia. At the request of Jacob Vanderveer, who now is about building a grist mill on his land on Brandywine Creek in the county of New Castle that we should grant him to make use of the waters of the said creek before his own land for the service of the said mill. We do hereby grant the same, he yielding & paying yearly to the proprietor, a half bushel of wheat. Signed Wm. Markham & John Goodson. (B2:52).

Notice. On 12 May 1688. By virtue of the commission granted by Wm. Penn, proprietary & governor of the province of Pennsylvania & territories annexed unto William Markham, hereto Thomas Ellis, John Goodson or any two of us, we send greetings. Whereas by virtue of a warrant from the Governor dated 8 May 1684 obtained by Jacob Vanderveer for the resurveying the land where he lives on Brandywine Creek according to a patent dated 24 Mar 1668/9 from Francis Lovelace, but by mistake or from other means the surveyor surveyed not only the land contained within the bounds of the aforesaid patent but also 2 small tracts of land lying contiguous & returned. But one tract nominated in the said patent of Governor Lovelace to be Anries Anderson by means the aforesaid Jacob Vanderveer obtained a patent dated 29 July 1685 for the said tracts as but on one tract and whereas a difference having arisen between Lucas & Erasmus Stedham, the 2 sons of Doctor Simon Stedham, dec. & Jacob Vanderveer about the right of the one small tract. Now is confirmed to Jacob Vanderveer. Signed Wm Markham & John Goodson. (B2:52).

Deed. On 2 Apr 1688. Jonas Askham of White Clay Creek, plater to Zachariah Vandercoolen of the town of New Castle. Jonas Askham for £20 granted to Zachariah Vandercoolen a tract of land being on the south side of White Clay Creek called Eastern bounded by White Clay Creek & a swamp containing 200 acres which said land was surveyed to Jonas Askham in right of Peter Clauson 8 June 1686. Signed Jonas Askham. Delivered in the presence of Emelus De Ring, Jan Bishk & Ro. French. Recorded 19 June 1688. (B2:54).

Deed. On 17 Dec 1685 Mathyas Deffoes of Christiana Creek, yeoman to Charles Pickering of Christiana Creek, planter. Whereas the dec. John Stalcop of the Christiana Creek in his life time for valuable consideration of 2 settlements or improvements made by Lassy Cornelius & Samuel Peterson before the land was granted to John Stalcop & for 350 guilders paid to John Stalcop by Lassy Cornelius & Samuel Peterson did by deed dated 2 Sept 1674 confirmed unto Lassy Cornelius & Samuel Peterson that land that was taken up before & also one half of the marsh lying between 2 corners of the said land & also one half of the woodland adjoining the same. Also John Stalcop by another deed dated 16 Apr 1675 for 700 guilders paid by Lassy Cornelius & Samuel Peterson granted another tract of land on the other side of Oleman's Creek, one half of the land according to patent. Lassy Cornelius for 1000 guilders by deed dated 2 July 1684 granted to Justa Anderson of New Castle, planter one half of the land bought of John Stalcop. Justa Anderson did make an exchange for another tract of land with Mathias Deffoes, so that Justa Anderson did grant all the land that he bought of Lassy Cornelius to Mathias Deffoes. Now Mathias Deffoes for 3000 guilders granted to Charles Pickering Signed Mathias Deffoes. Delivered in the presence of Wm. Guest & John White. Recorded 1 June 1688. (B2::55).

Patent. On 16 May 1688. William Markham, Thomas Ellis & John Goodson or any 2 of them, by virtue of the commission granted by William Penn to Thomas Jones. Whereas there is a tract of land called Goodspring lying both sides of Shellpott Creek in the County of New Castle bounded by a small run called Goodspring Run containing 100 acres surveyed 22 Sep 1680 by Richard ___ by order of Ephraim Herman unto Olle Olleson & by Henry Olleson, son & heir of Olle Olleson conveyed to Thomas Jones, who now requests confirmation. By virtue of commission confirm unto Thomas Jones the 100 acres & he paying 1 bushel of winter wheat yearly. Signed Wm. Markham & John Goodson. (B2:57).

Deed. On 16 Mar 11687. Edward Eglinton of Grear Manta's Creek in West Jersey to George Foreman of Chichester. Edward Eglinton for £10 granted to George Foreman 200 acres of land part of 400 acres lying together undivided between the said Edward Eglinton & Isaac Warner called Partners Adventure, lying on both sides a branch of Naaman's Creek bounded by the south branch of said creek containing 400 acres. Granted by warrant from the Governor on 22 Feb 1682 & surveyed by Ephraim Herman on 28 Dec 1683 to Edward Eglinton & Isaac Warner old renter. Signed Edward Eglinton. Delivered in the presence of Martin Houh, Edward Bezer & Isaac Warner. Recorded 19 June 1688. (B2:58).

Deed. On 22 June 1688. Reyneir Vandercoulin of the town of New Castle, innholder to Anthony Green of the town of New Castle. Reynier Vandercoulin for £120 granted to Anthony Green a lot of land in the town of New Castle bounded by the fence of Capt. Markham, the swamp commonly called Allrichs Swamp, a street & the market place. Signed Reynier Vandercoulin. Delivered in the presence of James Bradshaw & John White. Recorded 18 Sep 1688. (B2:60).

Deed. On 30 Aug 1688. Justus Anderson of the town of New Castle to George Fisher of the town of New Castle. Whereas there is 2 lots of land & 2 houses in the town of New Castle, the said land bounded on the SE by Mary's Street, SW with Hart Street, NW with Brewer's Street & NE with land surveyed for Joseph Burnham. Said lots were granted to Justus Anderson by John Smith & Mary his wife by deed dated 23 Feb 1687 & since on 3 Aug 1688 Justus Anderson granted on equal part of the said lots & also the new dwelling house to Hugh

MacGregory. Now Justus Anderson for a considerable sum of money granted to George Fisher all the house called The Kitchen with the said other half part of the 2 lots. Signed Justus Anderson. Delivered in the presence of Hugh MacGregory, John White & Wm. Sweatnam. Recorded 18 Se 1688. (B2:61).

Deed. On 22 Feb 1687/8. Edward Green of the county of New Castle, merchant to James Claypoole of the town of New Castle, surveyor. Edward Green for £12 granted to James Claypoole 2 lots situate at the northern most end of the town of New Castle, one bounded on SE by the river Delaware, W with the common & NE with a small creek being 64 feet in width & 300 feet in length. The other bounded on the W by a lot granted to Abraham Man, N the street called Dike Street, E by a lot formerly granted to James Walliam & S by the strand at the riverside, this lot being the 2nd from the town creek containing 60 feet in width & 300 feet length equal with the other adjoining lot which said lots were granted by patents from the commissioners to Arnoldus DeLagrange on 7 & 8 Oct 1685 & made over by him in open court at New Castle to Edward Green on 8 Dec 1687. Signed Edward Green. Delivered in the presence of James Newill, James Walliam & James Bradshaw. Recorded 23 Feb 1687. (B2:62).

Deed. On 19 June 1688. William Guest of the county of New Castle to Richard Mankin of the County of New Castle. William Guest for £10 granted to Richard Mankin a tract of land lying on the north side of one of the branches of Christianna Creek called White Clay Creek being part of a tract of land called Wedgeberry in the occupation of William Guest & granted to William Guest by patent from Governor Penn dated 9 Aug 1688, bounded by other land of William Guest & White Clay Creek being 200 acres. Signed William Guest. Delivered in the presence of John White. Recorded 19 June 1688. (B2:64).

Deed. On 16 Oct 1688. John Peirson of Augustine Creek in the county of New Castle, planter to Thomas Rothwell of the county of New Castle, husbandman. John Peirson for a valuable sum granted to Thomas Rothwell one half part of a tract of land on the north side of Augustine Creek now by the name of Canne Brach surveyed to John Peirson 24 Sep 1688, the said one half being 108 1/2 acres. Signed John Peirson. Delivered in the presence of Peter Bainton & James Claypoole. Recorded 17 Oct 1688. (B2:65).

Deed. On 3 Aug 1688. Justus Anderson of the town of New Castle to Hugh MacGregory of the town of New Castle. Justus Anderson for £40 granted to Hugh MacGregory all the new dwelling house that Justus Anderson lately bought of John Smith with the one moiety of 2 lots belonging to the house, the said house & land situated in the town of New Castle bounded on the SE with Mary's Street, SW with Hart Street, NW with Brewers Street & NE by the land surveyed for Joseph Burnham, the 2 lots being 124 feet in breadth & in length equal to the next lots. Excepting a little house called "The Kitchen" & the one moiety of the lots. Signed Justa Anderson. Delivered in the presence of John Latham & John White. Recorded 17 Oct 1688. (B2:67).

Acknowledged. John Street of Appoquinimy of the river Delaware, planter, has conveyed unto Robart Morton of the same river, planter all my right & interest & my wife Joan's interest in a tract of land lying on the branch of Appoquinimy Creek called Hangman's Creek, excepting 20 square foot of land where the boy Robert lies, for a burying place for me & my family which tract of land is belonging to a patent which is coming from New York, being for a sum of money already received, which said tract of land mentioned is to be acknowledged in open court by John Street & his wife Joan to Robart Morton with the penalty of 6000 lbs. of tobacco. Singed John Street & Joan Street. Delivered in the presence of Thomas Moore & Andries Cornelius. (B2:68).

Patent. On 1 Jan 1667. Richard Nicolls, Esq. principal commissioner from his majesty in New England, Governor under his Royal Highness James Duke of York & Albany & all his territories in the Americas & commander in chief of all the forces employed by his majesty to reduce the Dutch Nation and all their usurped lands under his obedience. Whereas there is a tract of land lying on Christiana Creek adjoining Swarton Nutton Island bounded on the N with the creek of the island, W with Christiana Creek, S with the main land & E with the meadow ground of said island containing 100 acres. Whereas there is also a small cottage with a backside lying in the town of New Castle bounded SW by the river, N by a house of Martin Garrets, NW by land taken up on the backside of the town & the highway. Now by virtue of authority unto me given, I have confirmed unto James Crawford the tract of land & the cottage for consideration for the good service performed by said James Crawford, soldier in hi majesties service at the town. James Crawford to pay 2 bushels of winter wheat yearly to persons of authority. Signed Richard Nicolls. Written by Mathias Nicolls, stewart. (B2:69).

Patent. On 16 Aug 1670. Francis Lovelace, Esq. one of the gentlemen of his Majesty's Honorable Privy Chamber & Governor General under his Royal Highness, James Duke of York & Albany & of all his territories in the Americas send greetings. Whereas there is a tract of land at New Castle lately purchased by Peter Allrichs from Mathias & Emelius DeRingh bounded on the W with land granted to Sergeant Erskin, N with the street, east with the market place & south with the lots of Mt. Thom: & the said Peter Allrichs. Know ye that by virtue of authority to me given by his Royal Highness, I thought it fit to grant & confirm said piece of land to Peter Allrichs, he paying 1 bushel of winter wheat to persons of authority. Signed Francis Lovelace at Fort James in New York. Recorded by Mathias Nicolls, stewart. (B2:70).

Deed. On 23 Aug 1683. Peter Allrichs of New Castle, merchant to Reyneir Vandercoolin. Peter Allrichs make over & assign to Reyneir Vandercoolin all right, title & interest of the with in mentioned patent [prior document]. Signed Peter Allrichs. Delivered in the presence of Wm. Markham & Jno. Moll.

Deed. On 29 Nov 1687. Hendrick Vandenburgh of the town of New Castle. Whereas Richard Nicolls, Governor, by patent dated 6 Jan 16__ in New York confirmed unto Sergeant John Erskin, Thomas Brown & Martin Garretson in common a tract of land lying in the county of New Castle lying on the south side of Christiana Creek bounded by said Creek, Swarton Nutton Island, a little spring called Bossie & Fearn Hook containing 500 acres, which to wit on the 1 Oct 1669, Francis Lovelace, Governor did by patent granted & confirmed unto John Erskin, Martin Garretson & Gisbert Derikson a tract of land lying on Christiana Creek bounded by land of Jan Classen containing 100 acres. Whereas Martin Garretson, who for years improved upon the land so granted by said patent being the lower most part next to Fearn Hook did on 6 Feb 1677/8 for valuable consideration granted to me, Hendrick Vandenburgh all his right & title in the land granted to him by the 2 patents & on 7 Jan 1678/9 was by me sold to Englebert Lot then of the town of New Castle, but late of Flat Bush on Long Island in the territory of New York, shoemaker, for 1700 guilders or £42. Now Hendrick Vandenburgh confirm unto Englebert Lot the said land. Memorandum. It being alleged that Martin Garretson did in his lifetime make a division & partition with John Erskin & Thomas Brown of his part of above said land. It is then before signing & sealing of this deed agreed on between Englebert Lot & Hendrick Vandenburgh the said division is lawfully proved by sufficient evidence to have been made & fully agreed on between said parties above named shall stand & remain good for the future. Signed Hend. Burgh. Delivered in the presence of Eph. Herman & William Neering. Recorded 9 Dec 1687. (B2:71).

Deed. On 30 Nov 1688. Edward Gibbs & Judah his wife, relict & adm. of James Cransford late of the town of New Castle, dec. to Robert Evans of the town of New Castle, innholder. Whereas there is lot of ground in the town of New Castle bounded to the S with the river, N with the house lately belonging to Martin Garrets (now in the tenure of Robert Evans), NW with the land taken up on the backside of town & by the highway, which said lot was granted & confirmed to James Cranford by patent from Governor Nicolls dated 1 Jan

1667. Now Edward Gibbs & Judah his wife in capacity as administrator of the estate of James Cranford, dec. for £12 12 shillings granted to Robert Evans the said lot. Signed Edward Gibbs & Judah Gibbs. Delivered in the presence of Hugh MacGregory & John White. Recorded 20 ___ 1688. (B2:73).

Deed. On 22 Mar 1687/8. Justa Anderson of the town of New Castle, yeoman to James Walliam & John Darby of the town of New Castle, gentlemen. Justa Anderson for valuable consideration granted to James Walliam & John Darby a lot in the town of New Castle being a moiety & easternmost of 2 lots granted by Edmund Andros then Governor of New York to John Moll by patent dated 17 Nov 1679 & the said John Moll made over to Justa Anderson in open court 21 Feb 1687/8. The said lot have the Warmers Street to the E, the remaining lot of Justa Anderson to the W, the lot of Samuel Land to the N & Hart Street to the S being 150 in length & 120 foot in breadth. Signed Justa Anderson. Delivered in the presence of Peter Allrichs & John Cann. Recorded 22 Mar 1687/8. (B2:75).

Deed. On 20 Dec 1688. William Guest of the county of New Castle to Alexander Crooker & John Donaldson both of the county of New Castle, merchants. William Guest for £20 12 shillings granted to Alexander Crooker & John Donaldson a tract of land being on Mill Creek being a branch of White Clay Creek called by the name of Wednesbury containing 500 acres provided that William Guest pay to Alexander Crooker & John Donaldson £22 12 shillings on 20 Dec 1689 at the town of New Castle & this deed shall become void, but if William Guest shall fail to pay the said sum at the time & place then this deed to be & remain in full force & William Guest shall immediately after the failure to pay said payment deliver possession of the said premises to Alexander Crooker & John Donaldson. Signed Wm. Guest. Delivered in the presence of Edward Gibbs & John White. Recorded 20 Dec 1688. (B2:76).

Deed. On 18 Dec 1688. Wolla Franson & Neils Neilson, sons & heirs of Wolla Franson & Neils Neilson, dec. late of the county of New Castle & Hofell Myara of the county of New Castle being purchaser & survivor from Marcus Lawrensen to Peter Boynton. Whereas there is a tract of land near Bird Creek Hook & now divided by consent & surveyed by James Claypoole & the said Myara helped to carry the chain bounded on the SW side of Honey Creek upon a point called Mill Point, a branch of Poplar Creek & the river being the land granted to Wolla Franson, Marcus Lawrensen & Neils Neilson by patent from Governor Edmund Andros, which said land was added to another tract of land adjoining it as appears in patent from Governor Lovelace dated 7 Apr 1673 to Wolla Franson, Neil Neilson, Peter Mounson & Marcus Lawrensen containing 300 acres. Said 700 acres was confirmed by Governor Andresson dated 15 Jan

1675 & the said Hofell Myara is vested into all the right of the above patents & lands from the aforesaid Marcus Lawrensen dated 21 Oct 1685. The said 400 acres is transported to Peter Boynton, as by a deed from Neils Neilson dated 20 July 1686 for 133 1/2 acres, from Wolla Franson by deed dated 14 July 1687 for 133 1/2 acres & from Thomas Clifton by deed dated 24 May 1686 for 133 acres & was confirmed to Thomas Clifton by deed from Hofell Myara, the said Myara having bought the said right from Marcus Lawrensen by deed dated 21 Oct 1685. Also Neils Neilson, son & heir of Neils Neilson, dec. did by deed dated 21 Mar 1688 granted all his right to the patent for 300 acres being 1/3 part to Peter Boynton. Signed Wolla Franson, Hofell Myara & Neils Neilson. Delivered in the presence of John Donaldson, Reyneir Vandercoolin & John Smith. Recorded 18 Dec 1688. (B2:77).

Deed. On 3 Dec 1688. Hugh MacGregory of the town of New Castle to John White. Whereas Hugh MacGregory by deed from Justa Anderson was confirmed a lot of land in the town of New Castle lately in the tenure of John Smith, the one moiety of 2 lots belonging to the house bounded by Mary's Street, Hart Street, Brewer's Street & land surveyed to Joseph Burnham with several conditions & covenants within the said deed as recorded in Book B Page 67 & 68. Now Hugh MacGregory for £40 granted to John White, one moiety of the said 2 lots. Signed Hugh MacGregory. Delivered in the presence of Rob. French, Geo. Fisher & Wm. Stockdale. Recorded 20 Dec 1688. (B2:79).

Deed. On 23 Feb 1687. John Smith & Mary his wife of the town of New Castle to Justa Anderson of the town of New Castle. John Smith for consideration of a certain lot confirmed to him by Justa Anderson & for a considerable sum of money to be paid granted to Justa Anderson al the 2 lots in the town of New Castle bounded by Mary's Street, Hart Street, Brewer's Street & land surveyed to Joseph Burnham. Signed John Smith & Mary Smith. Delivered in the presence of Richard Noble, James Read & Wm. Mann. Recorded 23 Feb 1687. (B2:79).

Deed. On 6 Sep 1688. Reyneir Vandercoolin of the town of New Castle to Capt. William Markham of Philadelphia. Reyneir Vandercoolin for £15 granted to Capt. William Markham a lot in the town of New Castle bounded by the swamp commonly called Allrichs Swamp, land of Doctor Gerrardus Wessells, the market place & land of Anthony Green. Signed Reyneir Vandercoolin. Delivered in the presence of James Pennington & John White. Recorded 18 Sep 1688. (B2:80).

Deed. On 26 Feb 1688/9. Derrick Vandenburgh, late of New York to George Hogg of the town of New Castle. Derrick Vandenburgh for £32 granted to George Hogg a piece of land in the town of New Castle bounded by the house &

ground of John Hendrickson, the house & ground late of Justa Anderson but now of John White, Front Street & the market place, being the same piece of land Derrick Vandenburgh bought of Justa Anderson by deed dated 20 Apr 1687. Signed Derrick Vandenburgh. Delivered in the presence of Hend. Burgh & John White. Recorded 12 Mar 1688/9. (B2:81).

Bond. On 17 Oct 1688. John Pearson of Augustine Creek, planter to Thomas Rothwell of Augustine Creek, husbandman. John Pearson is firmly bound to Thomas Rothwell for £10 John Pearson to pay the quit rents yearly on the 108 1/2 acres & to pay Thomas Rothwell 5 shillings yearly. When obligation is paid then this is void. Singed John Pearson. Delivered in the presence of John Grantam & James Claypoole. Recorded 17 Oct 1688. (B2:82).

Deed. On 23 Feb 1687. Justa Anderson of the town of New Castle to John Smith of the town of New Castle. Justa Anderson for the exchange of a certain house & lot in the town of New Castle confirm unto John Smith a lot of land in the town of New Castle bounded by the line drawn between 2 lots that Justa Anderson bought of John Moll, Hart Street, Minquaes Street, Samuel Lands lot containing in breadth 120 foot & in length 150 foot & also another lot of land in the town of New Castle bounded by Hay Street, the common, the land of Job Nettership, land of John Burgrave being one half part of 6 lots which Justa Anderson bought of John White being 352 1/2 feet in length & 181 1/2 feet in breadth. Signed Justa Anderson. Delivered in the presence of Richard Noble, James Reed & William Mann. Recorded 23 Feb 1687. (B2:83).

Deed. On 16 Oct 1688. Hans Peterson of Shilpot Creek, gentleman to Hendrich Anderson Smith of Crane Hook, husbandman. Whereas there is a tract of land lying at Crane Hook bounded by land of Hendrick Anderson Smith, land of Mathias Erickson & the Delaware River containing 100 acres, being the land Hans Peterson bought some years back from Mathias Lawson late of Crane Hook. Now Hans Peterson for £50 granted to Hendrick Anderson Smith the said tract. Signed Hans Peterson. Delivered in the presence of Thomas Peirson, Ro. French & Reynold Hawk. Recorded 16 Oct 1688. (B2:84).

Deed. On 11 Mar 1688/9. Henry Vandenburgh of the town of New Castle, merchant to Robert Ashton of St. George's Creek, yeoman. Henry Vandenburgh for £30 granted to Robert Ashton a tract of land called Doctor's Common lying on the south side of St. George's Creek, bounded by the creek, land formerly of Ann Whale now in actual possession of Robert Ashton & Company & Doctor's Swamp containing 160 acres being the land that Thomas Spry on 2 Feb 1678/9 granted to Jacob Young & by Jacob Young by deed dated 16 Feb 1686/7 granted to Henry Vandenburgh as recorded in New Castle Book B Page 4 & 5.

To better secure said land to Robert Ashton, Hannah Vandenburgh, wife of Henry Vandenburgh does voluntarily acknowledge the above to Robert Ashton. Signed Hendrick Vandenburgh & Anna Vandenburgh. Delivered in the presence of Wm. Stockdale, Jonas Askin. Recorded 15 Mar 1688/9. (B2:85).

Deed. On 1 July 1695 Charles Rumsey of Christiana Creek, yeoman to John Hussey late of Hamptown in New Hampshire near Pistatoway in New England, yeoman. Charles Rumsey for £200 granted to John Hussey a tract of land on the south side of Christiana Creek containing 340 acres which said tract is part of a greater tract bounded by _____ Creek containing 640 acres being part of a tract granted to John Arskin, Thomas Brown & Martin Garret by patent dated 1 Feb 1667. Whereas Jonas Arskin, son & heir of John Arskin granted 1/3 of said tract to Charles Rumsey & John Watkins written on the back of said patent dated 1 Mar 1680. John Watkins by deed dated 9 Jan 1684 conveyed to Charles Rumsey recorded in the county of New Castle, part where of being 300 acres was by deed dated 9 Apr 1687 granted to John Richardson 300 acres. Now Charles Rumsey granted to John Hussey 340 acres. Signed Charles Rumsey. Delivered in the presence of Cornelius Empson & John Donaldson. Recorded 6 Aug 1695. (B2:88).

Deed.. On 6 Aug 1695. John Richardson of Christiana Creek, yeoman to John Hussey, late of Hamptown in New Hampshire in New England, yeoman. John Richardson for £53 granted to John Hussey all his right & interest in 300 acres. Signed John Richardson. Delivered in the presence of David Lloyd & Cornelius Empson. Recorded 6 Aug 1695. (B2:91).

Letter of Attorney. On 16 Apr 1695. George Jaffrey of Portsmouth in New England, merchant appoint my trusty friend John Jaffrey to be my lawful attorney to collect such sums or debts due me. Signed George Jaffrey. Delivered in the presence of Benjamin Blacklidge, John Nest, Alexander Grant. The within John Nest & Alexander Grant, 2 of the witnesses to the with letter of attorney, did personally appear before me & made Solemn attestation that they did see George Jaffrey sign & seal the above letter of attorney on 27 May 1695. Signed John Beers. The within named Benjamin Blacklidge & Alexander Grant, 2 of the witnesses to the with mentioned letter of Attorney appeared Before me & made solemn attestation that they did see George Jaffry sign, seal & deliver the with letter of Attorney on 24 July 1695. Signed William Neering. (B2:91).

Release. On 24 Mar 1695. Paul Paulson of Christiana Creek having intermarried with Elisabeth, the daughter of Henry Lemons, late of Turkey Island in Christiana Creek, dec. have released & discharge Charles Rumsey &

Nicholas Lockyer, gentlemen, last guardians to the said Elizabeth of all manner or to be accountable for & by any reason for being guardian to said Elizabeth. Singed Paul Paulson. Delivered in the presence of John Hamilton & Grift Jones. (B2:92).

Deed. On 20 Sep 1694. Zachariah Vandercoulin of the town of New Castle to William Crosse of the New Castle. Zachariah Vandercoulin for valuable consideration granted to William Crosse a lot of land in the town of New Castle situated on Land Street bounded by land of William Crosse, land of Gisbert Derrickson containing in breadth 66 foot & 290 foot in length, which did formerly belong to Gisbert Derrickson & now to Emelius DeRingh, dec. but the said 66 foot of land in now in the possession of Zachariah Vandercoulin. Signed Zachariah Vandercoulin & Alehe Vandercoulin. Delivered in the presence of Jonas Arskin & John Smith. Recorded 18 Sep 1694. (B2:93).

Deed. On 28 May 1695. John Bisk of New Castle, tailor & Elizabeth his wife, William Crosse of New Castle, brasier & Thomas Jauvier & Sarah his wife the surviving daughter & heir of Mary the late wife of William Crosse of New Castle, by her former husband John Jourdain. Whereas Isaac Tine late of New Castle, husbandman dec. brother to Elizabeth the wife of John Bisk & Mary, the late wife of William Crosse, dec. was in his lifetime seized in a lot of land situated at the strand between the house & lot late of Justa Andries & Mathias & Emelius DeRingh in New Castle containing in breadth 60 foot & in length from the strand to the market place. Isaac Tine died without issue, after whose dec. the said lot descended to his sisters, Elizabeth & Mary as heirs at law. Whereas Mary before any partition of the premises was made for her part, died. So that part came to vested by way of survivorship in the said John Bisk & Elizabeth his wife, but in regard to the said Isaac Tine by his last will had given & bequeathed all the estate after his wife's death or marriage to his sisters Mary & Elizabeth equally & in case of their death to be divided between their children equally. Whereas Isaac Tine's wife being dead & his sister Mary being dead, having left their daughters named Mary, Jane & Sarah, 2 of whom being also dead & Sarah being party to this, surviving them to claim her part. Whereas John Bisk & Elizabeth his wife, William Crosse & Thomas Juavier & Sarah his wife with unanimous assent, with the assistance & direction of Edward Blake & Richard Reynolds being of the high court have made a perfect division of said lot in the manner following. John Bisk & Elizabeth, his wife, shall have the south side of said lot with the house & all the apple trees & £10 to be paid John Bisk. Thomas Jauvier & Sarah his wife shall enjoy 2/3 of the other moiety or north side of the lot & William Crosse shall have & hold during his natural life & after his death to the use of Thomas Jauvier & Sarah his wife the other 1/3 part. Signed John Bisk & Elizabeth Bisk. Delivered in the presence of Peter Jaquett

& John Smith. Recorded 6 Aug 1695. (B2:94).

Deed. On 18 Oct 1697. William Hunt of Philadelphia, shipwright to Richard Sharp of Boston, merchant. William Hunt for £490 granted to Richard Sharp the hull of the ship Merry, further [unreadable] before New Castle. To have the hull of the said ship Merry to dock & dispose of at his will & pleasure. Signed William Hunt. Delivered in the presence of Richard Reynolds & William Stone. (B2:98).

Deed. On 20 Sep 1696. John Day, owner of the brigantine called Josiah at anchor at New Castle in the river Delaware for £300 granted 1/4 share of the said brigantine. Signed John Day. Delivered in the presence of John Hamilton, Peter Goddin & James Claypoole. (B2:99).

Deed. On 17 Dec 1696. John Bisk of the town of New Castle & Elizabeth his wife to Benjamin Swett of the town of New Castle. John Bisk & Elizabeth, his wife for valuable consideration granted to Benjamin Swett1 house & piece of land towards the upper end of the town of New Castle bounded on the NE side with the lot of Reynier Vandercoulin except 5 foot from & 20 foot back already sold by John Bisk to Reynier Vandercoulin, on the SW with the lot of Benjamin Swett, SE with Front Street & NW with Land Street being chief part of 3 lots of ground as confirmed by patent from Governor Lovelace dated 8 Apr 1672 to Isaac Tine of the town of New Castle, since in the tenure of John Bisk, executor of the said Isaac Tine. Signed John Bisk & Elizabeth Bisk. Delivered in the presence of John Williams, John Smith & John Walker. Recorded 16 Mar 1696. (B2:100).

Deed. On 31 Mar 1696. John Bisk of the town of New Castle, tailor & William Spark of the province of Maryland & Margaret his wife, the daughter of Josiah Hamilton, late of New Castle, dec. to Benjamin Sweet of New Castle. John Bisk, William Spark & Margaret his wife for valuable consideration granted to Benjamin Swett a lot of ground in the town of New Castle being 30 foot in breadth & in length from sewer to street bounded by on the E with Front Street, W by Land Street, N by the land of John Bisk & south by land & house lately belonging to Josiah Hamilton, dec. which said lot was confirmed by Governor Lovelace on 8 Apr 1672 to Isaac Tine with other lots adjoining. Signed John Bisk, Elizabeth Bisk & William Sparks. Delivered in the presence of Lendorr Osterhaven, Jacob Allrichs, Henry Wright & Sarah Bisk. Recorded 15 June 1696. (B2:101).

Deed. On 16 June 1696. James Claypoole of the town of New Castle to Robert French of the town of New Castle, merchant. James Claypoole for £20 granted to Robert French 2 lots being at the northern most end of the town of New Castle bounded as expressed in 2 patents by commissioners of property both dated 7 July 1685 granted to Arnoldus Delagrange & from him in open court granted to Edward Green, who by a deed granted to James Claypoole. Signed James Claypoole. Delivered in the presence of William Houston & Edward Gibbs. Recorded 16 June 1696. (B2:102).

Deed. On 26 May 1693. Charles Pickering of the town of Philadelphia, merchant to Christiana Stalcop & John Stalcop of the county of New Castle, yeomen. Charles Pickering for £190 granted to Christiana & John Stalcop a tract of land lying on north side of Christiana Creek bounded by land of Christiana Stalcop containing 276 acres, also, a tract of land lying on the north side of Christiana Creek bounded by a small branch which lies between this & land of Christiana Stalcop, the widow Stalcop's land, land of Samuel Peterson, Christiana Creek containing 228 acres of land & 5 acres marsh, in whole being 509 acres, being the land Charles Pickering bought of Edward Gibbs, late sheriff by deed dated 12 Mar 1691. Signed Charles Pickering. Delivered in presence of Charles Landdos, Edward Gibbs & Peter Stalcop. Acknowledged by John Cann as attorney of Charles Pickering in open court 21 June 1693. (B2:103).

Deed. On 1 Jan 1694. Col. William Markham, Esq. Lt. Governor of the province of Pennsylvania to Jasper Yeates of the county of Chester, merchant. For the performance of a certain exchange agreed upon by him the said Col William Markham & Jasper Yeates: to wit Col. William Markham granted to Jasper Yeates a tract of land called Markham's Hope lying just below the town of New Castle bounded by the first neck of land below the point by the river & the marsh called Little Marsh, the Great Marsh, the highway to Maryland & Christiana Road containing 1078 acres, also a parcel of ground being at the south end of the town of New Castle containing 180 foot in breadth & in length in proportion to the adjoining lots bounded by E Front Street, W with Bank Street, N with the street leading from the river & S with the remaining parcel of ground belonging to Robert French, which said lands are in the possession of Col. William Markham by virtue of a warrant from William Penn dated 3 Jan 1682 directed to Ephraim Herman, then surveyor to survey & lay out to Col. Markham & confirmed to Col. William Markham by patent from William Penn dated 16 Dec 1689, recorded Philadelphia Book A, No. 1 Page 76 on 1 Dec 1694. Which the 2nd parcel is in possession of Col. Markham by virtue of a patent from the commissioners to Robert French, dated 5 May 1694, recorded in Philadelphia Book A. No. 1 Page 77 on 1 Dec 1694, & by virtue of a deed from Robert French dated 18 Aug 1694 to Col. William Markham as recorded in Philadelphia Book A No. 1 Page 77. And in exchange Jasper Yeates granted to Col. William Markham a lot of land on the Delaware River in the town of

Philadelphia containing 30 1/2 foot in breadth & 250 foot in length bounded by N by land of John Whitpins now Patrick Robinson, E with the River Delaware, S with the land of William Samptons now of Charles Reed & W with Delaware Front Street. Col. William Markham appoints Major John Donaldson to be his attorney to acknowledge said deed. Signed William Markham. Delivered in the presence of Phil. Richards, Samuel Peres & Patrick Robinson. Recorded 20 Mar 1694. (B2:106).

Deed. On 18 May 1697. Richard Carr, son & heir of Capt. John Carr, late of New Castle, dec. & George Oldfield intermarried with Petroeleas, the late widow of Capt. John Carr to Jasper Yeates of the county of New Castle. Richard Carr & George Oldfield for sum of money granted to Jasper Yeates all right & title in a tract of land. Signed Richard Carr & George Oldfield. Delivered in the presence of Peter Allrichs, John Donaldson & Adam Peterson. Recorded 18 may 1697. (B2:107).

Deed. On 3 Aug 1696. Richard Carr of Cecil County in Maryland, yeoman, son & heir of Richard Carr of New Castle, dec. to John Donaldson, Richard Hallywell & Robert French of the town of New Castle, merchants. Whereas Richard Nichols, Gov., by letter of patent dated 1 Jan 1667 granted to John Carr a tract of land lying neat the fort containing 150 acres, not long since in the tenure & occupation of Alex. _____ bounded on the S by the river, N & NE by land Garret B__, NW by a plantation called Landery & S SW by land lately belonging to John Nobber. Richard Carr for a valuable sum granted to John Donaldson, Richard Hallywell & Robert French the said parcel. Signed Richard Carr. Delivered in the presence of Cornelius Empson & Peter Allrichs. Recorded 17 Nov 1696. (B2:111).

Deed. On 31 Oct 1695 Mary Mayle of Appoquinimink Creek, widow to John Heally of the said place, husbandman. Mary Mayle for valuable consideration granted to John Heally a tract of land called The Cheuige, lying on the SE side of a branch of Appoquinimink Creek called Sassafras Creek bounded by land formerly belonging to David Jones, the said creek, the main road containing 500 acres from the certificate of surveyor which said tract of land was confirmed by patent from Gov. Frances Lovelace on 20 Feb 1672 to Timothy Love & Edward Sap & afterwards in open court on 8 Feb 1676 confirmed to John Walker, late of the said place, dec. but before his death by his last will & testament among other bequest gave & devised the said tract of land unto Dorothy his then wife, who intermarried with Walter Smith, which Walter Smith & Dorothy his wife by deed dated 20 Sep 1692 granted said land to Mary Mayle. Signed Mary Mayle. Delivered in the presence of Job England, Richard Cantwell & Benjamin Gumley. Recorded 17 Dec 1695. (B2:113).

Deed. On 16 Mar 1696. John Crawford of the county of New Castle, son & heir of James Crawford, dec. to Edward Gibbs of the same place, gentleman. John Crawford for £112 granted to Edward Gibbs all his right & title in a tract of land called Gerwick lying on the south side of St. George's Creek bounded by as expressed in patent dated 5 Nov 1675 from Edmund Andros, the Gov. of New York to James Crawford, now in the possession of Edward Gibbs & Judith his wife, mother of John Crawford, which said land & other premises be the said John Crawford's after the death of Judith, his mother. Which said tract of land, James Crawford, dec. devised & bequeathed to the said Judith during her natural life & immediate reversion to John Crawford. John Crawford granted to Edward Gibbs all right to said reversion of land at the death of his mother. Signed John Crawford. Delivered in the presence of John Ogle & Nath. Claypoole. Recorded 15 Mar 1696. (B2:116).

Deed. On 19 Nov 1695. John Healy of Appoquinimink Creek, husbandman to Richard Cantwell of the same place, gentleman. John Healy for valuable consideration granted to Richard Cantwell a tract of land called Poplar Hill, lying on Hangman's Creek a branch of Appoquinimink Creek & land of Robert Morton containing 200 acres. Signed John Healy. Delivered in the presence of James Read & Edward Gibbs. Recorded 19 Nov 1695. (B2:119).

Deed. On 18 Mar 1696/7. James Read of New Castle, yeoman to Helletye Anderson of the said county, widow. James Read for £130 granted to Helletye Anderson all that dwelling house & lot of land lying in New Castle bounded on the E with Front Street, W with Land Street & on N & S as specified in a patent dated 5 Jan 1667 granted by Richard Nicholls, Gov. of New York to Thomas Wollaston, whom the said James Read by virtue of a mean conveyances doth lay claim to the premises. Signed James Read. Delivered in the presence of David Lloyd & John Watts. Recorded 16 Mar 1696. (B2:120).

Release. On Mar 1696/7. Thomas Wollaston of the county of New Castle, son & heir of Thomas Wollaston, dec. to Helletye Anderson of the said county, widow. Thomas Wollaston for 6 shillings release all claim to a lot in the town of New Castle near the strand in the possession of Helletye Anderson by virtue of a deed from James Read of New Castle bounded by a house formerly belonging to Isam Swin, the house formerly of Michael Baron & the river. The said lot was granted to my late father, Thomas Wollaston by patent dated 1 Jan 1667. Singed Thomas Wollaston. Delivered in the presence of David Lloyd & John Watts. Recorded 16 Mar 1696. (B2:122).

Deed. On 17 Aug 1697. John Donaldson of the town of New Castle & Elizabeth his wife to Richard Bonsell, late of the county of Chester, yeoman &

John Wood of the county of Chester, yeoman. John Donaldson & Elizabeth his wife for £300 from Richard Bonsell & £100 from John Wood granted to Richard Bonsell & John Wood a tract of land called Good Land lying near the mouth of the Delaware River between Duck Creek & a great swamp & creek called Cedar Swamp & Creek bounded by land of Christopher Ellitt & ___ anl Woods, the Cypress Swamp & Thoroughfare Creek being a branch of Duck Creek containing 1200 acres. Signed John Donaldson & Elizabeth Donaldson. Delivered in the presence of Cornelius Empson, Joseph Wood & Benj. Gumley. Recorded 14 Sep 1697. (B2:124).

Deed. On 17 Aug 1697. John Donaldson of the town of New Castle, & Elizabeth his wife to Richard Bonsell & John Wood. John Donaldson & Elizabeth his wife for granted & confirmed to Richard Bonsell & John Wood 2 tracts of land bounded by land of John Taylor, a branch of Duck Creek & land of Christopher Ellit containing 430 acres & the other tract being near Duck Creek bounded by land of James Crawford, Thomas Bell & James Boewick containing 200 acres. Signed John Donaldson & Elizabeth Donaldson. Delivered in the presence of Cornelius Empson, Joseph Wood & Benj. Gumley. Recorded 14 Sep 1697. (B2:126).

Deed. On 15 Aug 1699. Hans Peterson of the county of New Castle to Charles Springer, Lucas Stedham, Olah Slooby, Gilbert Wallraven, Henry Evertson & Ollah Thomas. Hans Peterson for £35 granted to Charles Springer, Lucas Stedham, Olah Slooby, Gilbert Wallraven, Henry Evertson & Ollah Thomas, trustees & church wardens, a tract of land lying at Verdredee Hood containing 100 acres bounded by the river Delaware, land of Peter Mounce, land of Jacob Clement & 113 acres of marsh, for the use of the Sweeds Church. Signed Hans Peterson. Delivered in the presence of Peter Peterson & Jonas Wallraven. Recorded 15 Aug 1699. (B2:128).

Patent. On 12 Apr 1686. Thomas Lloyd, James Claypoole & Robert Turner or any 2 of us being appointed commissioners by William Penn, Governor to grant & sign warrants & patents for land. Whereas there is a piece of land in the county of New Castle bounded by a run called First Branch standing by the King's Road & land of William Markham containing 39 acres, granted by warrant from ourselves dated 25 Nov 1684 to Henry Vandenburgh in right of John Carolson & Susanna Henrickson, orphans of Hendrick Peterson Russenburgh. Henry Vandenburgh requesting us to confirm. We confirm to Henry Vandenburgh the 39 acres he paying 1/2 bushel of wheat yearly to persons of authority. Signed James Claypoole & Robert Turner. (B2:130).

Deed. On 3 July 1696. Henry Vandenburgh to John Watts. Henry

Vandenburgh for valuable consideration granted to John Watts the within tract. Signed Henry Vandenburgh. Delivered in the presence of Sylvester Garland & James Claypoole. Recorded 17 Nov 1696. (B2:131).

Deed. On 30 May 1698. Hester Watts, widow & executrix of the will of John Watts, butcher, dec. to Jasper Yeates of Upland, merchant. Hester Watts for 240 gallons of rum granted to Jasper Yeates the within mentioned tract of land containing 39 acres & bounded as expressed in the within patent [Patent from page 130]. Signed Hester Watts. Delivered in the presence of Joshua Hastings, Willaim Alloway & John Moore. Recorded 20 June 1698. (B2:132).

Deed. On 29 Aug 1698. Hypolitus Lefever of the town of New Castle, innholder to Joseph Pidgeon of Philadelphia, merchant. Hypolitus Lefever for £22 14 shillings granted to Joseph Pidgeon a lot in the town of New Castle bounded on the E with Front Street, W by Land Street, N with ground late of Henry Williams & S by ground of Mathias Vandenhayden. Signed Hypo. Lefever. Delivered in the presence of Richard Halliwell, Jasper Yeates & James Claypoole. Recorded 15 Aug 1699. (B2:133).

Deed. On 15 Feb 1686/7. Henry Evertson of Crane Hook to John Granthom of the county of New Castle. Henry Evertson for £20 granted to John Granthom a lot of land in Crane Hook bounded by lands of John Mattson, the river Delaware, land sold by Henry Evertson to Henry Vandenburgh being bounded as the line run by Thomas Peirson the late deputy surveyor. Henry Granthom. Delivered in the presence of Richard Noble, Hans Peterson & John White. Recorded 21 Apr 1687. (B2:134).

Deed. On 16 Mar 1696. Jacob Rotier of the county of New Castle to Reyneir Vandercoulin. Jacob Rotier for a competent sum of money granted to Reyneir Vandercoulin the within mentioned tract of land . Signed Jacob Rotier. Delivered in the presence of John Blanchard & Thomas Fauvier. Recorded 16 Mar 1696. (B2:135).

Deed. On 5 May 1693. James Read of New Castle, yeoman to John Heally of Maryland, yeoman. James Read for & in consideration of marriage intended & shortly to be had & solemnized between the said James Read & Ann Phiana, the daughter of Adam Peterson of Appoquinimink Creek & that Anna Phiana may be provided of a sufficient jointure in case she shall survive the said James Read, & for other good causes & considerations, James Read promise & granted to John Heally that James Read shall & will before the justices of the county of New Castle acknowledge & deliver an assurance & covenant of all the messuage & dwelling house & lot of land with improvements in New Castle, the true intent whereof between the parties shall be construed, intended to be the use & behoove of James Read during his life & the behoove of Anna Phiana fur & during her natural life. And after her dec. to the use & behoove of the heirs of the body of James Read on the body of Anna, lawfully begotten & for the default of such issue to the right heirs of James Read for ever. Provided always that if the marriage shall not take effect or be solemnized between the said James Read & Anna Phiana, then this conveyance shall be for the use of James Read. Signed James Read. Delivered in the presence of Edward Gibbs & James Claypoole. Recorded 16 Mar 1696. (B2:136).

Deed. On 16 Mar 1696/7. Erik Erickson of the county of New Castle to Reyneir Vandercoulin. Erik Erickson for valuable sum of money granted to Reyneir Vandercoulin one lot in Crane Hook bounded by the lot of Erik Erickson, land of Reyneir Vandercoulin & the marsh. Signed Erik Erickson. Delivered in the presence of John Ranels & John Smith. Recorded 16 Mar 1696. (B2:137).

Deed. On Mar 1696/7. Reyneir Vandercoulin of the county of New Castle to Mathias Vanderheyden of Cecil County in the province of Maryland. Reyneir Vandercoulin for a valuable sum of money granted to Mathias Vanderheyden a house & lot in the town of New Castle, likewise a 5 foot in breadth & 20 foot back taken out of the lot of John Bisk (now Benjamin Swett's lot) situated in the Front Street bounded by the lot of Moses Sherry & land of Benjamin Swett being in breadth 65 foot besides the 5 foot & in length according to other lots being the remaining part of a lot of ground formerly granted by patent from Governor Francis Lovelace dated 9 Apr 1669. Signed Reyneir Vandercoulin & Mary Vandercoulin. Recorded 16 Mar 1696. (B2:138).

Deed. On June 1696. Jacobus Allrichs of the town of New Castle to John Parris of Cecil County in the province of Maryland. Jacobus Allrichs for valuable consideration granted to John Parris a lot of ground in the town of New Castle on the south side of Otter Street containing in breadth 120 feet & in length 300 feet formerly granted by patent to John Foratt of the town of New Castle & now in the tenure of Jacobus Allrichs. Signed Jacobus Allrichs. Delivered in the presence of Humphrey Best & Robert Hutchinson. Recorded 16 June 1696. (B2:139).

Deed. On 19 Aug 1699. Nichols Lockyer of Swanneck in the county of New Castle & Elizabeth his wife to John Heally of Appoquinimink Creek. Nicholas Lockyer & Elizabeth his wife for 5 shillings granted to John Heally a tract of land being bounded by land formerly belonging to Peter DeWitt, the marsh that runs to the Horse Neck(or Peardehook), land of Durian Johnson commonly called Layman's Hook in breadth by the river 100 rods & into the woods 300 rods & also that tract of land in the county at Peardehook bounded by land formerly of John Sybranson, land of Barbara, then the widow of Peter Macland, dec. the river containing in breadth 520 rods in length 600 rod in Dutch measure. Also a tract of land Peardehook bounded by land of Earthman Hyne, land hertofor of Jacob Clauson & a small creek containing in length 500 rod & in breadth 25 rod. Also that tract of marshland lying between the marsh of James Holliday & the marsh of Bilchy Johnson between the river & Swanneck Creek, formerly the marsh of John Sybrant, Jr.. All said tracts of land were left in the tenure of Nicholas Lockyer & Elizabeth his wife but now by virtue of the statute for transferring uses into possession, are now in the actual possession of the said John Heally & all the estate right. That is to say that as to this to the use & behoove of Nicholas Lockyer & Elizabeth his wife during the terms of their natural lives & the life of the longer liver of them, & after their dec. to their heirs & as to concerning the before mentioned tracts of land to be & remain to the only use of Nicholas Lockyer & Elizabeth his wife. In last, it shall happen the said Elizabeth shall die in the lifetime of Nicholas Lockyer, that the said Elizabeth shall have free power by her will or as she shall think fit to give & devise any gift to such persons as she shall appoint & nominate to the value of £100 & that John Heally shall stand seized in the first mentioned tract of land, till the sum of £100 is paid to the true intent & purpose of these presents. Signed Nicholas Lockyer & Elizabeth Lockyer. Delivered in the presence of John Orton & Thomas Wollaston. Recorded 15 Aug 1696. (B2:140).

Deed. On 11 Mar 1697/8. James Read of the town of New Castle to John Richardson of the county of New Castle. James Read for £54 5 shillings granted to John Richardson one house & 2 lots in the town of New Castle bounded by the street called Wood Street, River Street, lands of John Watts & Otter Street being 235 foot in breadth & 332 foot in length. The same formerly belonging to Gerherd Johnson (alias) Smith & now in the tenure of James Read. Signed James Read. Delivered in the presence of John Donaldson, Joseph Wood & John Dunn. Recorded 15 Aug 1699. (B2143).

Deed. On 15 Aug 1699. Edward Gibbs of the county of New Castle to Mathias Erickson of the county of New Castle. Whereas there is a tract of land on the east side of Scott's Creek between the head of the same & the head of St. George's Creek bounded by Scott's Run crossing the King; road & land of Amos Nichols containing 200 acres surveyed & laid out to Amos Nichols 1 Apr 1686 & Amos Nichols conveyed the same to Edmund Perkins by deed dated 22 July 1686 & by Francis Luckins the lawful attorney of Edmund Perkins by deed dated 20 Apr 1687 granted said land to John Simm's of the county of New Castle, merchant. John Simms granted the land to Edward Gibbs. Now Edward

Gibbs for a valuable sum of money granted to Mathias Erickson all the said tract. Signed Edward Gibbs. Delivered in the presence of Thomas Peirson, Joseph Griffin & John Smith. Recorded 15 Aug 1699. (B2:144).

Deed. On 17 Aug 1699. Mathias Erickson of the county of New Castle to Jacobus Allrichs of the said county. Mathias Erickson for a competent sum of money granted to Jacobus Allrichs a tract of land formerly laid out to Hendrick Lemmon bounded by land of John Williams, by the road near the head of a run called Masters ___om's Runland which was formerly of Olah Powellson, & another tract of land since bought by Hendrick Lemmons containing 200 acres. Said tracts of land are more fully expressed in Patent dated 5 Aug 1687. Signed Mathias Erickson. Delivered in the presence of John Prow & William White. Recorded 15 Aug 1699. (B2:147).

Deed. On 15 Aug 1699. Joseph Wheeldon of ----. Whereas there is a tract of land containing 220 acres known by the name Dalton lying on the north side of Blackbird Creek bounded by land of Thomas Snelling formerly granted by patent dated 25 Mar 1676 by Governor Edmund Andros to John Barker, formerly of Blackbird Creek & since John Barker sold unto Isaac Wheeldon. Now Joseph Wheeldon & William Robinson, executors to the dec. Isaac Wheeldon of Blackbird Creek, for £8 granted to William Grant of Appoquinimink Creek all that tract of land bounded by land of Robert Hartuup, a beaver dam & a branch containing 220 acres. Signed Joseph Wheeldon & William Robinson. Delivered in the presence of John Heally & Adam Peterson. Recorded 15 Aug 1699. (B2:148).

Deed. On 15 Aug 1699. Joseph Clayton of the town of New Castle, carpenter to John Ogle of Turk Creek, planter. Joseph Clayton for a competent sum of money granted to John Ogle a tract of land lying on the east side of the main branch of Christiana Creek, land of Jonas Arskins & land of Andrew Tille containing 444 acres. Signed Joseph Clayton. Delivered in the presence of Cornelius Empson & John French. Recorded 15 Aug 1699. (B2:150).

Deed. On 18 Aug 1697. John Moll of Bohemia River in the province of Maryland, gent. to John Donaldson of the town of New Castle, merchant. John Moll for valuable consideration granted to John Donaldson a tract of land called The Acquittance bounded by the road that leads to Maryland, land of Peter Allrich & land of Ephraim Herman aforesaid dec. called Expected containing 200 acres granted by warrant from the Governor dated 23 Feb 1682 to John Moll. Signed John Moll. Delivered in the presence of Griffith Jones & Cornelius Empson. Recorded 17 Aug 1697. (B2:151).

Deed. On 16 Mar 1696. John Ogle of the County of New Castle, planter to John Crawford of the County of New Castle, planter. John Ogle for a competent sum of money granted to John Crawford one moiety or upper most half (adjoining the plantation of Thomas Ogle) of a tract of land called Two Brothers situated on the north side of White Clay Creek containing in whole 300 acres bounded as expressed in patent dated 26 Mar 1684 from William Penn, Gov. to Thomas Ogle & John Ogle, containing 150 acres. Signed John Ogle. Delivered in the presence of Robert Dyer & Sylvester Garland. Recorded 16 Mar 1696. (B2:153).

Deed. On 15 Feb 1697. Thomas Ogle for a competent sum of money granted to John Crawford the other moiety or the lower most half of the within mentioned 300 acres. Signed Thomas Ogle. Delivered in the presence of John Buckley & James Claypoole. Recorded 15 Feb 1697. (B2:153).

Deed. On 24 Jan 1697. Peter Godin of the county of New Castle, one of the heirs at law of John Forratt, late of the county, dec. to Christopher Hussey of the County of New Castle. Peter Godin for £46 granted to Christopher Hussey one house & piece of ground in the town of New Castle situated towards the south west end of the said town being bounded on the SE with the river, WSW with the house & lot of Peter Allrichs, NW with the house of Edward Blake, dec. & N with the house of Jacobus Allrichs being part of a lot of ground bought by the said John Forratt of John Moll by deed dated 16 Oct 1688. Signed Peter Godin. Delivered in the presence of Benjamin Swett, John Smith & John Ellis. Recorded 15 Feb 1697. (B2:154).

Deed. On 15 Feb 1697. Jonas Arskins of White Clay Creek, yeoman to Thomas Ogle of the said place, yeoman. Jonas Arskins for valuable consideration granted to Thomas Ogle a tract of land on the south side of White Clay Creek containing 200 acres bounded as expressed in a patent granted by the commissioners on 15 June 1688 to Jonas Arskins. Signed Jonas Arskins. Delivered in the presence of John Crawford & James Claypoole. Recorded 15 Feb 1697. (B2:155).

Deed. On 21 Nov 1699. John Mony of Cecil County in the province of Maryland, planter to Job Nanscoyre & John Nanscoyre of Appoquinimink Creek. John Mony for valuable consideration granted to Job Nanscoyre & John Nanscoyre 2 tracts of land situated at Appoquinimink bounded by the said Creek, land of Barnett Hendrickson, dec., land of Bryan O'Neal & land of Abraham Coffin containing 388 acres formerly surveyed in 2 tracts 188 acres surveyed for Jacob Fiana & 180 acres surveyed for Marris Daniel by virtue of a patent granted to John Bradburn, surveyed by Walter Wharton in 1671 & 1676 with a part of the marsh below Drayers Creek. Signed Robert Mony. Delivered in the presence of Isaac Vigoreux & Harman Allrichs. Recorded 21 Nov 1699. (B2:156).

Deed. On 20 Feb 1699. Mathias Erickson for a competent sum of money granted to Lymon Marsellottthe lower half of 200 acres of land on Scott's Run between a branch & St. George's Creek bounded by Scott's Run crossing the Kings Road, land of Amos Nicholls containing 200 acres, to have & hold the lower moiety or part. Signed Mathias Erickson. Delivered in the presence of Edward Braming & Elston Wallis. Recorded 20 Feb 1699. (B2:157).

Deed. On 15 Sep 1691. Cornelius Empson & Henry Vandenburgh of New Castle to Edward Gibbs. Cornelius Empson & Henry Vandenburgh for £20 granted to Edward Gibbs one half a certain tract of land situated on the south side of St. George's Creek being the upper half of the tract bounded as by patent from Edmond Andros, dated 5 Nov 1675. Signed Henry Vandenburgh & Cornelius Empson. Delivered in the presence of Peter Allrichs, John Cann, John Donaldson & Edward Blake. Recorded 15 Sep 1691. (B2:159).

Deed. On 31 Dec 1690. John Macarty of Blackbird Creek, planter to Richard Halliwell of the town of New Castle, merchant. John Macarty for £60 granted to Richard Halliwell all his tract of land situated on the north side of a creek called Hangman's Creek bounded by the land of Hemicus Williams, the creek & land of Edmond Cantwell containing 279 acres. Signed John Macarty. Delivered in the presence of John Simes & Richard Haes. On 31 Dec 1690. Ellinor Macarty, the wife of John do hereby freely give her consent to the within conveyance of land to the said Richard Halliwell & has appointed Edward Gibbs for her behalf to acknowledge said in open court. Signed Elinor Macarty. Delivered in the presence of John Simes & Richard Haes. Recorded 17 Mar 1690. (B2:159).

Deed. On 20 Mar 1698. Richard Halliwell for valuable consideration granted to Richard Cantwell the with tract of land. Signed Richard Halliwell. Delivered in the presence of Joseph Wood & John Smith. Recorded 21 mar 1698. (B2:161).

Deed. On 17 Dec 1689. John Darby & James Walliam both of the County of New Castle, gentlemen to John Donaldson of the town of New Castle, merchant. John Darby & James Walliam for a valuable sum of money granted to John Donaldson the within mentioned lot. Signed John Darby & James Walliam. Delivered in the presence of Peter Allrichs & John Cann. Recorded 15 Apr 1690. (B2:161).

Deed. On 23 Mar 1698. John Donaldson of the county of New Castle, gentleman to Mathias Vanderhayden of the province of Maryland, merchant. John Donaldson for a valuable sum granted to Mathias Vanderhayden the within mentioned lot. Signed John Donaldson. Delivered in the presence of Joseph Wood & Cornelius Empson. Recorded 25 Mar 1698. (B2:162).

Deed. On 21 Mar 1698/9. Brewer Sinnexen of Christiana Creek, husbandman to Thomas Ogle of White Clay Creek. Whereas there is a tract of land called Waterland situated on both side of White Clay Creek containing 300 acres confirmed to Brewer Sinnexen by patent dated 7 June 1686 & Brewer Sinnexen having sold out the said tract unto his son in law Christian Urianson & John Garnerall, that his part of the land on the north side of the said creek bounded by said creek & there remaining unto Brewer Sinnexen the land lying on the south of the said creek bounded by the creek containing 100 acres. Now Brewer Sinnexen for £12 12 shillings granted to Thomas Ogle the said tract of land on the south side of the creek. Signed Brewer Sinnexen. Delivered in the presence of John Richardson, Thomas Pierson & Richard Maankin. Recorded 21 Maar 1698. (B2:162).

Deed. On 23 mar 1698. John Champion of the county of New Castle to Edward Green of the county of New Castle. John Champion for £400 & 2 buckskins granted to Edward Green a tract of land being one half of 400 acres bounded by Pecks Creek, land of William Balls containing 400 acres. Signed John Champion. Delivered in the presence of Edward Gibbs, William Ball & Hyop. Lefever. Recorded 21 Mar 1698. (B2:164).

Deed. On 17 Nov 1696. Reynier Vandercoulin of the County of New Castle, yeoman to Cornelius Empson of the County of New Castle, gentleman. Reynier Vandercoulin for a competent sum granted to Cornelius Empson a parcel of land & a house in the town of New Castle bounded by the street fronting the market place, by a swamp, the river, the land of Edward Blake, dec. & Peter Allrichs & land of James Claypoole. Signed Reynier Vandercoulin. Delivered in the presence of P. Perdrain & Isaiah Lebahy. Recorded 17 Nov 1696. (B2:165).

Deed. On 4 June 1696. Henry Vandenburgh to John Donaldson of the town of New Castle, merchant. Henry Vandenburgh for valuable consideration granted to John Donaldson a tract of land lying toward the upper part of Red Lyon Run containing 440 acres bounded as expressed in patent granted by William Penn dated 30 July 1685 to John Harms & from him in open court Henry Vandenburgh. Signed Henry Vandenburgh. Delivered in the presence of John Hamilton & James Claypoole. Recorded 17 Nov 1696. (B2:166).

Deed. On 16 Nov 1689. John Moll formerly of the town of New Castle but now of the County of Cecil in the province of Maryland to Garret Janson (alias) Smith of the town of New Castle, farmer. John Moll for £20 & the remainder engaged to be paid according to a agreement dated 14 Aug 1689, granted to Garret Janson (als) Smith all my right & interest in a tract of land being at the back part of the town of New Castle bounded on the SE with Otter Street, NE with land of Huybert Hendricks, dec., NW with the cripple that divides this land from the land which was formerly called John Webber's land & SW with the King's Highway which goes to Christiana Creek & Swaart Nutton Island containing 6 or 7 acres as it now lies & this last year has been rented by the said Garret Jansen (als) Smith, which said parcel is part of greater quantity granted in a patent to John Moll from Governor Andros dated 25 Mar 1676. Signed John Moll & Christina Moll. Recorded 19 Nov 1689. (B2:166).

Deed. On 17 Nov 1696. James Read of the town of New Castle for a competent sum granted to John Richardson the within tract of land. Signed James Read. Delivered in the presence of George Lamb & John Lewden. Recorded 17 Nov 1696. (B2:168).

Deed. On 25 Oct 1689. William Markham of Philadelphia, gentleman to James Claypoole, clerk of the county of New Castle. William Markham for £30 granted to James Claypoole a lot of land in the town of New Castle bounded on the SW with the swamp commonly called Allrichs Swamp, SE with the house of Gerhardus Wessell, NE with the market place & NW with the land of Anthony Green, dec. containing 60 foot in breadth. Signed William Markham. Delivered in the presence of John Claypoole, Alexander Craber & John Test. Recorded 19 Nov 1689 by John Cann & Edward Blake, justices. (B2:168).

Deed. On 26 Apr 1692. Jacob Hendrickson of Salem County in river Delaware did on 7 Apr 1692 sell to Erick Anderson of the County of New Castle a tract of land lying in Brandywine Creek called Jacob's Land, bounded by land of Adam Stedham, land of Mathias Defoss containing 300 acres as surveyed by Thomas Pierson on 16 Mar 1684. Now Jacob Hendrickson granted to Erick Anderson the said 300 acres. Signed Jacob Hendrickson. Delivered in the presence of Urian Anderson, Peter Anderson & Thomas Pierson. I underwritten Hendrick Hendrickson, brother to Jacob Hendrickson do by these present acknowledge that the one half of the above mentioned land which I have formerly taken up with my brother that I have fully & absolutely given it over to my brothers whole & sole dispose & am content that he hath made sale to Erick Anderson of it. Signed Hendrick Hendrickson. Delivered in the presence of Lucas Stedham & James Bisch. Recorded 17 Sep 1695. (B2:169).

Deed. On 7 Oct 1695. John Willson of Appoquinimink Creek to Kenhelm Clark of Cecil County in the province of Maryland. John Willson for valuable consideration granted to Kenhelm Clark a tract of land called Mill Fork being on the north side of Drawyers Creek bounded by land of Thomas Sadler, land of Richard Ingelloes & Walkers Run containing with a small parcel of marsh, 111 acres. Signed John Wilson. Delivered in the presence of Sylvester Garland, Jacobus Allrichs & John Smith. Recorded 17 Sep 1695. (B2:170).

Deed. On 17 Oct 1695. Wybrough Walker, adm. & widow of John Walker, late of the town of New Castle to John Wilson of Appoqiniimink Creek. Wybrough Walker for valuable consideration paid to her late husband granted to John Wilson a tract of land called Mill Fork being in the northside of Drawyers Creek bounded by land of Thomas Sadler, land of Richard Ingelloes & Walkers Run containing 111 acres. Signed Wybrough Walker. Delivered in the presence of Sylvester Garland, Jacobus Allrichs & John Smith. Recorded 17 Sep 1695. (B2:172).

Deed. On 16 Apr 1698. Andrew Cork of the town of New Castle & Alchee his wife to Joseph Griffin of the town of New Castle. Andrew Cork & Alchee his wife for a sum of silver money granted to Joseph Griffin one house & lot of land in the town of New Castle being formerly the dwelling house of Zachary Vandercoulin & now in the tenure of the said Andrew Cork bounded on the SE with Beaver Street, NW with Otter Street, SW with a lot now in the possession of Sylvester Garland & NE a lot now in the possession of Cornelius Kettle containing in breadth 60 foot & 300 foot in length being the one half of a parcel of land granted by patent from Governor Penn to Zacharias Vandercoulin dated 26 June 1691 with the privilege of the well in the lot of Cornelius Kettle. Signed Andrew Cork & Alchee Cork. Delivered in the presence of Richard Halliwell & Benjamin Swett. Recorded 16 May 1699. (B2:173).

Deed. On 16 May 1699. Robert Hartop of Blackbird Creek to Richard Cantwell of Appoquinimink Creek, gentleman. Robert Hartop for a competent sum granted to Richard Cantwell a tract of land between Appoquinimink Creek & Blackbird Creek bounded by other land of Richard Cantwell containing 250 acres. Signed Robert Hartop. Delivered in the presence of John Heally & William Burrows. Recorded 16 May 1699. (B2:174).

Deed. On 20 Sep 1694. Zacharias Vandercoulin of the town of New Castle to Reyneir Vandercoulin of the town of New Castle. Zacharias Vandercoulin for a valuable sum granted to Reynier Vandercoulin a house & lot of land in the town of New Castle bounded on the W with the lot of John Bisk, S with the main river containing in length 315 foot & in breadth 58 foot. Signed Zacharias

Vandercoulin & Alchee Vandercoulin. Delivered in the presence of Leond. _otterhaven & William Cracksee. Recorded 18 Sep 1694. (B2:175).

Deed. On 19 Sep 1694. Christian Jurianson of the county of New Castle to Neal Cook of the County of New Castle. Christian Jurianson for valuable consideration granted to Neal Cook a tract of land containing 100 acres situated on the north side of White Clay Creek bounded a run called Dividing Run & White Clay Creek. Signed Christian Jurianson. Delivered in the presence of Robert Hutchison & John Smith. Recorded 19 Sep 1694. (B2:176).

Deed. On 6 Aug 1695. James White, son & heir of John White late of the town of Philadelphia, dec. to John Lewden of Christiana Creek, weaver. James White for valuable consideration granted to John Lewden a tract of land containing 435 acres being called Fishing Place, situate on the SE side of the southern most branch of Christiana Creek bounded by Eilly's Run, Spry's Run & a swamp also over said creek 16 acres of marsh for hay. Signed James White. Delivered in the presence of Mary Parson, Alice White, John Donaldson & Cornelius Empson. Recorded 6 Aug 1695. (B2:177).

Deed. On 5 Nov 1694. William Price, Sr. of Elk River in Cecil County in the province of Maryland to John Healy of the above county & province. William Price for consideration already received, granted to John Healy a tract of land called Poplar Hill situated on Hangmans Creek it being one of the branches of Appoquinimink Creek bounded by land of Robert Morton containing 200 acres. Signed William Price & Margaret Price. Delivered in the presence of John Wilson & William Burrows. Recorded 6 Aug 1695. (B2:178).

Deed. On 18 Aug 1697. Richard Carr, son & heir of Capt. John Carr, dec. & George Oldfield & Peternella his wife to Mathias Vanderheyden of the province of Maryland, gent. Richard Carr, George Oldfield & Peternella his wife for a valuable sum granted to Mathias Vanderheyden a lot with housing in the town of New Castle on the north side of the street called Hart Street containing in length 233 foot, the said lot & premises having on the northside the lot of Edmond Cantwell & in breadth next to the lot of Johannes Dehaes 60 foot. Signed Richard Carr, George Oldfield & Peternella Oldfield. Delivered in the presence of John Smith & George Lamb. Recorded 14 Sep 1697. (B2:179).

Deed. On 19 Mar 1694/5. John Moll of the county of Cecil in the province of Maryland to Hans Hanson of New Castle County, farmer. John Moll for £225, £30 in hand paid, the remainder assured to be paid by 4 obligations & a mortgage dated this day, & also for more other weighty reasons & considerations granted to Hans Hanson a tract of land called the Exchange, lying between the Delaware River & a great swamp called Dragons Swamp adjoining the land belonging to the estate of Henry Ward, dec. bounded by Dragon Swamp, and of Ward, Beaver Dam Branch & the eastside of the head of Dragons Creek containing 1000 acres as appears by the original patent granted to John Moll by dated 8 Aug 1679 by Edmond Andros (then Governor). Signed John Moll. Delivered in the presence of George Moore & John Wilson. Recorded 19 Mar 1694. (B2:1179).

Deed. On 10 Mar 1694. Thomas Ogle of the county of New Castle to Edward Gibbs of the County of New Castle. Whereas there is a tract of land called Windsor lying on the southside of St. George's Creek containing 280 acres granted to George Moore by patent from Governor Edmund Andros dated 5 Nov 1675 & said George Moore conveyed the said land to James Crawford by deed as recorded in the county of New Castle in folio. 12 & James Crawford having giver unto his daughter Mary Crawford 100 acres of the aforementioned land by his last will & testament proved 22 Feb 1682/3. Know ye that Thomas Ogle in right of his wife Mary to the aforementioned land for £10 granted to Edward Gibbs the whole 100 acres bounded by a branch of Doctors Swamp, land of Edward Gibbs & near the head of another branch that divides this from the rest of the aforementioned tract. Signed Thomas Ogle. Delivered in the presence of Edward Hillington & Thomas Brason. Recorded 19 Mar 1694. (B2:182).

Deed. On 20 July 1695. Cornelius Post of the County of New Castle to John Ellis of the town of New Castle. Cornelius Post for valuable consideration granted to John Ellis a house & lot of land being on the SW end of the town of New Castle bounded on NE with the lot of John Grantham, SW with the lot of Doctor Samuel Perry being 30 foot in breadth & 300 foot in length. Signed Cornelius Post. Delivered in the presence of James Bursgrave & John Smith. Recorded 16 June 1696. (B2:182).

Deed. On 16 June 1696. Reynier Vandercoulin of the county of New Castle to John Thompson of the County of Cecil in the province of Maryland. Reynier Vandercoulin for £84 granted to John Thompson a house & lot in the town of New Castle bounded on the S by the market place, NE by house & lot of John Walker, SW by land of Ambrose Baker NW with Brewer Street being in breadth 30 foot, which was by Cornelius Derrickson of the town of New Castle, cooper, conveyed in open court 23 Mar 1693 to Reynier Vandercoulin. Signed Reynier Vandercoulin & Margaret Vandercoulin. Delivered in the presence of Adam Peterson & James Read. Recorded 16 June 1696. (B2:183).

Deed. On 20 Mar 1696. Henry Vandenburgh for £27 10 shillings granted to

Henry Evertson a tract of land & dwelling house situated at St. George's Creek now in the possession of Olla Ollson containing 100 acres. Signed Henry Vandenburgh. Delivered in the presence of Mathias Erickson & James Claypoole. Recorded 14 Sep 1697. (B2:184).

Deed. On 17 Aug 1697. William Pattison of the County of New Castle, yeoman to Thomas Rothwell of the County of New Castle, yeoman. William Pattison for a competent sum of money granted to Thomas Rothwell a tract of land bounded by Augustine Creek, land lately belonging to Casparas Herman, dec. the remaining part of William Pattison's land & Appoquinmink Road containing 100 acres. Signed William Pattison. Delivered in the presence of John Moll & Benjamin Gumley. Recorded 14 Sep 1699. (B2:185).

Deed. On 16 Sep 1697. Walter Scott of Cecil County in the province of Maryland, cordwainer to Christian Urinson of the county of New Castle. J. Walter Scott for £40 granted to Christian Urinson a tract of land called Maidstone bounded the point of the fork of St. George's Creek containing 400 acres as by a patent from Governor Edmund Andros to John Scott, whose son & heir I am, dated 15 Jan 1673. Signed Walter Scott. Delivered in the presence of Wessell Allrichs & John Smith. Recorded 17 Aug 1697. (B2:185).

Deed. On 21 June 1692. Peter Baynton of the County of New Castle to Thomas Nixson of the County of New Castle, planter. Peter Baynton for £30 paid & secured to be paid granted to Thomas Nixson a tract of land situated in the Bought on the west side of Delaware River bounded on the SW by land of Baynton, E with Bought Creek, Poplar Branch & the river Delaware formerly belonging to Neils Neilson & came by right of Peter Baynton as by deed from Neilson dated 20 July 1686 recorded in Book A Page 120 being part of a patent formerly granted by Governor Edmund Andros dated 15 Jan 1675 & entered in the records of New Castle in the year 1678 granted to Neils Neilson, Alias Franson & Marcus Lawrence containing 150 acres. Signed Peter Baynton. Delivered in the presence of John Grubb & William White. Recorded 21 June 1692. (B2:186).

Deed. On 14 Oct 1693. Thomas Nixson of the County of New Castle to Joseph Perkins late of New England, husbandman. Thomas Nixson for £65 granted to Joseph Perkins a tract of land being on the Bought bounded by land of Peter Baynton, Bought Creek at its beginning & the River Delaware being part of a patent formerly granted by Governor Edmund Andros dated 15 Jan 1675 recorded in the record of patent in New Castle in 1678 & was formerly granted to Woola Franson, Neils Neilson & Marcus Lawrenson being part of the said patent became right of said Thomas Nixson by deed dated 21 June 1692.

Signed Thomas Nixson & Grace Nixson. Delivered in the presence of Arthur Cooke, John Morrey & Ebenezer Perkins. Recorded 19 Dec 1693. (B2:188).

Deed. On 14 Oct 1693. Peter Baynton of the County of Chester to Ebenezer Perkins, late of New England, husbandman. Peter Baynton for £140 granted to Ebenezer Perkins a tract of land lying in the Bought bounded on the NE by the land of Thomas Nixson, SW by land of William Poole & the main river containing near 200 acres, being part of a patent formerly granted by Sir Edmund Andros dated 15 Jan 1675 to Woola Franson, Neils Neilson & Marcus Lawrenson being part of said patent came to Peter Baynton by deed recorded in New Castle Book A Page 88 & page 120 & in Book B Page 15, one in the tenure of Peter Baynton. Justis Grub is desired by the said Baynton to acknowledge this deed the next court held at New Castle as his attorney. Signed Peter Baynton. Delivered in the presence of Joseph Perkins, William Hearne & Thomas Nixson. Recorded 19 Dec 1693. (B2:190)..

Deed. On 21 June 1698. Roger Wotten of the town of New Castle, yeoman to John Donaldson of New Castle, merchant. Roger Wotten for a competent sum of money granted to John Donaldson a tract of land in the town of New Castle bounded on S & E by 2 streets, N & W by a piece of marsh, adjoining specified in a patent dated 1 Oct 1672 granted by Francis Lovelace, Governor to Hybert Hendrickson. Signed Roger Wotten. Delivered in the presence of John Moore & James Claypoole. Recorded 21 June 1698. (B2:191).

Deed. On 20 Sep 1682. Richard Hudden of Drawyers Creek, planter for valuable consideration granted to Henry Vanderburgh of the town of New Castle, merchant a tract of land situated at 2nd Drawyers Creek containing 200 acres adjoining the land of John Walker called Green Spring. Signed Richard Hudden. Delivered in the presence of William Grant & Henry Hollingsworth. Recorded 20 Sep 1692. (B2:192).

Deed. On 19 Sep 1694. Henry Vanderburgh for valuable consideration granted to Henry Williams all his right & title to within mentioned tract of land. Signed Henry Vanderburgh. Delivered in the presence of Edward Lillington & John Bisck. Recorded 18 Sep 1694. (B2:193).

Deed. On 2 Oct 1694. John Bolton for valuable consideration granted to Charles Crowe a tract of land containing 150 acres being half of a tract called Chesterfield near Appoquinimink adjoining the land of Hans Hanson, the other half belonging to John Cox. Singed John Bolton. Delivered in the presence of Cornelius Empson & James Claypoole. Recorded 2 Oct 1694. (B2:193).

Deed. On 16 Nov 1698. Nathaniel Janes of the Province of West New Jersey for a competent sum of money granted to John Clementson of Verdretigh Hook a tract of land lying in the county of New Castle containing 165 1/2 acres & bounded as by a patent dated 11 Feb 1688/9 granted by the commissioners to John Nelson. Signed Nathaniel Janes. Delivered in the presence of Peter Godin & John Donaldson. Recorded 21 Mar 1698. (B2:194).

Deed. On 21 Feb 1698. John Grantham (son & heir of John Grantham, deceased) of White Clay Creek to Robert French of the town of New Castle, merchant. John Grantham for £80 granted to Robert French a tract of land lying on the north side of White Clay Creek bounded by the Creek, land of Thomas Wollaston called Bishops Castle, Cross Peck Creek & land of Brewer Sinnexsen containing 161 1/4 acres. Singed John Grantham. Delivered in the presence of John Robinson & Richard Halliwell. Recorded 21 Feb 1698. (B2:194).

Deed. On 21 June 1698. Thomas Sawyer of the County of New Castle to Benjamin Cox of the County. Thomas Sawyer for £16 granted to Benjamin Cox a tract of land lying on the east side of Red Clay Creek called the name of Red Meadow bounded by the land of George Hogg, land of John Cox, land of Thomas Child containing 322 acres excepting 2 or 3 acres of land what mines or timber William Guest shall make use of on same & what mines & timber Cornelius Empson shall make use of in any of the remaining part. Signed Thomas Sawyer. Delivered in the presence of Robert Hutchinson & John Smith. Recorded 21 June 1698. (B2:195).

Deed. On 16 Aug 1698. Benjamin Cox for in consideration of a competent sum granted to Benony Empson all his right to the within mentioned tract of land. Signed Benjamin Cox. Delivered in the presence of John Donaldson & Richard Halliwell. Recorded 16 Aug 1698. (B2:196).

Deed. On 18 June 1695. Isaac Wheeldon, attorney of Joseph Holden of Cape May in West New Jersey to Joseph Alman of Duck Creek, planter. Isaac Wheeldon for valuable consideration granted to Joseph Alman a tract of land containing 286 acres situated on the south side of Blackbird's Creek bounded as specified in the patent from the Proprietor dated 1684. Signed Isaac Wheeldon. Delivered in the presence of Adam Johnson & Samuel Levis. Recorded 18 June 1695. (B2:197).

Deed. On 21 June 1695. Joseph Alman of the County of New Castle, gentleman to Thomas Graham of the County of New Castle, gentleman. Joseph Alman for £30 granted to Thomas Graham the within mentioned tract of land. Signed Joseph Alman. Delivered in the presence of John Donaldson & Isaac

Wheeldon. Recorded 16 Aug 1698. (B2:198).

Deed. On 1 Dec 1691. Richard Darkin & Jacob Decow, son & heir apparent of Isaac Decow to Robert Ashton. Richard Darkin & Jacob Decow for £60 granted to Robert Ashton the one half of a tract of land called Chelsey situated at the mouth of St. George's Creek which said plantation was bought in partnership by Isaac & Jacob Decow, Robert Ashton & Richard Darkin of Rowlif Anderson & Jacob Artson as by deed dated 20 Oct 1686 recorded in Book A Page 134. Signed Richard Darkin & Jacob Decow. Delivered in the presence of John Richardson, Edward Blake & John Hayls. Recorded 20 Dec 1692. (B2:198).

Deed. On 20 Aug 1700. Abraham Decow, son of Jacob Decow & Thomas England intermarried with Hannah, daughter of Jacob Decow, the sole heirs of Jacob Decow, dec. to Robert Ashton of the county of New Castle, yeoman. Abraham Decow & Thomas England & Hannah his wife for £70 granted to Robert Ashton the 1/4 part of a tract of land called Chelsey situated at the mouth of St. George's Creek divided to Jacob Decow in his lifetime which said tract of land was bought in partnership of Isaac & Jacob Decow, Robert Ashton & Richard Darkin of Rowliff Anderson & Jacob Artson as by deed dated 20 Oct 1686 recorded in Book A Page 134. Signed Abraham Decow, Thomas England & Hannah England. Delivered in the presence of Cornelius Empson & Sylvester Garland. (B2:199).

Deed. On 21 Aug 1691. Edward Green of the County of New Castle, merchant to John Scott of St. George's Creek, planter. Edward Green for a valuable sum of money granted to John Scott a tract of land situated on the head branches of St George's Creek bounded by the land of John Darby, Herman's Road, Maryland Road & Back Creek containing 2500 acres which said tract of land was by the court of New Castle granted to several persons who legally took up & possessed & the same conveyed to me, Edward Green. Signed Edward Green. Delivered in the presence of Robert Wotten & John Watts. (B2:200).

Deed. On 18 Aug 1702. Joseph Hanson of Dragons Swamp, planter to John Boyer. Whereas there is a tract of land called Bowerly situated on the northside of Dragon Swamp being part of the land called the Exchange bounded by the head of Dragon Swamp, the mouth of a branch called Beaver Dam & land of Joseph Scott containing 100 acres as by a survey made by Thomas Peirson dated 4 Nov 1701. Now Joseph Hanson in right of the will of my father, Hans Hanson, dec. for love & affection that I bear my brother in law, John Boyer granted to John Boyer the said 100 acres. Signed Joseph Hanson. Delivered in the presence of Christopher White & Thomas Peirson. Recorded 18 Aug 1702. (B2:204)..

Deed. On 21 May 1702. John Gyesbertson of the County of Monmouth in the province of East New Jersey to Isaih Gooding of the County of New Castle. John Gyerbertson for £90 granted to Isaih Gooding all the just eighth part of all that tract of land lying on the Delaware River called Augustina bounded by Appoquinimink Creek, the Delaware River, St. Augustine Creek, the land formerly sold to William Pattison, the Kings Road & land of Edward Green containing 350 acres which said whole tract of land containing 2809 acres. John Gyesbertson appoint John Smith of the town of New Castle his lawful attorney to acknowledge this deed to Isaih Gooding. Signed John Gyesbertson. Delivered in the presence of Sylvester Garland & Nicholas Lockyer. Recorded 18 Aug 1702. (B2:205).

Deed. On 20 June 1692. Mary Block of Swanwick, widow to her daughter Barbara Hicky. Mary Block for great love & good will voluntarily given & granted to her daughter Barbara Hickey & by persons confirmed to the children lawfully begotten of the body of her daughter, Barbara to be equally divided among them & the survivors of them all her plantation at Swanwick aforesaid with the 1/3 part of all cattle, utensils & moveable which shall remain on the plantation & Mary Block restoring to herself during her natural life the uses of said premises to be intrusted to the care & management of Peter Allrichs & John Donaldson during the minority of the eldest son of the said children, to be equally divided amongst them, the eldest son, Cornelius Maslander at the age of 21 to take possession of all said premises until William Maslander comes to age, who enjoy the same equally & they are to pay unto rest as they come of age an equal proportion of the value by the advise & consent of Peter Allrichs & John Donaldson. Signed Mary Block. Delivered in the presence of Jan Harms & John Adams. Recorded 21 June 1692. (B2:207).

Deed. On 16 July 1702. Adam Hike & William Maslander, both of Swanhook, husband to Joseph Wood of the town of New Castle, gentleman. Adam Hyke & William Maslander for £30 granted to Joseph Wood all right they have in a tract of land situated on the backside of Swanhook bounded by Swanhook Marsh, land of Cornelius Kettle & Adam Hykes, Swanhook Road, the kings road to Christiana ferry containing 50 acres of fast land being in the possession of Adam Hykes & William Maslander by virtue of a deed of gift from Mary Block, widow, dec. dated 20 June 1692. Signed Adam Hyke & William Maslander. Delivered in the presence of Harmanus Allrichs & Thomas Land. Recorded 19 Aug 1702. (B2:209).

Deed. On 14 Feb 1706. Paul Thomas of the County of New Castle, husbandman & Hylike his wife, daughter & co-heir of John Bowyer, late of the town of New Castle, dec. to Joseph Wood of the town of New Castle, gentleman. Paul Thomas & Hylike his wife for £5 granted to Joseph Wood all that lot in the town of New Castle bounded on the N by a lot lately belonging to Adam Beldiydge, W & S by land of Joseph Wood & Front Street. Signed Paul Thomas & Hylike Thomas. Delivered in the presence of Henry Garrotson, Reynier Vandercoulin & William Guest. Recorded 22 Feb 1706. (B2:212).

Note: Page 215 & 216 are missing.

Deed. On 2 Nov 1701. Olla Stooby of West New Jersey, mortham (?) to Cornelius Kettle of Swanhook, husbandman. Olla Stooby for £65 granted to Cornelius Kettle a tract of land being part of a patent granted to Edmund Cantwell & Johannes Dehaes dated 15 Jan 1675 situated near the town of New Castle bounded by land of Richard Halliwell, the river & land formerly of Mary Block containing 90 acres. Signed Olla Stooby. Delivered in the presence of Sylvester Garland & John French. Recorded 18 Aug 1702. (B2:217).

Deed. On 13 May 1702. Thomas Gardiner of Burlington in the province of West New Jersey, merchant & Elizabeth his wife (heretofore the wife of William Frampton, late of Philadelphia, merchant, dec.) to Alexander Avant, late of Freehold in the province of East New Jersey & now of Appoquinimy, yeoman. Whereas John Taylor, late of Appoquinimy by virtue of a patent granted from William Penn, Governor & dated 26 Mar 1684 to John Taylor a tract of land called Larkford Hall situate on the southwest side of 2nd Drawyers Creek bounded by Walkers branch, Ferodons branch containing 620 acres as recorded in New Castle Book A Page 9 & 93. Whereas John Taylor in his lifetime did agree with Edward Green of the County of New Castle, merchant to sell all the said tract called Larkford to Edward Green, with Edward Green paying £100. Whereas Edward Green paid & the said John Taylor died before executing the conveyance. Jane Taylor, widow & administrix of the estate of John Taylor, her deceased husband by deed dated 22 Oct 1685 confirmed the said land to Edward Green as recorded in Book A Page 90. Edward Green by deed dated 6 May 1686 granted & confirmed to William Frampton in his lifetime. Whereas William Frampton in his lifetime & at the time of his death was seized of the said Larkford Hall, & by his will dated 9 Sep 1686 did appoint Elizabeth, then his wife & now the wife of Thomas Gardiner, to be executrix of the said will, empowering her to dispose of his estate to the uses of the said will & soon after died. Which said will was proved at Philadelphia 8 Nov 1686. Now Thomas Gardiner & Elizabeth his wife for £63 granted to Alexander Adams all the aforesaid tract called Larkford Hall. Thomas Gardiner & Elizabeth his wife have appointed Cornelius Empson their attorney to deliver this deed in open court. Signed Thomas Gardiner & Elizabeth Gardiner. Delivered in the presence of Abraham Bickby, Thomas Grubb & Thomas

Rowell. Recorded 18 Aug 1702. (B2:218).

Patent. On 1 Oct 1669. Francis Lovelace, Esq. one of the Gentleman of his Majesties Honorable Privy Chamber, Governor General under his Royal Highness, James, Duke of York & Albany & all his territories in the Americas to John Arskin. Whereas there is a house & garden at New Castle now in the tenure of Sergeant John Arskin being in breadth 60 foot bounded by land of John Henry Jones & land of Martin Garrottson & also a tract of land west of the town bounded by land of Captain Carr, the swamp, & the river containing 7 acres & also a tract of land in the town given him by Robert Catt containing about 6 acres bounded by land of Garret Garrettson, land belonging to Reyneir Vandercoulin. Now confirmed unto John Arskin, he paying one bushel of winter wheat yearly to persons of authority. Signed Francis Lovelace at Fort James in New York. Recorded by Mathias Nicolls. (B2:224).

Deed. On 26 Aug 1682. Jonas Arskin, son & heir of John Arskin, dec. to John Moll of the town of New Castle. Jonas Arskin for valuable consideration granted to John Moll a piece of land first granted to Sir Robert Carr to John Arskin containing 6 acres bounded by land of Garret Garrettson, the highway & land which was formerly of Reyneir Vandercoulin excepting out of the said 6 acres 4 lots next to the land of Garret Garrettson made over to John Dehaes & Ephraim Herman, executors of Martin Rosamond & mentioned on the other side so that all the remaining of 6 acres is hereby made over to John Moll. Signed Jonas Arskin & Jane Arskin. Delivered in the presence of Ephraim Herman, John Ogle & Sam Land. This assignment of Jonas & his mother to John Moll was by them acknowledged in court 5 Sep 1682. (B2:225).

Note: The piece of land of 7 acres lying to the west of the town, mentioned in the within patent was on 7 June 1670 granted by John Arskin & Jane his wife to Peter Allrichs & since by Peter Allrichs granted to Anthony Bryant, who is the possessor there of. 3 May 1682 Which attests. Ephraim Herman, clerk. Out of the piece of land of 6 acres granted by Sir Robert Carr mentioned in the with patent, John Arskin, the son & heir of John Arskin has sold over to Johannes DeHaes & Ephraim Herman as executors of the estate of Martin Rosamond, dec. & for the use of the heirs of Rosamond 4 lots of land lying together next to the land of Garret Janson. 3 May 1682. Recorded at the request of George Daykin. 3 Feb 1708. (B2:226).

Agreement. On 5 Dec 1709. Whereas George Dakeyne has repeatedly requested of me a grant of a small tract of land containing about 1/2 doz acres near the town of New Castle in consideration of his services not yet fully satisfied, I do hereby certify that I have agreed that the said George Dakeyne shall have the said land confirmed unto him on a reasonable rent as soon as he has cleared off his bond to the proprietary & shall in the meantime continue in quiet possession thereof. Signed James Logan. Recorded 4 Mar 1709/10. (B2:226).

Deed. On 19 Mar 1700/1. Edward Cole of the town of New Castle, cooper & Hermann his wife to Allicia Baker of the town of New Castle, widow & Adam Ika of Swanwick. Edward Cole & Herman his wife for £113 17 shillings 8 pence granted to Allicia Baker & Adam Ika all interest in real estate mentioned in the will made by Ambrose Baker, dec. to his daughter Hermana Baker, now intermarried with Edward Cole. Signed Edward Cole & Hermana Cole. Delivered in the presence of John Brewster, George Moore & Richard Reynolds. Recorded 13 Mar 1709/10. (B2:226).

Affirmation. In March 1706, Richard Reynolds upon his oath & John Brewster upon his oath solemn affirmation declare that they saw Edward Cole & Hermana his wife sign, seal & deliver this instrument as their deed & that they with George Moore subscribed their names as witnesses. Taken before Richard Halliwell, the above oath & affirmation was endorsed on the backside of the before recorded deed. (B2:227).

Deed. On 11 Mar 1709/10. Edward Cole of New Castle, cooper to Garratte Ike, widow & late wife & executrix of Adam Ike, late of the county of New Castle, yeoman. Edward Cole for good causes & consideration have granted & released to Garratte Ike all manner of actions as well real as personal suits, quarrels, debts, trespasses, complaints & debates whatsoever which I the said Edward Cole had or anytime hereafter may have against Garratte Ike or the executors of Adam Ike for or by reason of any matter or cause or thing what so ever from the beginning of the world to the day of the day of these presents. Also all the estate right, title & interest, I the said Edward Cole now have or at anytime might have in a claim to a plantation lying in Swanwick formerly the inheritance of Ambrose Baker, dec & the said lots in New Castle sold by the said Adam Ike to Samuel Silsbee, Mary Scott & Jonathan Savage. Signed Edward Cole. Delivered in the presence of Samuel Silsbee & Joseph Wood. Recorded 11 Mar 1609/10. (B2:227).

Deed. On 20 Feb 1702. Joseph Moore of the county of New Castle & Anna Maria his wife, daughter & heirs of Cornelius Yoras, late of the county, dec. to James Sinnexen of the said county who intermarried in Dorcas Harmanson, one of the daughters & co-heirs of John Harmanson and Anna Harmonson the other daughter & co-heir of John Harmanson. Joseph Moore & Anna Maria his wife for a competent sum of money paid by James Sinnexen & Dorcas Harmanson on behalf of Anna Harmanson have granted to James Sinnexen & Dorcas his wife & Anna Harmanson all estate right & interest which they the said Joseph Moore & Anna Maria his wife now have in a lot of land situated in the town of New Castle, the inheritance of Cornelius Yoras, dec. & late in the tenure of Joseph Davies. Signed Joseph Moore & Anna Maria Moore. Delivered in the presence of Joseph Wood & Grif Jones. Recorded 1 June 1703. (B2:229).

Patent. On 11 Feb 1688/9. William Markham, Secretary Thomas Ellis & John Goodson, commissioners of property to Henry Toarson, old renter, son & heir of Olla Ollason. Whereas there is a tract of land bounded by the land of Charles Peterson, the river & a point called Stone Point containing 165 1/2 acres granted by virtue of a warrant of resurveyed from the commissioners directed to the chief surveyor of the town & county of New Castle to resurveyed the land belonging to Verdritige Hook, resurveyed & let out to (according to a former survey made by Edmund Cantwell) on 10 Nov 1688 the whole containing 827 1/2 acres & by request of the inhabitants thereof divided into 5 plantations according to the district settlements of the present inhabitants thereof unto Henry Toarson, old renter, son & heir of Olla Ollason, who had right from John Hinderson (from a patent granted by Francis Lovelace unto Olla Ollason, Neil Neils Sr., Hendrick Neilson, Mathias Neilson & Neils Neilson Jr. dated 16 May 1670) the said 165 1/2 acres & the said Henry Toarson requesting confirmation of said tract. We the commissioners now confirm unto Henry Toarson the 165 1/2 acres & he paying one bushel of winter wheat per each 100 acres to persons of authority yearly. Signed William Markham & John Goodson. Recorded 27 Jan 1703. (B2:230).

Deed On 20 Apr 1703. Henry Toarson, late of Stone Hook in the county of New Castle & now of Morris River in the province of West New Jersey, husbandman & Stephen Toarson of the county of New Castle, husbandman to Mathias Toarson. Henry Toarson for £30 & Stephen Toarson for £6 granted to Mathias Toarson all their two sixth parts (divided or to be divided) containing 27 1/2 & 1/2 part of an acre each, the said parts being one sixth part of a tract of land containing 165 1/2 acres situated in Verditige Hook being bounded by the river the Manor of Rockland, land of John & Peter Mounce & land formerly belonging to Charles Peterson & now of Edward Beeson. Which said 165 1/2 acres was granted to Henry Toarson by the commissioners by patent dated 11 Feb 1688/9. Where unto relation being had theirs being 2 sixth parts of 20 acres of marsh laid out for Henry Toarson, Jacob Clemens, John & Peter Mounce lying on the west side of the Delaware River bounded by Island Creek & the fast land being the 1/3 part of 60 acres of marsh laid out 9 Apr 1690 by virtue of a warrant dated 17 Feb 1689. Said 165 1/2 acres of land & 20 acres of marsh with the consent of Henry Toarson, John Toarson, Margaret their sister,

Mathias Toarson, Olla Toarson & Stephen Toarson heir brothers is divided: one sixth part to Henry Toarson, two sixth parts to John Toarson (one sixth part being by right of Margaret his sister) one sixth part Mathias Toarson, one sixth part to John Toarson by right of Olla Toarson & one other sixth part to Mathias Toarson by right of Stephen Toarson. Signed Henry Toarson & Stephen Toarson. Delivered in the presence of Hugh Owen, Cirily Baldwin & Hugh Bawden. Recorded 18 May 1703. (B2:232).

Power of Attorney. On 20 May 1699. Adam Baldridge of the City of New York, merchant have made & appointed William Hall of Salem in West New Jersey my true & lawful attorney to recover debts & monies owed & to look after & manage my plantation I lately bought of John Budd & all servants, Negroes, stock of cattle, horses & hogs. Signed Adam Baldridge. Philadelphia 22 May 1699. Personally appeared before me, the above, Adam Baldridge, who did in my presence sign, seal & deliver the above power of attorney & acknowledge the same to be his act & deed. Certified under my hand. Anthony Morris, Justice. Recorded 15 Oct 1703. (B2:236).

Power of Attorney. On 23 July 1703. Abraham Brewster of the County of New Castle appoint my loving father, John Brewster of the said place my attorney to recover all debts & monies due me & to sell, let or dispose of all or any of my lands, goods of estate. Signed Abraham Brewster. Delivered in the presence of James Coatts & R. D:haes. Recorded 17 Nov 1703. (B2:237).

Deed. On 19 Aug 1702. John Vance of Salem in the province of West New Jersey, millwright to John Sawtell of Philadelphia, baker. John Vance for £27 granted to John Sawtell all that tract of land situated on the south side of Shilpot Creek bounded by the creek containing 200 acres, now in the possession of John Vance by virtue of a patent of confirmation from William Penn, Governor dated 26 Sep 1701 & recorded in Philadelphia. John Vance has appointed George Lowder his attorney to acknowledge this deed in open court. Signed John Vance. Delivered in the presence of Samuel Hedge & Jo. Woodrooffe. Recorded 2 Dec 1703. (B2:239).

Deed. On 28 May 1702. Roliff Dehaes of the town of New Castle, merchant have sold to Herman Allrichs of the same place, merchant, one equal eighth part of my sloop named the Sarah, which was built at New Castle aforesaid by Henry William of the said place, shipwright, together with the equal eighth part of all her rigging appurtenances where with she was furnished at her departure from the port of New Castle on the 16 May this instant. Signed R. D:haes. Delivered in the presence of Sylvester Garland & John Smith. Recorded 3 Dec 1703. (B2:242).

Deed. On 18 Aug 1703. John Cann of White Clay Creek, yeoman to John Ball of White Clay Creek, husbandman. John Cann for £12 granted to John Ball a tract of land being part of a tract of 400 acres called the New Deligue situate on the west side of one of the branches of White Clay Creek commonly called Mill Creek between the said Mill Creek & the land of William Ball, Joseph Barnes bounded by Mill Creek, land of William Ball, land of Governor Widow Thomas & Benjamin Thomas containing 202 acres. Signed John Cann. Delivered in the presence of Joseph Griffin & George Read. Recorded 13 Dec 1703. (B2:243).

Deed. On 5 July 1703. John Smith & Sarah his wife of their own free will have bound themselves, apprentices & servants unto John Neeve of Chester marinor with him to dwell & serve from the day of the date hereto fore & during the full term of 4 years each of them. John Neeve to provide for his servants sufficient meat, drink, apparel, washing, lodging & other necessaries fit & convenient for them during their term. Signed John Smith & Sarah Smith. Delivered in the presence of Rebekah Shippen & Samuel Trewolla. John & Sarah Smith appeared before me on 3 July 1703 & acknowledged that they put themselves servants to John Neeve of their own free wills without force. Signed Edward Shippen. Recorded 13 Dec 1703. (B2:247).

Power of Attorney. On 15 Jan 1702/3. James Dyre of the City of New York, merchant for good cause appoint my friend Capt. Richard Halliwell of the town of New Castle to be my lawful attorney to sell all my right & title in a tract of land in the county of New Castle. Signed James Dyre. Delivered in the presence of James Poutts, William Dyre & Thomas Nevell. Recorded 22 Feb 1703. The deed related to this is recorded on page 316. (B2:248).

Deed. On 29 Nov 1698. Joseph Davis of town of New Castle, & Lucretia his wife to Leonard Osterhaven of Philadelphia. Joseph Davis & Lucretia his wife for £20 granted to Leonard Osterhaven all their right & interest in one house & lot situated in the town of New Castle bounded on SE by Front Street, NE with the burying ground, NW with the market place & SW with house & lot of Thomas January being formerly the dwelling house of Emelius DeRingh. Signed Joseph Davis & Lucretia Davis. Delivered in the presence of Jan Bisck & John Smith. Recorded 16 Mar 1703. (B2:249).

Deed. On 17 June 1701. Susannah Osterhaven for £60 granted to John Brewster a part of a lot in the Front Street adjoining the ground of Thomas Janvier containing in breadth 27 foot 9 1/3 in & behind next the market place 23 foot 4 in & in length equal to the other lots. Signed Susannah Osterhaven. Delivered in the presence of George Hogg & Jacobus Allrichs. Recorded 20 Mar 1703. (B2:249).

Receipt. Received this 23 Mar 1699 of Susannah Osterhaven, executrix & administrator of Leonard Osterhaven, late of Philadelphia, the sum of £4 4 shillings 10 pence being the last payment & in full for all my interest, right, title & claim to one house & lot in the town of Newcastle bequeathed to my wife, Lucretia by her father Emelius DeRingh, dec. Signed Joseph Davis. Delivered in the presence of John Lumby & John Smith. (B2:250).

Receipt. On 19 June 1700 received of John Brewster the full sum of £28 14 shillings 7 pence being in part of pay of £60 for the house & lot I sold to John Brewster. Signed Susannah Osterhaven. Delivered in the presence of George Hogg & Abraham Decow. (B2:251).

Obligation. On 18 June 1700. I, oblige me & my heirs to pay to James & Hercules Coutts the sum of £5 6 shillings 7 pence at or before 10 Nov this date. Signed John Brewster. Receipt. On 4 Dec 1700 received the full contents hereof. Signed James & Hercules Coutt. (B2:251).

Receipt. On 10 Apr 1701. Received from John Brewster the full sum of £13 10 shillings 10 pence it being part of a greater sum due me by his obligation for that lot where he now dwells. Signed Susannah Osterhaven. Testes: Stephen Jackson & Elizabeth Clemens. (B2:251).

New Castle on 10 Apr 1701, John Brewster pay to Elizabeth Clemens or to her order the sum of £3 17 shillings 4 pence when I make over the deed for that lot that thou hast bought from me & her receipt shall discharge thee for so much from thy friend. Signed Susannah Osterhaven. Testes: Stephen Jackson. Accepted for me John Brewster. Friend John Brewster please pay the contents of the within note to Stephen Jackson & his receipt shall discharge thee from they friend. Signed Elizabeth Clemens. Philadelphia 28 June 1701. (B2:251).

Receipt. On 7 May 1702. Received of John Brewster the sum of £5 6 shillings being in part of pay for the house & lot bought of me. Signed Susannah Osterhaven. Testes: Jan Bisck & John Brett. (B2:252).

Receipt On 4 July 1701 received the full sum of £3 19 shillings for the use of Elizabeth Clemison of Philadelphia. Received by Stephen Jackson. (B2:252).

Receipt. On 17 June 1701 Received of John Brewster, £6 5 shillings 8 pence being the last & in full satisfaction in payment for a house & lot bought by John Brewster of me, Susannah Osterhaven being in the town of New Castle. Signed Susannah Osterhaven. Delivered in the presence of Thomas Fauvier & Benjamin Swett. All the above receipts & notes on were recorded 20 Mar 1703.

(B2:252).

Deed. On 19 Nov 1703. John Guest of Philadelphia, Esq. & Susannah his wife to Evan Rice of the County of New Castle, gentleman. Whereas there is a tract of land situated on the northside of White Clay Creek bounded by a run called Middle Run containing 400 acres part of 1000 acres formerly surveyed to William Welsh, dec. late father of the said Susannah by virtue of a warrant from William Penn, who by his patent dated 23 Oct 1701 confirmed said 1000 acres to John Guest & Susannah his wife as recorded in Philadelphia Book A Vol 2 Page 123. Now John Guest & Susannah his wife for £100 granted to Evan Rice the above described 400 acres. Signed John Guest & Susannah Guest. Delivered in the presence of Thomas Tresse, Anthony Stevens & David Lloyd. Recorded 24 Mar 1703. (B2:252).

Deed. On 13 May 1704. Robert French of town of New Castle, merchant to Richard Buckley. Robert French for £5 formerly paid by Richard Beacham & £22 now paid by Richard Buckley granted to Richard Buckley a tract of land bounded by Perkins Creek at Paret Hook joining the land of Nicholas Lockyer. Signed Robert French. Delivered in the presence of Richard Reynolds & William Houston. Recorded 30 Mar 1704. (B2:257).

Sheriff's Deed. On 4 Mar 1703. John French, High Sheriff of the County of New Castle to James Coutts of New Castle, Esq. Whereas James Askew at the court of common pleas on 18 May last past recovered against Joseph Clayton, late of the County, carpenter the sum of £9 4 shillings 9 pence & damages to be levied on the lands of Joseph Clayton in the county of New Castle. Whereas for the value of £13 14 shillings I have seized a tract of land of the aforesaid Joseph Clayton. Now I, the said sheriff according to a writ & for £13 14 shillings granted to James Coutts a tract of land (being part of a greater tract belonging to Joseph Clayton) containing 50 acres situated on the west side of White Clay Creek, opposite the land of John Guest, Esq. & other land of Joseph Clayton. Signed John French. Delivered in the presence of R. Dehaes & William Touge. Recorded 9 Jun 1704. (B2:258).

Deed. On 16 Sep 1701. Maurice Liston of the County of New Castle, planter to Robert French of the City of Philadelphia, merchant. Maurice Liston for £50 granted to Robert French a tract of land on the northeast side of Duck Creek bounded by land of John Mackenzy, dec., a bridge & the old landing resurveyed for Robert French by warrant dated 15 July 1701 & containing 503 acres. Said land is free on incumbencies except 3 years of arrears of quit rent. Signed Maurice Liston. Delivered in the presence of Cornelius Empson & John Hussey. Recorded 23 June 1704. (B2:260).

Deed. On 18 Aug 1701. Nathaniel Puckle of the City of Philadelphia, mariner to Robert French of the same place, merchant. Nathaniel Puckle for £21 granted to Robert French a tract of land on the north side of Drawyers Creek bounded by land of James Smothers, a marsh, Hogg branch containing 256 acres. Signed Nathaniel Puckle. Delivered in the presence of William Trent & William Houston. Recorded 23 June 1704. (B2:262).

Deed. On 17 June 1701. Sigfriedus Allrichs, Hermanus Allrichs, Jacobus Allrichs & Wessell Allrichs for a valuable sum of money granted to Robert French a tract of land situated near the foot dike in the town of New Castle bounded by Dike Street & the street which goes over the Broad Dike. Signed Sigfriedus Allrichs, Hermanus Allrichs, Jacobus Allrichs & Wessell Allrichs. Delivered in the presence of T. Clarke & John Donaldson. Recorded 23 June 1704. (B2:264).

Deed. On 15 Oct 1700. Jacobus Allrichs of the County of New Castle to Peter Anderson of the same County. Jacobus Allrichs for £9 granted to Peter Anderson a tract of land bounded by the King's Road near the dwelling house of Peter Anderson, land of Jacobus Allrichs & land formerly belonging to Peter Anderson containing 23 acres. Signed Jacobus Allrichs. Delivered in the presence of Peter Mounce, John Smith & James Anderson. Recorded 28 July 1704. (B2:265).

Deed. On 20 Apr 1703. Robert French of New Castle, merchant to David Miller of White Clay Creek. Robert French for valuable consideration granted to David Miller a tract of land situated on the south side of White Clay Creek bounded by land of Andrew Tilly & the creek containing 300 acres. Signed Robert French. Delivered in the presence of James Coutts & Roeloffe Dehaes. Recorded 28 July 1704. (B2:266).

Deed. On 7 Aug 1703. Valantine Hollingsworth, Sr. of the County of New Castle, yeoman to George Jackson of Philadelphia, yeoman. Valantine Hollingsworth for £35 granted to George Jackson a piece of land situated in the Manor of Racksland bounded by land of William Sharples, Shilpot Creek, land of Valantine Hollingsworth containing 200 acres & 10 acres of marsh lying in Reedy Hook marsh fronting the Delaware River bounded by land of George Robinson & land of Has Peterson.. Signed Valantine Hollingsworth. Delivered in the presence of Phillip Gilbert & John Robinson. Recorded 28 July 1704. (B2:268).

Deed. On 16 Nov 1696. Paul Paulson of Christiana Creek, husbandman to Peter Anderson of Christiana Creek. Whereas there is a tract of land called

Poplar Neck situated on the north side of Red Lyon Creek containing 220 acres & also a tract of marsh on the south side of said creek containing 25 acres granted by the court of New Castle to his father, Oele Paulson & laid out by survey of Edphraim Herman dated 2 Oct 1682. His father having sold the same unto Hendrick Lemmons of Crane Hook as by deed dated 26 June 1685. Hendrick Lemmon died, possessed of the same. Now Paul Paulson in right of his wife Elizabeth, only daughter & survivor of the children on Hendrick Lemmons & for £18 granted to Paul Anderson the aforesaid tract of land bounded by land of John Williams, Little Run & the King's Road containing 220 acre & the marsh situated on the south side of Red Lyon Creek bounded by land of John Williams containing 25 acres. Signed Paul Paulson & Elizabeth Paulson. Delivered in the presence of Gwen Morgan, Thomas Pierson, Walter Hughlis, Amos Nichols, Jr. Recorded 10 Aug 1704. (B2:269).

Deed. On 5 July 1703. Thomas Lawrence, notary by royal authority admitted & sworn in London do hereby certify that I have seen certain letters of patents granted by our Sovereign Lady Queen Anne under the broad seal of England dated 24 June in the 2nd year of her majesties reign. Where in among others is a instead the name of Thomas Janvier, who the born beyond seas is made her majesties liege & subject and is held to be reputed & taken as subject born in this kingdom of England & may purchase, but, sell & dispose of land in this kingdom or any other of her majesties dominions as freely & peaceably & entirely as a subject born in this kingdom. Signed Thomas Lawrence, Notary. Recorded 23 Aug 1704. (B2:272).

Bond. On 19 Dec 1702. I, Isaac Gervaize of London, merchant do hereby assign & transfer to David Straughan of Stafford County, planter all the right & title I have of Thomson & John Dimpy. That is to say 5 years service of each to serve in any lawful employment according to the customs of the country. The said service to begin 14 Apr 1702. Signed Isaac Gervaize. Witness Mathew Perkins. Recorded 11 Sep 1704. (B2:273).

Deed. On 15 Aug 1704. Peter Jacquett of the county of New Castle & Mary his wife to Benjamin Swett, John Hussey, Jr. & Frederick Hussey of the town of New Castle. Peter Jacquatt for valuable consideration granted to Benjamin Swett, John Hussey, Jr. & Frederick Hussey a tract of land bounded by Christiana Creek containing 30 acres. Signed Peter Jacquatt & Mary Jacquatt. Delivered in the presence of George Dakeyne, Chris. Hussey & Peter Anderson. Recorded 12 Sep 1704. (B2:273).

Patent. On 15 Jan 1675. Edmund Andros, Esq., Governor under his Royal Highness, James Duke of York & Albany & his territories of America to John

Scott. Whereas there a tract of land situated at the first dividing of St. George's Creek called Maidstone, which by virtue of a warrant has been surveyed & laid out to John Scott bounded by branches of the creek containing 400 acres as surveyed by Capt. Edmund Cantwell. Now by virtue of the commission & authority I have, confirmed to John Scott the said 400 acres & he paying 4 bushels of winter wheat to persons of authority, yearly. Signed Edmund Andros. Examined by Mathias Nicolls, Sec. Recorded 20 Sep 1704. (B2:275).

Deed. On 21 Jan 1700. Christian Urinson, John Scott & Jarvis Scott all of the County of New Castle to Urin Anderson of the said County. Christian Urinson, John Scott & Jarvis Scott for valuable consideration granted to Urin Anderson all the within mentioned tract of land (page 1185 & 186 for Walter Scotts Deed). Signed Christian Urinson, John Scott & Jarvis Scott. Delivered in the presence of Joseph Clayton & John Smith. Recorded 20 Sep 1704. (B2:277).

Virginia. On 25 Aug 1703. Exchange for £7 14 shillings 6 pence. At forty days ... sight of this my first exchange, my second & third not paid, pay or cause to be paid to Mr. Francis Lynch or order the sum of £7 14 shillings 6 pence it being for like value received of him here for the use of the ship Laurell & place it to account of the same from your humble servant. William Bushel. To Alderman Thomas. Sweettin & Company merchant in Liverpool. Recorded 26 Sep 1704. Endorsed on the back by Francis Lynch. (B2:278).

Deed. On 12 Aug 1701. John Colwart of New Castle, wheelwright to Francis Land of Christiana Creek, yeoman. John Colwart for £40 granted to Francis Land a house & lot in the town of New Castle fronting the market place containing in breadth 60 foot & in length as the other lots adjoining the land of John Thompson & land of Ambrose Baker, dec. The intent is that John Colwart is to pay Francis Land £4 before 12 Aug 1702, £4 before 12 Aug 1703 & £44 before 12 Aug 1704, then this present deed will be void. Signed John Colwart. Delivered in the presence of George Hogg & James Claypoole. Then received of John Colwart the just sum of £44 it being in full for the within mortgage. Signed Francis Land. Delivered in the presence of Charles Springer & John Healey. Recorded 16 Aug 1704. (B2:278).

Deed. On 17 June 1701. John Williams of the County of New Castle & Elinor his wife to Cornelius Kettle of Swanwick. John Williams & Elinor his wife for £50 granted to Cornelius Kettle a plantation situated at Swanwick formerly the land of Peter DeWitt bounded by land of John Barretson, the river & the King's Road to Christiana containing 62 acres. Signed John Williams & Elinor DeWitt alias Williams. Delivered in the presence of R. Dehaes & Sara Dehaes. Recorded 13 Apr 1705. (B2:280).

Deed. On 27 July 1691 Casparus Herman of Cecil County in the province of Maryland, gentleman & brother to Ephraim Herman late of New Castle, dec. eldest son & heir of Augustine Herman, late of Bohemia in Cecil County in the province of Maryland, dec. to Elizabeth Herman, relict & administrix of Ephraim Herman. Casparus Herman for valuable consideration granted to Elizabeth Herman all interest in 3 lots of land in the town of New Castle, 2 of them fronting the river & the other on the back part of the town, likewise 400 acres situated on Appoquinimink Creek about 5 miles from town in partnership with Johannes Dehaes, & another tract near Duck Creek containing 1800 acres & all right & interest to all & every thing that belonged to Ephraim Herman in his lifetime or at the time of his death & since then which might belong to him Casparus Herman by the reason of the death of the said Ephraim Herman & the nearness of kin of the said Casparus Herman. Signed C. August Herman. Delivered in the presence of Andrew Gravenraet, John Donaldson & James Claypoole. Acknowledged by Edward Gibbs, attorney for Casparus Herman & delivered to John Donaldson in right of Elizabeth his wife, the relict of Ephraim Herman, dec. in open court 20 Sep 1692. Recorded 18 Apr 1705. (B2:281).

Deed. On 20 Mar 1692. John Donaldson of New Castle, merchant & Elizabeth his wife to John Cann of the said place, merchant. John Donaldson & Elizabeth his wife for valuable consideration granted to John Cann the dwelling house & ground fronting the river, also one lot situated between the lots of Thomas Spry, dec. & the lots of Nicholas Daniel, likewise 400 acres 5 miles from town, one parcel on Appoquinimink Creek in partnership with Johannes Dehaes & another tract near Duck Creek containing 1800 acres. Signed John Donaldson & Elizabeth Donaldson. Delivered in the presence of John Claypoole & Edward Killington. Recorded 19 Apr 1705. (B2:285).

Deed. On 21 Mar 1692. John Cann of the town of New Castle, merchant. to John Donaldson of the County of New Castle & Elizabeth his wife. John Cann for valuable consideration granted to John Donaldson the dwelling house & ground fronting the river, also one lot situated between the lots of Thomas Spry, dec. & the lots of Nicholas Daniel, likewise 400 acres 5 miles from town, one parcel on Appoquinimink Creek in partnership with Johannes Dehaes & another tract near Duck Creek containing 1800 acres. Signed John Cann. Delivered in presence of Edward Blake & Ch. Rumsey. Recorded 19 Apr 1705. (B2:286).

Deed. On 8 Nov 1701. John Donaldson of the town of New Castle, merchant to Robert French of the City of Philadelphia, merchant. John Donaldson for £1400 granted to Robert French 2 lots of ground in the town of New Castle fronting the river Delaware containing in breadth 120 foot & in length 300 foot & bounded on the NE by the lot belonging to the heirs of John Hermanson, SW with the house & lot of John Cann with bolting mills & also one new clock & clock case with 1/4 part of a mill called Naaman's Creek Mill situated on the northeast side of Naaman's Creek & bought from Jasper Yeates by deed dated 15 Dec 1698. John Donaldson is bound to Robert French for £2800 & this obligation is such that John Donaldson is to pay Robert French said sum & when paid this deed is to be void. Signed John Donaldson. Delivered in the presence of Richard Halliwell & Thomas Kanyon both of the county of New Castle, merchants & Hugh Hagg. Recorded 20 Apr 1705. (B2:287).

Deed. On 23 Nov 1703 Evert Evertson of the County of New Castle, yeoman to Edward Edwards of the County of Philadelphia, yeoman. Evert Evertson for £45 granted to Edward Edward's tract of land on St. George's Creek bounded by land of Mathias Screekes, land of Herman Allrichs & land of Darby containing 200 acres. Signed Evert Evertson. Delivered in the presence of Nicolas Lockyer, John Baron & William Tonge. Receipt. Received of Edward Edwards £25 on 25 Nov 1703. Recorded 23 Apr 1705. (B2:292).

Deed. On 4 Sep 1704. Peter Mainardo of Chester County, carpenter & Peternella his wife, one of the daughters of John Carr, late of New Castle, dec. & John Bristow of Chester County, gentleman, & Anne his wife, the other daughter of John Carr, dec. Whereas John Carr by his last will & testament dated 30 Jan 1675 did give & bequeath to his wife & children all his estate to be equally divided amongst them. And whereas Richard Carr of Cecil County in the province of Maryland, yeoman, son & heir of John Carr dec. by deed dated 3 Aug 1696 granted to John Donaldson, Richard Halliwell & Robert French all of New Castle, merchants a piece of meadow situated near the fort containing 150 acres, since in the tenure of Alexander Hiniosa bounded on the S by the river, N by land lately in the possession of Garret Vansneering, NW by the plantation commonly called The Landery & SW by land lately belonging to John Webber. Now Peter Mainardo & Peternella his wife & John Bristow & Anne his wife, daughters of John Carr, dec. for £20 granted to Richard Halliwell & Robert French & the heirs of John Donaldson, dec. all their interest & right to the within mentioned land. Peter Mainardo & Peternella his wife & John Bristow & Anne his wife have appointed Samuel Loman of New Castle, gentleman to by their lawful attorney to acknowledge this in open court. Signed Peter Mainardo, Peternella Mainardo, John Bristow & Anne Bristow. Delivered in the presence of John French & William Tonge. Recorded 27 Apr 1704. (B2:297).

Power of Attorney. On 4 Nov 1702 John Roe of Calbot County in the province of Maryland, yeoman, appoint Robert French of New Castle, merchant, & Richard Reynolds of New Castle, yeoman, my true & lawful attorneys to recover any such monies, wares or merchandise & things due me. Signed John Roe. Delivered in the presence of Joseph Wood & William Tonge. Recorded 28 Apr 1705. (B2:301).

Declaration. On 28 Nov 1702. James Logan, Receiver General of the Province of Pennsylvania by virtue of a commission from William Penn, Governor, to George Dakeyne of the County of New Castle. Whereas the Governor by commission dated 29 Oct last appointed me his receiver general of all his rent due him out of the said province with full power to appoint deputies to demand the same becoming due. Due to the Proprietary within the county of New Castle, I have debuted & appointed George Dakeyne to be the collector in said county. Signed James Logan. Recorded 8 May 1705. (B2:302).

Deed. On 14 May 1705 Alexander Adams of Appoquinimink Creek to Peter King of Drawyers Creek. Whereas there is a tract of land situated on the south side of the Maryland road from Reeden Island commonly called The Holt bounded by the aforementioned road, land of John Rice, land of Alexander Adams, land of Cornelius King & Appoquinimink Road containing 256 acres. Now Alexander Adams for £35 granted to Peter King the above mentioned land. Signed Alexander Adams. Delivered in the presence of Francois King & John Rice. Recorded 22 May 1705. (B2:303).

Deed. On 14 May 1705 Alexander Adams of Appoquinimink Creek to Jacob King of Drawyers Creek. Whereas there is a tract of land situated on the northside of Drawyers Creek being part of a tract of land called Larksford Hall bounded by Walkers branch land of Cornelius King, land of Alexander Adams & the marsh containing 150 acres. Alexander Adams for £40 granted to Jacob King all the aforementioned land. Signed Alexander Adams. Delivered in the presence of Francois King & John Rice. Recorded 22 May 1705. (B2:306).

Deed. On 14 May 1705 Alexander Adams of Appoquinimink Creek, yeoman to Cornelius King of Drawyers Creek (son in law of Marinna DeWitt of the aforesaid place & county, late deceased). Whereas there is 2 tracts of land surveyed for Cornelius King, the first tract bounded by Walkers branch & land of Jacob King containing 150 acres & another tract bounded by the King's Road to Appquinimink containing 60 acres. Now Alexander Adams for £35 granted to Cornelius King the aforementioned 2 tracts. Signed Alexander Adams. Delivered in the presence of Francois King & John Rice. Recorded 25 May 1705. (B2:309).

Deed. On 15 May 1705. John Nancoim of New Castle, planter to Richard Hambly of Appoquinimink, blacksmith. John Nancoim for £18 granted to

Richard Hambly a tract of land being the upper part of that tract taken up by virtue of a warrant & laid out for Maurice Daniels called Drummer's Neck on the north west side of Appoquinimink Creek & conveyed from person to person & now in the actual possession of John Nancoim, the said land bounded by the creek, land of Barnard Hendrickson, land of Jacob Fiaen which said tract having been surveyed to 180 acres out of which land the said John Nancoim has sold to Richard Hambley 100 acres between 2 valleys joining to the Mill Land bounded by the land of Jacob Fiaens containing 100 acres. Signed John Nancoim. Delivered in the presence of William Stone, Samuel Griffing & William Carden. Recorded 26 May 1705. (B2:312).

Deed. On 18 May 1705. Richard Hambly of the County of New Castle to Jacob Reall of the aforesaid place. Richard Hambly for £29 granted to Jacob Reall a mill dam & 1 acre of land situated upon Mill Fork on the south side of Drawyers Creek. Signed Richard Hambly. Delivered in the presence of John Jawert, William Williams & William Dyre. Recorded 26 May 1705. (B2:313)

Deed. On 17 May 1705. John Nancoim of Saint Anns Appoquinimy in the county of New Castle, planter to William Carden of the parish & county aforesaid, husbandman. John Nanciom for £15 10 shillings granted to William Carden a tract of land called New Saxony lying on Drawyers Creek bounded by Walkers branch containing 150 acres of land confirmed by patent dated 26 Mar 1684. Signed John Nancoim. Delivered in the presence of James Askew, Robert Thorold & Richard Hambly. Recorded 27 May 1705. (B2:314).

Deed. On 12 Jan 1702. Kenhelm Clark of the County of New Castle to Jacob Reall of the County of New Castle. Kenhelm Clark for £47 10 shillings granted to Jacob Reall a tract of land called Mill Fork, situated on the north side of Drawyers Creek bounded by land of Thomas Sadler, land of Richard Ingelloes, Walkers Run & Drawyers Creek containing with a small part of marsh, 111 acres. Signed Kenhelm Clark. Delivered in the presence of Robert Wotten, John Smith & Benjamin Charrier. Recorded May 1705. (B2:315).

Deed. On 16 May 1705. Joseph Griffin of the town of New Castle, blacksmith, & Sarah his wife to John Hussey, Sr., farmer, George Hogg, Sr., cordwainer & Benjamin Swett, tanner, of the town of New Castle. Joseph Griffin for £59 granted to John Hussey, Sr., George Hogg, Sr. & Benjamin Swett one house & lot in the town of New Castle, which said lot being grated to Zacharias Vandercoulin from Governor Penn by patent dated 26 June 1691 & one containing in breadth 120 foot & in length 300 foot bounded on the SE with Beaver Street, NW with Otter Street, SW with land of Roeloffe Dehaes & NE with land of John Richardson, Sr the said lot being the same lot Joseph Griffin purchases of Andrew Cork & Cornelius Kettle by 2 deeds dated 16 Apr 1698 & 20 May 1703. Andrew Cork & Cornelius Kettle being possessed of the said lot by virtue of the will of Zacharias Vandercoulin dated 2 Nov 1694. Signed Joseph Griffin & Sarah Griffin. Delivered in the presence of George Harlan, Joseph England, George Robinson & John Gregg. Recorded May 1705. (B2:317).

Deed. On 17 Aug 1702. James Logan of Philadelphia to John Gregg of the County of New Castle, yeoman. Whereas the Honorable William Penn, Esq. Governor in this province to the same belonging by a grant or patent under his had dated 23 Oct 1701 for the considerations mentioned granted to his only daughter, Letitia Penn, a tract of land called Manor of Staining, situated on the south side of Brandywine Creek by Burroughs Run containing 15,500 acres. Whereas Letitia Penn by her letter of attorney dated 31 Oct 1701 did appoint Edward Pennington of Philadelphia, gentleman (since deceased) & me the said James Logan jointly her attorneys giving us the full power to give, grant & sell to such persons & upon such terms as her attorneys should seem met, all her manor's lands. Now James Logan for £40 granted to John Gregg a tract of land part of the Manor aforesaid containing 200 acres, & John Gregg to pay 2 silver shillings yearly to the said James Logan on behalf of Letitia Penn on 1 Mar in the town of Chester. Signed James Logan. Delivered in the presence of Jacob Taylor & Thomas Grey. James Logan has appoint George Hogg my attorney to acknowledge this deed in the county court in New Castle. Signed James Logan. Delivered in the presence of Jacob Taylor & Thomas Grey. Recorded May 1705. (B2:319).

Deed. On 1 Jan 1703. Richard Halliwell of the town of New Castle, merchant to George Dakeyne of the town of New Castle, surveyor. Whereas William Penn by patent dated 22 July 1684 recorded in New Castle Book A Page 22 granted to Hendrick Vandenburgh late of New Castle, merchant a tract of land called Poplar Neck situated on the north side of Red Lyon branch bounded by land of Oalla Paulson containing 200 acres. Whereas Hendrick Vandenburgh by his deed of sale on the back of said patent dated 22 June 1686 granted to William Dyre of the province. Whereas Anna Vandenburgh, wife of Hendrick Vandenburgh by her hand endorsed also upon the back of said patent did voluntarily consent to the said sale. Whereas Major William Dyer by his last will & testament dated 20 Feb 1687/8 amongst other things did give & bequeath to his youngest son, James Dyre 200 acres of land lying in the county of New Castle about 7 miles from the town of New Castle bounded as described above. Whereas James Dyre by his Letter of Attorney dated 15 Jan 1702/3 appointed his honorable friend Capt. Richard Halliwell to be his lawful attorney to sell such land. Now Richard Halliwell for £40 granted to George Dakeyne the said tract of 200 acres. Signed Richard Halliwell. Delivered in the presence of Richard Cantwell & William Tonge. Recorded May 1705. (B2:322).

Deed. On 20 Aug 1705. Sigfridus Allrichs, yeoman, Harmanus Allrichs, merchant, Jacobus Allrichs, yeoman & Wessell Allrichs, goldsmith, all of the county of New Castle to Peter Hanson of the County of New Castle, yeoman. Sigfriedus, Harmanus, Jacobus & Wessell Allrichs for £20 in hand paid granted to Peter Hanson all that western island of Anakaninck with the County of New Castle containing 200 acres also the meadow ground adjoining the said island situated on the west side of Red Lyon Creek which said island & marsh above said is part of 2 islands & marsh with other premises granted by Alexander D'hinoyossa by authority of Burger Masters of the City of Amsterdam, director over the south river in New Netherland with the worshipful the council thereof to Peter Allrichs, gentleman, father of Sigfridus, Harmanus, Jacobus & Wessell Allrichs by deed dated 2 June 1664. Signed Sigfridus Allrichs, Harmanus Allrichs, Jacobus Allrichs & Wessell Allrichs. Delivered in the presence of Joseph Wood, R. Clarke & Sylvester Garland. Recorded 18 Dec 1705. (B2:326).

Deed. On 23 Aug 1705. John Wood of Duck Creek, husbandman to Robert Marsh of the County of Kent in the province of Maryland. Whereas there is a tract of land called Good Land containing 1280 acres situated on the north side of Duck Creek near the thoroughfare formerly belonging to Ephraim Harman, late dec. as by 2 patents from Sir Edmund Andros, Governor of New York, one granted to Ephraim Harman dated 24 Sep 1680 for 500 acres & the other granted to Lawrence Cock dated 14 Oct 1680 for 700 acres, residue of the said 1280 acres & 2 deeds of enforcement from Lawrence Cock to Ephraim Harman one dated 14 Oct 1680 & the other dated 4 Apr 1682 for the said 700 acres reference for the said patents & deeds to the records of New Castle in Liberty C from page 1114 to129. Whereas Richard Bonsall of Darby in the County of Chester, husbandman, late deceased, purchaser of 3/4 part of the said tract of land & John Wood purchaser of 1/4 part of said tract purchased the said land of Major John Donaldson, merchant of the town of New Castle, late deceased & Elizabeth his wife relict of the aforementioned Ephraim Harman as by deed 17 Aug 1697. Whereas there is a piece of the aforementioned 1/4 part belonging to John Wood bounded by the Marsh next to Duck Creek, land of Hugh Marsh, land of Richard Bonsall, land of William Dixson & John Cox containing 100 acres & another tract of land bounded by land of James Crawford, Thomas Bell & James Beswicks, land of Thomas Bell & land of James Crawford containing 200 acres known by the name of Venture, granted by patent from the commissioners of property dated 12 Apr 1686. Now John Wood for £140 granted to Robert Marsh the 2 tracts of land. Signed John Wood. Delivered in the presence of James Crawford & Thomas Pierson. Acknowledged in open court 23 Aug 1705. (B2:329).

Deed. On 23 Aug 1705. John Wood of Duck Creek, husbandman to Robert Marsh of the County of Kent in the province of Maryland. Whereas there is a tract of land called Good Land containing 1280 acres situated on the north side of Duck Creek near the thoroughfare formerly belonging to Ephraim Harman, late dec. as by 2 patents from Sir Edmund Andros, Governor of New York, one granted to Ephraim Harman dated 24 Sep 1680 for 500 acres & the other granted to Lawrence Cock dated 14 Oct 1680 for 700 acres, residue of the said 1280 acres & 2 deeds of enforcement from Lawrence Cock to Ephraim Harman one dated 14 Oct 1680 & the other dated 4 Apr 1682 for the said 700 acres reference for the said patents & deeds to the records of New Castle in Liber C from page 1114 to129. Whereas Richard Bonsall of Darby in the County of Chester, husbandman, late deceased, purchaser of 3/4 part of the said tract of land & John Wood purchaser of 1/4 part of said tract purchased the said land of Major John Donaldson, merchant of the town of New Castle, late deceased & Elizabeth his wife relict of the aforementioned Ephraim Harman as by deed 17 Aug 1697. Whereas there is a piece of the aforementioned 1/4 part belonging to John Wood bounded by the marsh, land of Richard Bonsall containing 120 acres. Now John Wood for £140 granted to Robert Marsh the 120 acres of land. Signed John Wood. Delivered in the presence of James Crawford & Thomas Pierson. Recorded 20 Mar 1705. (B2:332).

To the Honorable William Penn, Esq. Absolute Proprietary & Governor of the Province of Pennsylvania & Territories. May it please your honor. That whereas the members of assembly for the lower counties did request your honor on behalf of the inhabitants of this town that you would be pleased to grant the Bank to such persons as have lots fronting the river at the yearly quit rent of 1 bushel of winter wheat for each 60 foot in breadth & 600 foot in length from the now Front Street, improving the same with good wharves in 7 years after the date of the first grant or else the same to revert to your honor to be granted to such persons as will comply with the same in the time prefix. (which your honor was pleased to promise should be done) we therefore on behalf of ourselves & the rest of the town concerned do further request that the same may be confirmed by some order or writing under your hand to your commissioners that warrants maybe granted & the same to be laid out & patented to such persons as shall desire the same & we shall as in duly bound ever pray. Richard Halliwell & Joseph Wood. Granted as here requested. William Penn. 31 Oct 1701. Recorded 20 Mar 1705. (B2:336).

Patent. On 1 Jan 1667. Richard Nicolls, Esq. principal commissioner from his majesty in New England, Governor under his Royal Highness James Duke of York & Albany & all his territories in the Americas & commander in chief of all the forces employed by his majesty to reduce the Dutch Nation and all their usurped lands under his obedience. Whereas there is a tract of land lying on Christiana Creek adjoining Swarton Nutton Island & Fearn Hook containing 500 acres bounded on the N with Christiana Creek, W with Nutton Island, S with a little spring called Bessies & E by Fearn Hook. Now Richard Nicolls granted to John Erskin, Thomas Browne & Martin Gerrits to be equally divided between them. They paying 5 bushels of winter wheat to persons of authority yearly. Signed Richard Nicolls. Written by Mathias Nicolls. Recorded 20 Mar 1705. (B2:336).

Deed. On 29 Jan 1705/6. Nicholas Dering of Philadelphia, tailor to Andrew Cork of the town of New Castle, cordwainer. Nicholas Dering for £15 10 shillings granted to Andrew Cork a tract of land situated in the town of New Castle bounded on NE by land of Robert French, E with the Delaware River, S with the town marsh & N with the Back Street or however the same may be bounded or reputed to be grounded late in the tenure of Mathias Dering, late of New Castle, dec., uncle of the said Nicholas & for lack of ____ descended to the said Nicholas. Signed Nicholas Dering. Delivered in the presence of Thomas Oekly & Samuel Weaver. Recorded 8 Apr 1706. (B2:338).

Patent. On 1 Jan 1667. Richard Nicolls, Esq. principal commissioner from his majesty in New England, Governor under his Royal Highness James Duke of York & Albany & all his territories in the Americas & commander in chief of all the forces employed by his majesty to reduce the Dutch Nation and all their usurped lands under his obedience. Whereas there was a grant made to Alexander Dhiniosa, late Governor at Delaware to Mattys Eschelsen for a piece of land next to Jurian Jansons containing along the river side eastward 25 rod & from thence going northwest into the woods 600 rod. Now for confirmation to Mattys Eschelsen the afore mentioned tract of land & he paying 1 bushel of winter wheat to persons of authority yearly. Signed Richard Nicolls. Written Mathias Nicolls. Recorded 1706. (B2:340).

Deed. On 29 Nov 1684. Artman Hayne & Matty his wife for good consideration granted all out interest in the within mentioned patent to William & John Peterson, both the sons of Matty my wife by her late husband Peter Mathyson. Matty my wife does further agree that William & John Peterson shall have possession of said when either William or John shall attain the age of 21 years. Signed Artman Hayne & Matty Hayne. Delivered in the presence of Charles Rumley & John White. Recorded 23 May 1706. (B3:341).

Deed. On 22 May 1706. John Hussey, Sr. of the county of New Castle, farmer to his loving sons, namely John & Jedediah Hussey. John Hussey, Sr. for love & good will granted to John & Jedediah Hussey all the plantation where I now dwell except for those particulars mentioned as follows: 150 acres of land being part of my plantation bounded by the creek which makes Black Walnut Island, my plantation & the town common & further I reserve to my own disposal all my beds, bedding, & all my household stuff. The rest of my estate real & personal shall go to my 2 sons to be divided equally excepting the right of survivorship, provided by 2 sons shall provide for me at all times whatever I shall require for my comfortable subsistence during the time of my natural life. And for non performance of any part of the conditions, I reserve the right, authority & pleasure to dispose of all or any of said premises for my comfortable lively hood. Signed John Hussey. Delivered in the presence of Caleb Offley & Benjamin Swett. Recorded 12 June 1706. (B2:341).

Deed. On 3 Apr 1706. Joseph Davis of Philadelphia, barber to John Brewster of New Castle, baker. Joseph Davis for £25 granted to John Brewster all his full part & share of a lot situated in the town of New Castle containing 11 foot 1 inch in breadth fronting the river & bounded on the S with the lot of Thomas Janvier, W with the market place & N with the church yard with his share in the bank or water lot, which said part or share of said lot was granted by Nicholas Dering of Philadelphia, tailor, son & heir of Emelius Dering, late of New Castle, dec (to whom as also to Mathias Dering, dec. the aforesaid lot was by Francis Lovelace granted by patent dated 7 Apr 1673 granted & confirmed) by his deed dated 8 Dec 1705 granted to Joseph Davis. Signed Joseph Davis. Delivered in the presence of George Dakeyne & William Guest. Recorded 13 June 1706. (B2:343).

Deed. On 20 Apr 1694. John Walker of the town of New Castle to John Wilson of the County of New Castle. John Walker for valuable consideration granted to John Wilson a tract of land called Oxmelter situated on the south west side of 2nd Drawyers Creek bounded by the creek, Smothers branch, Land of Smothers, John Walkers land called Exeter & the marsh containing 300 acres. Signed John Walker. Delivered in the presence of Sylvester Garland, Roeloffe Dehaes & John Smith. Recorded 27 June 1706. (B2:348).

Deed. On 20 Mar 1693. John Cox of Brandywine Creek in the county of New Castle to Job Nancoim. John Cox for consideration granted to Job Nanscoim the moiety or half part of 300 acres being 150 acres bounded by land of Andrew Peterson, Mill branch, Appoquinimink Creek containing 150 acres. John Cox will forever defend & likewise from John Boulton & his heirs. Signed John Cox. Delivered in the presence of William Guest & John Wilson.

Recorded 14 Aug 1706. (B2:350).

Deed. On 20 Aug 1700. John Richardson of the County of New Castle, yeoman to Powell Barnes of New Castle, turner. John Richardson for valuable consideration granted to Powell Barnes a piece of ground in the town of New Castle bounded on the N with land of Cornelius Kettle, SW with the house & lot of John Walker, dec. now in the tenure of Powell Barnes, SE with the market place & NW with Beaver Street containing 50 foot in breadth. Signed John Richardson. Delivered in the presence of Hip. Lefever & John Smith. Acknowledged in open court 20 Aug 1700. (B2:351).

Deed. On --- Paul Barnes for £24 16 shillings paid to John Grantham granted to Robert Bryant the within lot. Signed Paul Barnes. Delivered in the presence of John Cann & Thomas Land. (B2:351).

Deed. On Nov 1705. Margaret Heath & William Douglas in right of his wife the lawful executors of the last will & testament of Robert Bryant, late deceased, to Peter Juloes of the town of New Castle, hatter. Margaret Heath & William Douglas for £24 granted to Peter Juloes the within mentioned lot. William Douglas do appoint by beloved wife, Ann Douglas by lawful attorney to deliver this in open court. Signed Margaret Heath, William Douglas & Ann Douglas. Delivered in the presence of John Heally, George Douglas & Wessell Allrichs. Acknowledged in open court 10 Nov 1705. (B2:352).

Articles of Agreement. On 9 May 1695. Made between William Guest & Thomas Sawer, that William Guest shall have liberty from time to time and at all times hereafter for ever to dig upon a certain hill or knowledge of ground for _____ glass or other metals whatsoever he shall find there & carry away to his own use forever, the hill containing 2 or 3 acres and William Guest shall have occasion for any timber to build for the securing of the said or for a shelter he shall get what he wants on the said Sawers land. Upon consideration, William Guest has paid Sawer £12 10 shillings & it is further agreed on that if William Guest does not find there worth his labor & charge sufficient trial, that the said agree that he shall have liberty to get anywhere else on his land to make him satisfaction & Thomas Sawer shall at any time where there is required make William Guest a firm deed for same liberty. Signed Thomas Sawer. Delivered in the presence of Samuel Barker & Ann Barker.

Deed. On 25 Oct 1705. William Guest of Red Lyon Creek do assign & make over to Nicholas Hall upon George Harlans old plantation in New Castle County all my rights & interest in the with deed. Signed William Guest. Delivered in the presence of John Hatton & Mary Hatton. Acknowledge in court 21 Feb 1705. (B2:353).

Deed. On 6 July 1681. Mathias DeRing of the town of New Castle for the consideration of the half of a lot at New Castle exchanged with my brother Emelius DeRing & for other good reasons. I have granted & exchanged to my brother, Emelius DeRing all my right to all the ground as in the within mentioned patent. Signed Mathias DeRing. Delivered in the presence of John Hendrickson, Elder & Eglsbert Vanmer. (B2:354).

Deed. On 19 June 1701. Joseph Moore to Joseph England & Rebecca his wife. Whereas there is a tract of land situated on Duck Creek containing 600 acres, late in the tenure of Joseph Moore & by him sold (but no conveyed) to his excellency William Penn, Esq. Governor & the said tract of 600 acres having been granted by patent to Joseph England & Rebecca his wife. Now Joseph Moore for good causes granted & surrendered to Joseph England & Rebecca his wife the 600 acres. Signed Joseph Moore. Delivered in the presence of John Heally, Thomas Clarke & Thomas Grey. Acknowledge in court 17 June 1701. (B2:355).

Deed. On 21 Feb 1705. John Heally of Appoquinimink, Esq. to William Williams of the same place, yeoman. John Heally for £40 granted to William Williams all that tract of land called Barns Dale situated on the south side of the main branch of Appoquinimink Creek bounded by land of John Walker containing 300 acres. Signed John Heally. Delivered in the presence of Nicholas Lockyer, William Grant & Elston Wallis. Acknowledged in court 21 Feb 1705. (B2:357).

Deed. On 5 Sep 1682. John Nomers of White Clay Creek, planter to Joseph Barnes of White Clay Creek. John Nomers for a certain sum of money granted to Joseph Barnes a tract of land being part of a patent granted by Sir Edmund Andross, Governor to the said John Nomers dated 25 Mar 1676. The land sold is situated on the north side of a branch of Christiana Creek called White Clay Creek bounded by the land of Wallraven Johnson & Charles Rumley, the creek, the said John Nomers granted one half part on the north side of the creek to Thomas Wolleston & the rest of the land of the said patent on the south side of the creek the said John Nomers reserves for himself so that the one half of the land on the north side of the creek is made over to Joseph Barnes containing 100 acres. Signed John Nomers. Delivered in the presence of John Moll & Johannes Dehaes. Recorded 16 Nov 1705. (B2:363).

Letter of Attorney. On 25 Sep 1704. Joseph Osborne of the town of East Hampton in the county of Suffolk on the Island of Nassau in the province of

New York have appointed my beloved brother, Jonathan Osborne of Cape May in the province of West New Jersey to be my lawful attorney for me & in my name to sign & deliver such deeds shall be needful upon the sale of my right & interest which is one third part of a tract of land at Appoquiniminy which land did formerly belong to my brother, Bezeliell Osborne, dec. Signed Joseph Osborne. Delivered in the presence of Ebenezer Leach & William Schellinks. On 25 Sep 1704, Joseph Osborne, the subscriber came personally before us, Josiah Hobart & John Wheeler, 2 of her Majesties Justices of the Peace in East Hampton for the county of Suffolk & did voluntarily acknowledge the above instrument to be his act & deed. Signed Jos. Hobart & John Wheeler. Recorded 22 Jan 1706. (B2:364).

Letter of Attorney. On 13 July 1704. Jonathan Osborne of Cape May County in West New Jersey & Josiah Standburrough of Elizabeth Town in East Jersey do appoint our well beloved friend Mr. Richard Renalds of the county of New Castle to be our lawful attorney to make over in open court all title to John Heally of Appoquinimink Creek a tract of land situated on the southeast side of the said creek formerly know to be the land of Bazaliell Osborne, also we appoint our attorney to recover all debts due to us in the county but more particularly all the debts due us from John Heally be a bond dated 12 July 1704 & upon payment discharge said debt. Signed Jon. Osborne & Josiah Standborough. Delivered in the presence of Richard Sewell & Hans Hanson. Recorded 22 Jan 1706. (B2:365).

Deed. On 13 July 1704. Jonathan Osborne both in my own right & the lawful attorney of Joseph Osborne & Josiah Standburrough by right of his wife Elizabeth to John Heally of Appoquinimink Creek. Whereas there is a tract of land on the southeast side of Appoquinimink Creek bounded on the NW with the creek, SW with the land of Robert Money but now in the actual possession of Isaac Viguree & on the opposite 2 sides with the woods containing 400 acres, granted by patent from Governor Lovelace to Robert Tallant, who assigned it over to Lewis Johnson & Lewis Johnson assigned it over to Bazaliell Osborne & the said Bazaliell in his last will & testament amongst other bequests did give & bequeath the said tract of land to Jonathan Osborne, Joseph Osborne & Elizabeth the wife of Bazaliell Osborne. Now Jonathan Osborne both is his right & lawful attorney for Joseph Osborne & Josiah Standborough in right of his wife, the said Elizabeth, for valuable consideration granted to John Heally the said tract of land. Signed Jonathan Osborne & Josiah Standburrough. Delivered in the presence of Richard Sewell & Hans Hanson. Recorded 23 Jan 1706. (B2:366).

Deed. On 22 Feb 1705. Roeloffe Dehaes of New Castle, merchant & Sarah his wife to Richard Cantwell of Appoquinimy, gentleman. Roeloffe Dehaes & Sarah his wife for £225 granted to Richard Cantwell all the house & lot of land in the town of New Castle near the riverside between the lots belonging to Reyer Mill & Claes Peterson Smith containing 62 foot in breadth & 300 foot in length formerly granted & confirmed by Edmund Andros, Esq., Governor General, dec. by patent dated 29 Sep 1677 to Justa Andries & afterwards Justa Andries granted to the said John Williams Neering of the town of New Castle, merchant by deed dated 17 Apr 1678 & by John Williams Neering by his last will & testament dated 4 June 1698 bequeathed to Sarah his eldest daughter. Signed R. Dehaes & Sarah Dehaes. Delivered in the presence of James Coutts & Charles Springer. Be it remembered that Roeloffe Dehaes & Sarah his wife for consideration above mentioned granted & conveyed to Richard Cantwell all their right & title to the said bank or water lot belonging to the above lot. Signed R. Dehaes & Sarah Dehaes. Delivered in the presence of Richard Halliwell, John French & William Tonge. Recorded 23 Jan 1706. (B2:368).

Deed. On 5 Feb 1705. Joseph Hanson of the County of New Castle, husbandman to Joseph Wood of the town of New Castle, gentleman. Joseph Hanson for £102 granted to Joseph Wood a tract of land situated on the north side of the main branch of St. George's Creek bounded by the Marshy branch & land of John Darby containing 350 acres. Signed Joseph Hanson. Delivered in the presence of Joseph Griffin & Samuel Vans. Recorded 24 Jan 1706. (B2:372).

Receipt. On 25 Mar 1706. Received then of Joseph Wood £102 being the consideration mentioned. Signed Joseph Hanson. Delivered in the presence of Henry Williams & John Land. (B2:373).

Deed. On 16 Feb 1704. Thomas Gill Johnson of West New Jersey, yeoman & Elizabeth his wife, daughter & Co-heir of John Bowyer, late of the town of New Castle, dec. to Joseph Wood of Darby in the county of Chester, gentleman. Thomas Gill Johnson & Elizabeth his wife for £5 granted to Joseph Wood all that lot of land situated in the town of New Castle bounded by the lot lately belonging to Adam Bardrige Besterly, a lot of Joseph Wood, Front Street & also the bank lot. Signed Thomas Gill Johnson & Elizabeth Gill Johnson. Delivered in the presence of Elston Wallis & William Tonge. Recorded 24 Jan 1706. (B2:373).

Deed. On 21 Nov 1705. Joseph McGregory of the County of Salem in the province of West New Jersey, husbandman to Christopher White of White Clay Creek, husbandman. Whereas there is a tract of land called Switzerland lying on the north side of White Clay Creek bounded by land of Charles Rumsey, land of Thomas Woollastone, land of Joseph Cookson, land of Joseph Cookson & John Smith, land of Richard Smith & by land Joseph Barnes bought of Charles Rumsey containing 200 acres surveyed 13 Sep 1682 by Ephraim Herman, surveyor. Now Joseph McGregory for £20 granted to Christopher White all the said parcel of land. Signed Joseph McGregory. Delivered in the presence of Francis Land & Henry Williams. Recorded 24 Jan 1706. (B2:375).

Deed. On 20 Apr 1703. Olla Toarson, late of the County of New Castle & now of Morris River in the province of West New Jersey, husbandman to John Toarson of the County of New Castle, husbandman. Olla Toarson for £5 granted to John Toarson all my 6th part of half an acre, 1/6th part of 27 acres, 1/6th part of a tract divided or to be divided situated in Verditige Hook in the county of New Castle bounded by the river, the Manor of Rocklands, land of John & Peter Mounce & land formerly belonging to Charles Peterson & now to Edward Beeson containing 165 1/2 acres which was resurveyed & divided according to a former survey made by Edmund Cantwell on 10 Nov 1688 by virtue of a warrant from the commissioners dated 30 May 1688 being the fifth part of the whole tract of land containing 827 1/2 acres, which by request & agreement by the inhabitants were divided into 5 plantations according to the settlement of the then inhabitants. Said 165 1/2 acres was one of the plantations which was granted to Henry Toarson by patent from the commissioners at Philadelphia dated 11 Feb 1688/9. Also all his 1/6th part in 20 acres being one third part of a marsh granted to Henry Toarson, Jacob Clements & John & Peter Mounce bounded by the river, joining the fast land of Veritige Hook a creek called Island Creek being laid out for 60 acres on 9 Apr 1690 by virtue of a warrant dated 17 Feb 1689. Which said 165 1/2 acres of land & 20 acres of land are by consents of said Henry Toarson, the said John Toarson, Margaret their sister, Mathias Toarson, Olla Toarson & Stephen Toarson, their brothers is thus divided, 1/6th part to Henry Toarson, 1/6th part to John Roarson, 1/6h part to John Toarson by right of his sister Margaret, 1/6th part to Mathias Toarson, 1/6th part to John Toarson by right of Olla Toarson & 1/6th part to Stephen Toarson. Olla Toarson do covenant to & with the said John Toarson that the said 27 1/2 acres, 1/6th part of 1/2 acre & 1/6 part of 20 acres of marsh are hereby granted to John Toarson to the proper use forever against him the said Olla Toarson, against Edmund Cantwell, against all & every other person whatsoever claiming any interest to the same. Olla Toarson has appointed Thomas Jones, his father in law to deliver these presents in open court. Signed Olla Toarson. Delivered in the presence of Hugh Owen, Cicily Baldwin & Hugh Bowden. Recorded 26 Jan 1706. (B2:378).

Deed. On 14 Aug 1704. John Cann of the County of New Castle to Cornelius Empson & Richard Empson both of the County, gentlemen. John Cann for £12 granted to Cornelius Empson & Richard Empson a tract of land situated on White Clay Creek bounded by the Mill Creek, the road that goes to John Cann's house, White Clay Creek, land of Abraham Mann & the King's Road containing 12 acres. Signed John Cann. Delivered in the presence of Francis Land & Brian McDonald. Recorded 25 Jan 1706. (B2:381).

Deed. William Maslander of Swanwick, yeoman to Roeloffe Dehaes of New Castle, merchant. Whereas there is a tract of land situated at Swanwick bounded by land of Joseph Wood, the road that leads from New Castle to Christiana Ferry, Maslander's land, Delaware Bay & land of Adam Hykey containing 270 acres lately belonging to Mary Block, late of Swanwick, widow, deceased. Now William Maslander for £87 granted to Roeloffe Dehaes 2 full third parts of the said land. Signed William Maslander. Delivered in the presence of Richard Reynolds & William Tonge. Receipt. On 15 Dec 1705, then received of Roeloffe Dehaes the sum of 87R the full consideration money within mentioned. Signed William Maslander. Delivered in the presence of Francis Allen & William Tonge. Recorded 25 Jan 1706. (B2:383).

Deed. On 16 Aug 1705. Powell Garretson of White Clay Creek, yeoman to Samuel Lowman of New Castle, Esq. Powell Garretson for £6 5 shillings granted to Samuel Lowman a tract of land lying on White Clay Creek containing 50 acres being part of a tract of land granted to Powell Garretson by a warrant from the commissioners dated 28 Jan 1701 adjoining the Welsh Tract bounded by land of Jonas Arskin, land of Powell Garretson, land of Samuel Lowman & White Clay Creek. Signed Powell Garretson. Delivered in the presence of Roeloffe Dehaes & Elston Wallis. Recorded 25 Jan 1706. (B2:386).

Mortgage. On 10 Oct 1706. Jonas Arskin of the County of New Castle to Sylvester Garland of the county of New Castle, merchant. Jonas Arskin for £80 granted to Sylvester Garland a tract of land bounded by White Clay Creek, land now or late of Andrew Tillies containing 200 acres which said tract of land is commonly known by the name of Oakburne being situated on the south side of White Clay Creek. Provided Jonas Arskins shall pay or cause to be paid to Sylvester Garland the sum of £80 on 1 May 1709 with lawful interest then this shall be void. Signed Jonas Arskin. Delivered in the presence of John Heally & Charles Springer. Recorded 27 Jan 1706. (B2:389).

Deed. On 20 Dec 1706. William Osburne of Appoquinimink Creek, house carpenter, Paul Garretson of White Clay Creek, yeoman & Elizabeth his wife, Morgan Patton of the same place & Hannah his wife & Rachel Harris of the same place, spinster to Edward Williams of Appoquinimink Creek, yeoman.

Whereas by virtue of a warrant there was laid out to Thomas Harris, late of Duck Creek, yeoman, dec & William Osburne a tract of land called the Exchange situated on the main branch of Duck Creek bounded by the creek laid out for 700 acres as by survey dated 1684. Whereas the said Thomas Harris by his last will & testament dated 10 July 1690 among other things contained did devise & bequeath to his 3 daughters, Elizabeth, Hannah & Rachel all his share & portion of the said 700 acres. Now William Osborne, Paul Garretson & Elizabeth his wife, Morgan Patent & Hannah his wife & Rachel Harris for £40 granted to Edward Williams the above said land. Signed William Osborne, Paul Garretson, Elizabeth Garretson, Morgan Patton, Hannah Patton & Rachel Harris. Delivered in the presence of John Ogle, Elizabeth Ogle & Elston Wallis. Recorded 27 Jan 1706. (B2:392).

Letter of Attorney. On 1 Jan 1706. Paul Garretson & Elizabeth his wife, Morgan Patton & Hannah his wife & Rachel Harris have appointed our true & lawful friend, John Ogle our lawful attorney to acknowledge in open court a deed for a tract of land lying on Duck Creek sold to Edward Williams. Signed Paul Garretson, Elizabeth Garretson, Morgan Patton, Hannah Patton & Rachel Harris. Delivered in the presence of James Askew, Jonas Arskin & Elston Wallis. (B2:396).

Deed. On 16 Aug 1706. William Rakestraw, late of Oxfordshire in the kingdom of England & now in Philadelphia, yeoman to John Cann of White Clay Creek, yeoman. Whereas there is a tract of land on the west side of the Delaware River nigh onto the upper end of Bread & Cheese Island on the north side of White Clay Creek which divides this from the land of John Edmundson which by virtue of a warrant has been laid out for Wallraven Johnson DeFox & Charles Rumsey by patent from Edmund Andros, Esq. late Governor of New York, dated 25 Mar 1676 bounded by the creek, land of John Edmundson containing 570 acres. Whereas Wallraven Johnson DeFox by assignment on the backside of the patent dated 24 May 1679 granted all his right to said land to Charles Rumsey. Whereas Charles Rumsey by granted to John Cann, late of White Clay Creek, dec., father of the above John, 60 acres lying on the upper or west end of the said whole tract & likewise granted to John Watkins & Samuel Barker 300 acres of land then in the possession of John Cann, dec. & also conveyed to John Moll, late of New Castle, dec. 210 acres the residue of the 570 acres. Whereas John Moll by deed dated 20 Apr 1685 granted to William Rakestraw the aforesaid 210 acres. Now William Rakestraw for £45 granted to John Cann all the said 210 acres. William Rakestraw appointed Joseph Wood of New Castle, his lawful attorney to deliver this in open court. Signed William Rakestraw. Delivered in the presence of Richard Halliwell, Joseph Wood & John Childe. Recorded 29 Jan 1706. (B2:397).

Deed. On 22 Aug 1706. John Hussey of the County of New Castle to his loving son, Christopher Hussey. John Hussey for the love & goodwill he bears to his son, Christopher Hussey, granted to said son, Christopher a tract of land lying on the westerly side of my plantation bounded by my plantation, the town common, the ground adjoining to the creek which makes Black Walnut Island containing 150 acres. Signed John Hussey. Delivered in the presence of Kenhelme Clarke & Benjamin Swett. John Hussey does appoint his trust friend Benjamin Swett to be his attorney to deliver this to open court. Signed John Hussey. Delivered in the presence of Kenhelme Clarke & William Cooper. Recorded 31 Jan 1706. (B2:401)..

Deed. On 21 Aug 1705. Martha Wolleston of White Clay Creek, widow, Thomas Wolleston of White Clay Creek, yeoman & John Hendrick of Christiana Hundred, yeoman to Cornelius Empson of the County of New Castle, gentleman & Richard Empson of the said county, gentleman. Martha Wolleston, Thomas Wolleston & John Hendrick for £40 granted to Cornelius & Richard Empson a tract of land being the full moiety or half part of a tract of land lying on White Clay Creek near Christian Kill bounded by land of Hans Bones, land of James Crawford, the run at the head of Bread & Cheese Island containing ___ acres, which said tract was granted by patent from the commissioners of Richard Nicolls to Sergeant Thomas Wolleston, dec., John Ogle, John Hendrick & Harman Johnson dated Feb 1666 & confirmed since by Richard Nicolls by patent dated 1 Aug 1668. Signed John Hendrick. Delivered in the presence of Charles Springer & John Richardson, Jr. Recorded 31 Jan 1706. (B2:403).

Deed. On 15 Nov 1706. John Heally of Appoquinimy, yeoman to Cornelius Claus Cooper of Orange County in the province of New York, yeoman. John Heally for £130 granted to Cornelius Claus Cooper all that tract of land being on the south side of Appoquinimink Creek commonly called New England Mans Land being the land of Bazeliell Osborne containing 400 acres. Signed John Heally. Delivered in the presence of Robert Ashton & William Tonge. Recorded 31 Jan 1706. (B2:405).

Deed. On 4 Nov 1706. John Guest of White Clay Creek, Esq. to Richard Wolleston of the County of New Castle, yeoman. John Guest for £102 12 shillings granted to Richard Wolleston a tract of land bounded by White Clay Creek, land of James Claypoole, land Thomas Pierson, Peck Creek, land of Thomas Wollestons & land of James Anderson containing 342 acres which said tract is part of a tract of land granted by the commissioners of property by patent dated 1 Dec 1702 to John Guest. Signed John Guest. Delivered in the presence of Richard Reynolds & William Tonge. Recorded 31 Jan 1706. (B2:408).

Deed. On 17 Aug 1705. Hannah Ellis of the town of New Castle, widow to George Dakeyne of the said county, surveyor. Hannah Ellis for £12 granted to George Dakeyne a house & lot being on the southwest end of the town of New Castle adjoining the lots of George Dakeyne containing 30 foot & 300 foot in length, which said lot is part of a tract of land granted by patent from Francis Lovelace, late Governor General, dated 1 Oct 1669 to Sergeant John Askew, said Askew sold this house & lot to Henry Vandenburgh & Vandenburgh sold same to Cornelius Post. Cornelius Post conveyed it to John Ellis by deed dated 22 July 1695 & John Ellis by his last will & testament gives Hannah Ellis his wife full power to sell & dispose of said house & lot for the good of her & the children. Hannah Ellis appointed her beloved friend William Tonge to be her lawful attorney to make over the said lot to George Dakeyne. Signed Hannah Ellis. Delivered in the presence of Edward Thomas Nowell, Robert Marley & Robert Dyre. Recorded 5 Feb 1706. (B2:411).

Deed. On 23 Sep 1703. John Crawford of the County of New Castle, yeoman, son & heir of James Crawford, late of said county, yeoman, deceased, James Crawford, the other son of the deceased, Thomas Ogle of the County, yeoman & Mary his wife, the only daughter of the said deceased. Whereas James Miller of the town of New Castle, mariner became seized of a certain tenement & other buildings belonging to a lot in the town of New Castle bounded by the Delaware River, the house formerly belonging to Martin Garrets, land taken up at the backside of town & the highway, which said lot did belong to James Crawford in his lifetime by virtue of patent from Gov. Nichols dated 1 Jan 1667 & were sold by the relict & administratrix of the said James Crawford to Robert Evans, from whom the said James Miller claims & holds the same. Now John Crawford, James Crawford, Thomas Ogle & Mary his wife for £25 granted & released to James Miller the said tract of land. John, James & Thomas have appointed John French to deliver this in court. Signed John Crawford, James Crawford, Thomas Ogle & Mary Ogle. Delivered in the presence of Grimstone Boude, Henry Brooke & Thomas Grey. Recorded 6 Feb 1706. (B2:413).

Deed. On 1 Jan 1703. Richard Halliwell of the town of New Castle, merchant to George Dakeyne of the town of New Castle, surveyor. Whereas William Penn, Gov. by patent dated 22 July 1684 recorded in New Castle Book A Page 22, granted to Hendrick Vandenburgh, late of New Castle, merchant, a tract of land called Poplar Neck situated on the northside of Red Lyon Branch bounded by the road, land of Oele Paulson, Red Lyon branch containing 200 acres. Whereas Hendrick Vandenburgh by deed on the back of said patent dated 22 June 1686 granted to Major William Dyre the said tract of land. Whereas Anna Vandenburgh, wife of Hendrick Vandenburgh by her instrument also on the back of said patent did voluntarily consent to sail sale. Whereas Major William

Dyre by his last will & testament dated 20 Feb 1687/8 amongst other things did bequeath to his youngest son, James Dyre, 200 acres lying about 7 miles from the town of New Castle. Whereas James Dyre by his Letter of Attorney dated 15 Jan 1702/3 appointed his honored friend, Captain Richard Halliwell to be his lawful attorney to sell & convey said tract of land. Now Richard Halliwell for £40 granted to George Dakeyne the said 200 acres. Signed Richard Halliwell. Delivered in the presence of Richard Cantwell & William Tonge. Letter of Attorney recorded page 248. Acknowledged in court 15 May 1705. (B2:416).

Deed. On 12 Aug 1706. John Heally of Appoquinimy, yeoman to Nicholas Lockyer of Swanwick, yeoman. Whereas Nicholas Lockyer & Elizabeth, his late wife by their deed dated 19 Aug 1699 made between them & John Heally for the consideration mentioned granted to John Heally a tract of land bounded by land formerly of Peter DeWitt, the marsh, Horse Neck or Peerdehook & land of Urian Johnson commonly called the Laymakers Hook containing in breadth 100 rod & the tract of meadow land in Peered Hook bounded by land of John Sybranson, land of Barbara, then widow of Peter Maslander, dec. containing in breadth 25 rod & 600 rod in length & all that tract of land situated at Peerde Hook bounded by land of Arman Hayne, land belonging to Jacob Clawson & a small creek containing 500 rod in length & 25 rod in breadth & all that tract of marsh land lying between the marsh of James Hallyday, marsh of Bilchy Johnson, being between the creek & river upon Swanwick side being formerly the marsh of John Sybrans, Jr., all which tracts of land were then or late in the tenure of Nicholas Lockyer & Elizabeth his wife, but by virtue of the statute for transferring uses into possessions were then in the actual possession of John Heally & in the same deed expressed with this further covenant, likewise that in case it should happen said Elizabeth should die & depart this life in the lifetime of Nicholas Lockyer, that then the said Elizabeth should have the full power by her last will & testament as she should think fit to devise & bequeath any gift or legacy to such persons as she should appoint to the value of £100 & said John Heally should stand seized of the said land until the sum of £100 should be paid. Whereas Elizabeth did happen to depart this life in the lifetime of Nicholas Lockyer & did by her last will & testament did bequeath to Andrew Peterson, others the children of Adam Peterson, late of the County of New Castle, dec. the sum of £100 to be equally divided between them which said Nicholas Lockyer has since paid or secured the payment thereof to the said Andrew Peterson & other children of Adam Peterson. Now John Heally for £100 (in the will mentioned) granted & surrendered to Nicholas Lockyer all the said tracts of land. Signed John Heally. Delivered in the presence of William Guest & Richard Reynolds. Recorded 9 Feb 1706. (B2:419).

Deed. On 8 Mar 1705. Derrick Vanderburgh in the province of New York, mason, & Rymereth his wife & Isaac Goodwin of Reeden Island in the county of New Castle, yeoman to Peter Jacobs of New York, mason. Derrick Vanderburgh, Rymereth his wife & Isaac Goodwin for £54 granted to Peter Jacobs all that tract of land near Reeden Island known by the name Pipe Stave Neck bounded by the head of a branch of Augustine Creek, land of Peter Shykers containing 150 acres & also 50 acres of another tract situated near Reeden Island in a neck of land commonly called Long Neck known by the name of the Home lot to be taken out of the north east side of the said Long Neck said tracts are part of a tract formerly belonging to Casparus Augustine Herman, dec. containing 3209 acres surveyed by James Claypoole, surveyor by virtue of a warrant from William Penn dated 23 Feb 1682 to Casparus Augustine Herman. Casparus Herman & Katherine his wife by deed dated 9 May 1694 sold said tract to John Hanson, Baronet Joosten, Johannes Van Ekelen, William Hanson, Johannes Hanson, Isaac Goodwin & Johannes Smart, which said land is part of the 3 eighth parts of the aforesaid tract of land divided & laid out for John Hanson by Thomas Pierson, surveyor by joint consent of the purchasers & afterwards John Hanson by his last will & testament dated 10 Oct 1700 bequeathed the said land to the above named Rymereth & Geartroy [other spellings - Gatrick], late wife of the said Isaac Goodwin. Signed Derrick Vanderburgh, Rymereth Vanderburgh & Isaac Goodwin [also spell Gooding]. Delivered in the presence of D. Provoast, Jr., Andries Abraham, Abraham Brasher, John Stewart & Hans Hanson. New York. 17 Sep 1706. Then appeared before me, David Provoast, one of her majesties Justices of the Peace for the City & County of New York, the above named Derrick Vanderburgh, Esq. & Rymereth his wife & did declare this the above instrument to be their voluntary act & deed. Signed D. Provoast. Recorded 27 Feb 1706. (B2:423).

Deed. On 4 Oct 1706. John Guest of the City of Philadelphia, Esq. to John Martin of the same, merchant. Whereas William Penn, Gov. by patent dated 11 Aug 1702 confirmed to John Guest a tract of land containing 1250 acres & patent in recorded in Book A Vol. 2 Page 348. Now John Guest for £200 granted to John Martin a tract of land being part of the 1250 acres bounded by White Clay Creek, land of John Kings now Neal Cooks, land of the London Company & land of Thomas Pierson containing 600 acres. Signed John Guest. Delivered in the presence of Thomas Story, Maurice Little & George Lowther. Recorded 6 Mar 1706. (B2:428).

Deed. On 26 Dec 1706. John Martin of the City of Philadelphia, merchant to Richard Dowse of the same city, merchant. John Martin for £140 granted to Richard Dowse all that tract of land of White Clay Creek bounded by the creek, land of John Kings but now of Neal Cooks, land of John Guest, land of the London Company & land belonging to Thomas Pierson containing 600 acres.

John Martin does appoint George Lowther to be his attorney to deliver this in open court. Signed John Martin. Delivered in the presence of Mary Johnston & George Lowther. Recorded 6 Mar 1706. (B2:432).

Release. I clear all accounts with Euron Anderson & hereby do discharge him from all accounts, debts, dues & demands preceding the date hereof. Signed James Coutts & Hercules Coutts. New Castle 14 Apr 1701. (B2:435).

Deed. On 11 Nov 1706. Paul Barnes of the town of New Castle, turner & Penelope his wife to Erick Erickson of Crane Hook, yeoman. Paul Barnes & Penelope his wife for £45 granted to Erick Erickson all the estate right & title in one full fifth part or share of a tract of land lying near the mouth of Crane Hook, the inheritance of Reynier Vandercoulin & now or late in the possession of Swan Colesbury & Powell Paulson as also one full fifth share in the island & marsh adjoining the same. Signed Paul Barnes & Penelope Barnes. Delivered in the presence of John Colvert & William Tonge. Recorded 28 June 1707. (B2:435).

Deed. On 21 Apr 1707. Richard Dowle of the City of Philadelphia, merchant to Toby Leech of Cheltenham in the county of Philadelphia, gentleman. Richard Dowle for £200 granted to Toby Leech all that tract of land bounded by White Clay Creek, land of Neal Cook, Muddy Run, land of John Kings now Neal Cooks & land of John Guest, Esq. (whereof this was formerly part), land of the London Company & land of Thomas Pierson containing 600 acres. Richard Dowle has appointed Thomas Clark of Philadelphia, gentleman, his attorney to deliver in open court. Signed Richard Dowle. Delivered in the presence of Abell Tuder, William Cocker & John Leech. Recorded 16 July 1707. (B2:437).

Sheriff's Deed. On 19 May 1707. John French, Sheriff to John Greenwater. Whereas George Lamb of New Castle, yeoman at the court of common pleas 21 May 1706 recovered a debt of £8 6 shillings & £6 17 shillings & 9 pence in damages against Phillip Vessell, late of the County, yeoman. John French, sheriff, seized a tract of land on the east side of Scotts Run between the Canne Branch & St. George's Creek containing 100 acres being one moiety of a tract of land formerly conveyed by Edward Gibbs, dec. by his deed dated 15 Aug 11699 to Mathias Erickson. Now John French, sheriff, for £35 granted to John Greenwater the 100 acres. Signed John French, sheriff. Delivered in the presence of William Tonge & Elston Wallis. Acknowledged in open court 15 May 1707. (B2:442).

Mortgage. On 22 May 1707. Nathaniel Russell of Blackbird's Creek, yeoman to Jane Pearl of the same place, widow. Nathaniel Russell for £20 granted to

Jane Pearl all that tract of land situated in Duck Creek Hundred bounded by a swamp containing 290 1/2 acres which said land was by patent dated 26 May 1701 to Nathaniel Russell which said tract of land Robert Colby was formerly seized & sold the same to Joseph Holden, who sold the same to George Russell, who dying possessed of the premises, the right of inheritance to the same descended to his sons, Nathaniel, John, Jacob & George as by patent dated 25 Sep 1701. Provided always the true intent & meaning of the said parties to these present that if Nathaniel Russell pay or cause to be paid to Jane Pearl £20 with lawful interest with in 2 years after the date here, then this deed to cease & be void. Signed Nathaniel Russell. Delivered in the presence of William Williams & Elston Wallis. Recorded 23 Sep 1707. (B2:445).

Mortgage. On 22 Aug 1707. Paul Paulson of the County of New Castle, & Elizabeth his wife to Jane Pearl of Philadelphia, widow. Paul Paulson & Elizabeth his wife for £100 granted to Jane Pearl a tract of land called Turks Island situated at the mouth of Christiana Creek bounded by Crane Hook land & land of Jacob Clawson containing 200 acres, granted by virtue of a warrant dated 5 Jan 1678 to Henry Lemmon & confirmed by patent dated 5 Nov 1685. Provided that Paul Paulson & Elizabeth his wife pay to Jane Pearl £100 plus lawful interest on 24 Aug 1711, the full interest being paid yearly, then this deed by void. Signed Paul Paulson & Elizabeth Paulson. Delivered in the presence of Robert French & Elston Wallis. Recorded 20 Sep 1707. (B2:447).

Sheriff's Deed. On 19 Aug 1707. John French, Sheriff to John Steele of the county of New Castle, yeoman. Whereas Robert Hutchinson of the said county, yeoman, in the court of Common Pleas dated 18 Feb last recovered against Joseph Moore, late of said county, wheelwright the debt of £7 & £3 5 shillings damages. John French, sheriff seized a tract of land on Christiana Creek bounded by Reec Thomas, land of Abraham Brewster & land of John Ogle containing 252 acres. John French, Sheriff, for £42 granted to John Steele all the said tract of land. Signed John French, sheriff. Delivered in the presence of George Lowther & Elston Wallis. Recorded 1 Oct 1707. (B2:450).

Deed. On 27 mar 1707. John Guest of the City of Philadelphia, Esq. & Susannah his wife to Robert Jones of the County of Chester, millwright. Whereas there is a tract of land situated on the NE side of White Clay Creek bounded by a great hill near the creek, bounded by land of Joseph Moore & other land of John Guest containing 258 acres part of a tract of land called The Hop Yard which the present commissioners of property by patent dated 19 Apr 1703 granted to John Guest as recorded in Philadelphia Book A Vol 2 Page 506. Now John Guest & Susannah his wife for £50 granted to Robert Jones the said 258 acres. John Guest & Susannah his wife have appointed William James &

Richard Halliwell their attorneys to deliver this deed in court. Signed John Guest & Susannah Guest. Delivered in the presence of John Grog, Henry Lewis & John Powell. Recorded 14 Oct 1707. (B2:454).

Deed. On 19 May 1707. John Cann of White Clay Creek, yeoman to William Cann of White Clay Creek, yeoman. John Cann for £100 granted to William Cann a tract of land situated near the upper end of Bread & Cheese Island on the north side of White Clay Creek which has been laid out by warrant for Wallraven Johnson Defoe & Charles Rumsey containing 210 acres, being lately granted by William Rakestraw of Philadelphia, yeoman by deed dated 16 Aug 1706 to John Cann, said tract being part of a tract of 570 acres granted by Edmund Andros, Esq. late Gov. of New York dated 25 Mar 1676 unto Wallraven Johnson Defoe & Charles Rumsey. Signed John Cann. Delivered in the presence of William Bennett, Christian Stillman & William Tonge. Recorded 14 Nov 1707. (B2:457).

Letter of Attorney. On 22 Aug 1707, John Cann of the county of New Castle, yeoman appoint my trusty friend, Richard Reynolds my lawful attorney to acknowledge a deed for a tract of land on White Clay Creek now in the possession of William Cann to the said William Cann. Signed John Cann. Delivered in the presence of Peter Cocks & Matthi. Ebertson. (B2:460).

Deed. On 16 Aug 1706. Harman Allrichs of the County of New Castle, merchant to Ellis Humphreys of St. George's Creek, yeoman. Whereas there is a tract of land situated on the south side of St. George's Creek bounded by Doctor's Swamp & land of Bernard Egberts containing 100 acres, which said tract was granted by Edward Blay of Cecil County in the province of Maryland & Anne his wife to Thomas Thaxstone of Cecil County in the province of Maryland by deed dated 22 Apr 1702. Thomas Thaxstone by deed dated 28 Nov 1702 granted the said tract to Harman Allrichs. Now Harmans Allrichs for £20 granted to Ellis Humphrey all the said tract of land containing 100 acres. Signed Harman Allrichs. Delivered in the presence of William Tonge & Elston Wallis. Acknowledged in open court 22 May 1705. (B2:560).

Deed. On 8 Mar 1693. Ambrose Baker of the town of New Castle to Martin Martinson of the county of New Castle. Ambrose Baker for a consideration granted to Martin Martinson a lot in the town of New Castle bounded on the S with the market place, W with the land of Ambrose Baker, N with Brewer Street & W with the house & lot of Cornelius Derrickson containing in breadth 120 foot & in length 169 foot. Signed Ambrose Baker. Delivered in the presence of John Ellis, Henry Vandenburgh & John Smith. Acknowledged in court 23 Mar 1693. (B2:564).

Deed. On 23 Mar 1693. John Biske of the town of New Castle to John Hendrickson of the County of New Castle. John Biske for valuable consideration granted to John Hendrickson a 1 lot in the town of New Castle bounded on the S with St. Maries Street, SW with a lot formerly belonging to John Mandy, NW with Brewer Street & NE with the lot of John Biske containing in breadth 60 foot & in length 160 foot. Signed John Biske. Delivered in the presence of Martin Martinson & John Smith. Acknowledged in court 23 Mar 1693. (B2:464).

Deed. On 19 May 1697. John Hendrickson for valuable consideration granted to Adam Hay the lot within mentioned. Signed John Hendrickson. Delivered in the presence of Mary Claypoole & James Claypoole. (B2:465).

Articles of Agreement. On 18 Mar 1707. John Hussey of the County of New Castle, planter to his brother Jedidiah Hussey. John & Jedidiah Hussey now stand possessed in a plantation by a deed from their honored father, dated 22 May 1706. Whereas plantation lying undivided. Now to the division shall be made between the parties. It is agreed upon the John Hussey do agree with Jedidiah Hussey that Jedidiah Hussey shall from hence forth hold a tract of land being part of the plantation bounded by the commons & also half the mill the said Jedidiah being at half the charge to keep it in repair likewise the marsh & half the cripple & Jedidiah Hussey do freely agree with the said John Hussey that he shall enjoy the residue of plantation. Signed John Hussey & Jedidiah Hussey. Delivered in the presence of William Douglas, Sarah Swett & Benjamin Swett. (B2:466).

Deed. On 6 Mar 1706. Richard Cantwell of Appoquinimy, gentleman & Henry Garretson of the same place, gentleman & Elizabeth his wife, daughter of Edmund Cantwell, late of Appoquinimy, gentleman, dec. to Henry Land of the County of New Castle, yeoman. Whereas Edmund Cantwell in his lifetime in consideration of a certain execution of the Court at New Castle in the year of 1684 against Edmund Cantwell, for the sum of £12 besides the cost of the suite of one Evert Henricks by Samuel Land, the then sheriff on behalf of Edmund Cantwell paid & discharged, the said Edmund Cantwell did agree to & with Samuel Land in his lifetime to sell to Samuel Land a house & lot in the town of New Castle bounded by lot of Samuel Land, a lot laid out for Walter Wharton, Land Street & Minguaes Street containing in breadth 60 foot & in length 300 foot, which said lot was by Walter Wharton laid lot for Johannes Dehaes, late of the County of New Castle dec. 10 Aug 1676 & since that purchased by Edmund Cantwell but not be him conveyed to Samuel Land. Whereas Richard Cantwell & Henry Garretson & Elizabeth his wife, Richard & Elizabeth being the only daughter & son of Edmund Cantwell, dec. for consideration conveyed & confirmed said lot to Samuel Land. Signed Richard Cantwell, Henry Garretson & Elizabeth Garretson. Delivered in the presence of John Heally & John French. Acknowledged in court 22 May 1707. (B2:468).

Deed. On 20 Nov 1704. Urian Anderson of St.George's Creek, planter to Peter Johnsogoe of St. George's Creek. Whereas there is a tract of land on the south side of the main branch of St. George's Creek formerly surveyed for George Geady bounded by the mouth of Joy Run, land of John Jervises containing 200 acres granted by warrant from Gov. Penn dated 8 Aug 1684 & Whereas William Broxen & Elizabeth his wife of Cecil County in the province of Maryland, being the late relict of George Geady did by deed dated 16 Nov 1703 granted to Urian Anderson the aforementioned land. Now Urian Anderson for £20 granted to Peter Johnsogoe the said tract of land. Signed Urian Anderson. Delivered in the presence of Fra. Allen & Erick Erickson. Acknowledged in court 21 Nov 1704. (B2:470).

Deed. On 30 Nov 1702. Timothy Atkinson of the County of Glouster in the province of West New Jersey, yeoman to Thomas Babb of the County of New Castle, husbandman. Timothy Atkinson for £30 granted to Thomas Babb a tract of land situated in the Manor of Rockland bounded by Stone Creek containing 200 acres with 20 acres of marsh. Timothy Atkinson has appointed Benjamin Swett his lawful attorney to deliver this deed in court. Signed Timothy Atkinson. Delivered in the presence of William Druett, Joseph Perkins, Reuben Ford, Hugh Bawden. Recorded 20 Aug 1707. Hugh Bawden of Chester County, school master, makes oath that he was present & saw Timothy Atkinson seal this deed to the within named Thomas Babbs & the above named Joseph Perkins, dec. & Reuben Ford did then subscribe their names as witnessed. Hugh Bawden being attested before me, Philip Roman. Acknowledged in court 21 Aug 1707. (B2:473).

Discharge. On 5 Apr 1708. I do hereby discharge Edward Jeoffreys from all accounts, dues & demands preceding the date hereof having received full satisfaction for the same. Signed Ja. Coutts. Witnesses: Robert Ronnald & John French. (B2:475).

Survey. By virtue of a warrant from the court of New Castle, laid out for Wolla Paulson a tract of land called Poplar Neck situated on the west side of Delaware River in the woods back of John Williams land, formerly called Mr. Tom's Plantation bounded by land of John Williams, the Little Run, the King's Road containing 220 acres of fast land & then also surveyed by above order for Wolla Paulson a piece of marsh lying on the south side of Red Lyon Creek bounded by the path that goes by John Williams now plantation, the creek containing 28 acres of hay ground. Surveyed 2 Oct 1682. Signed Ephraim Herman. Recorded at the request of Peter Anderson. Recorded 24 Apr 1708. (B2:476).

Letter of Attorney. On 6 Apr 1708. John Richards of the City of Philadelphia, slaughterer, have appointed my beloved wife, Susannah Richards to be my lawful attorney for me in my name to ask demand & require from all persons whom it may or shall concern with the province & territories thereon depending, East & West New Jersey, Virginia & Maryland or elsewhere in the Americas all sums of money now or shall grow due me. Signed John Richards. Delivered in the presence of Nathaniel Poole, Joshua Ballings, Samuel Weaver, Joseph Griffin & Kenhelme Clark. On 19 May 1708 Kenhelm Clark declared that at the City of Philadelphia he did then & there see the above John Richards sign & deliver this above written power of attorney to his wife Susannah Richards & that he deed see Joseph Griffen sign & evidence to the same. Signed John Healy & Isaac Gooding. (B2:477).

Deed. On 8 May 1708. Adam Hyke of the County of New Castle, yeoman to Jonathan Savage of the town of New Castle, carpenter. Adam Hyke for £14 10 shillings granted to Jonathon Savage's lot of land in the town of New Castle bounded by land belonging to Solomon Hyke, Brewers Street, other lot of Adam Hyke & the market place, heretofore the inheritance of Ambrose Baker by patent dated 12 Apr 1686 in Philadelphia. And by Ambrose Baker given by his last will to his daughter Harmina who intermarried with Edward Cole did sell said lot to Adam Hyke by deed dated 19 Feb 1701. Signed Adam Hyke. Delivered in the presence of John Wood, Peter Jacquett & Joseph Wood. Acknowledged in court 20 May 1708. (B2:478).

Deed. On 12 May 1708. George Dakeyne of the County of New Castle, surveyor to Phillip Truax of East Jersey in the township of Freehold, yeoman. George Dakeyne for £52 10 shillings granted to Phillip Truax a tract of land bounded by St. George's Creek & land of Robert Darby containing 228 acres. Which said tract was granted by the court at New Castle to Hans Marcuson in 1684 & by Hans Marcuson by deed dated 10 May 1707 sold to George Dakeyne. George Dakeyne shall protect said deed from claims from Richard Garrot & his heirs & against Hans Marcuson & his heirs. Signed George Dakeyne. Delivered in the presence of Jonas Arskins, John Ogle & Elston Wallis. Acknowledged in court 20 May 1708. (B2:482).

Deed. On 17 Aug 1703. John Bowyer of the County of New Castle to Henry Parker. John Bowyer for £100 granted to Henry Parker one half part of a plantation being lately the plantation of Joseph Hanson, the one half containing 200 acres being the northernmost part of 400 acres sold to John Bowyer by deed dated 17 Feb 1701. Signed John Bowyer. Delivered in the presence of John Grantham & John Smith. Acknowledged in court 18 Aug 1703. (B2:486).

Deed. On 10 Oct 1705. John Cocks of the County of New Castle, yeoman to John Warford of the County of New Castle, laborer. John Cocks for £45 granted to John Warford a tract of land lying between St. George's Creek & Dragon Swamp bounded by Dragons Swamp & John Cocks Road containing 110 acres being part of a greater tract granted by patent from Edmund Andros, Esq. to Jacob Young of the County of New Castle being 1280 acres & John Cocks purchased of Jacob Young 854 acres by deed dated 20 Nov 1700. Signed John Cocks. Delivered in the presence of Mary Druett, George Dakeyne & Thomas Dakeyne. Acknowledged in court 20 May 1708. (B2:487).

Lease & Release. On 4 & 5 July 1678. William Penn, late of Bickmersworth in the County of Hertford now of Berminghurst in the county of Sussex, Esq., Gaven Laury of London, merchant, Nicholas Lucas of Hertford in the County of Hartford, maulster & Edward Bylllinge of Westminster of the county of Middlesex, gentleman to Samuel Norris of London, gentleman, Abraham Goodoune of Spittlefield in the parish of Strepney in the County of Middlesex, silk weaver, Appollo Morris of Castle Salem in the County of Corks in the kingdom of Ireland, gentleman, Thomas Davis of Brandon in the county aforesaid, clothier, William Steele of Corke, merchant & John Dennis & Samuel Dennis both of Corke, aforesaid in the kingdom of Ireland, joiners. Whereas the King's dearest brother, James Duke of York being by virtue of the King's grant by letter of patent under the great seal of England dated 20 Mar in the 16th year of his reign seized on amongst other things all that tract of land adjacent to New England & lying & being to the west of Long Island & Manhall Island, part of the said main land now of England beginning at Sr. Croix mentioned to be granted to the said Duke of York by patent by letters of patent, bounded on the east by the main sea & part by Hudson River & upon the river Delaware extending southward to the main ocean as far as Cape May and the mouth of Delaware Bay to the north with the northern most branch of the River Delaware. Whereas James Duke of York by several deeds of dated 23 & 24 June 1664 for consideration conveyed to John Lord Berkley, Barren of Stratten & George Carterett of Saltrum in the county of Devon, knight & Barron all that said tract of land then after to be called New Cesaria or New Jersey. Whereas afterwards, John Lord Berkley granted & conveyed all his part in the said tract to William Penn, Gaven Laury, Nicholas Lucas, & others who there in became seized a whole undivided moiety of half part of all said premises granted to John Lord Berkley & George Carterett, joint tenants which said whole was divided into 100 equal parts. Whereas by deed dated 1 July 1676 made between George Carterett to William Penn, Gaven Laury, Nicholas Lucas, Edward Byllinge in the high court of Chancery of England in performance of said agreement which for better partition agreed to be made, the said Edward Byllinge, William Penn, Gaven Laury & Nicholas Lucas by consent appointed Edward Byllinge to convey to George Carterett all the easternly part of share of the said tract of land extending along the sea coast & the river called Hudson from the east side of a harbor lying on the southern part of the tract of land & commonly called Little Egg Harbor to the part of the said river called Hudson which is being called the North Partition, the southern most partition called the Southern Partition. Whereas by virtue of a deed dated 1 July 1676 between George Carteret of Saltrum in the County of Devon, knight & Baronet & William Penn, Gaven Laury, Nicholas Lucas & Edward Byllinge, said William Penn, Gaven Laury, Nicholas Lucas & Edward Byllinge became seized in a large tract of land agreed to be called West New Jersey. Now Edward Byllinge with consent & appoint from William Penn, Gaven Laury & Nicholas Lucas for £50 from each, granted to Samuel Norris, Abraham Goodoune, Appollo Morris, Thomas Davis, William Steele, John Dennis & Samuel Dennis, one full equal ninetieth part of the said ninety equal undivided hundred parts of said premises called West New Jersey. Signed William Penn & Gaven Laury, in the presence of John Burley & Bemam Griffith. Signed Nicholas Lucas & Ed. Byllinge, in the presence of Harvert Springett, John Collett & Bemam Griffith. (B:1).

Lease & Release. On 2 Mar 1676. William Penn, late of Bickmersworth in the County of Hertford now of Berminghurst in the county of Sussex, Esq., Gaven Laury of London, merchant, Nicholas Lucas of Hertford in the County of Hartford, maulster & Edward Byllinge of Westminster of the county of Middlesex, gentleman to William Ogle of Grey's Inn in the County of Middlesex, Esq., William Royden of London, merchant & Nicholas Lax of Nappomiginth in the county of Middlesex, merchant. Edward Byllinge, by appointment of the said William Penn, Nicholas Lucas for full satisfaction of £116 13 shillings 4 pence paid by William Ogle, the same amount from William Royden & the same from Nicholas Lax, said Edward Byllinge granted to William Ogle, William Royden & Nicholas Lax one full equal undivided ninetieth part of the said 90 parts of 100. Signed William Penn, Gaven Laury, Nicholas Lucas & Edward Byllinge. Delivered in the presence of John Burley, Ben. Griffith & Harbart Springett. (B:7).

Lease & Release.. On 31 Jan 1682 & 1 Feb 1682. William Welsh of London, merchant to John Vanlaere of London, merchant. Whereas by virtue of a deed dated 1 July 1676 made between George Carteret of Saltrum in the county of Devon, knight & Baronet to William Penn, late of Ruckmarsworth in the county of Hartford, Esq., Gaven Laury of London, merchant & Nicholas Lucas of Hertford, maltster & Edward Byllinge of Westminster in the county of

Middlesex, gentleman, they the said William Penn, Gaven Laury, Nicholas Lucas & Edward Byllinge became seized in fee subject to several trusts in that great part of land on the parts of Americas agreed to be called West New Jersey. Said land was divided in to 100 equal undivided parts to be divided in trust for John Edridge of Shadwell in the County of Middlesex, tanner, Edmond Warner, citizen & pooulterer of London in fee to whom the same has been conveyed accordingly & as to the other 90 equal undivided hundred parts now called West New Jersey, the same were in trust for the said Edward Byllinge in fee. Whereas the said William Penn has by Laury for the consideration mentioned conveyed all that tract of land called West New Jersey. one deed dated 15 Apr 1681 & made between the said William Penn, Edward Byllinge & Gaven Whereas on 1 & 2 Sep 1681, made between Edward Byllinge, Gaven Laury & Nicholas Lucas to William Welsh. They the said Gaven Laury & Nicholas Lucas granted one full equal undivided ninetieth part of the said 90 parts of 100. Now William Welsh of £125 granted to John Vanlaere in his actual possession, now being by virtue of a lease & release granted to John Vanlaere a tract of land containing 5000 acres lying in the province or tract of land called West New Jersey. (B:12).

Lease & Release. On 6 & 7 June 1681. William Penn, late of Bickmersworth in the County of Hertford now of Berminghurst in the county of Sussex, Esq., Gaven Laury of London, merchant, Nicholas Lucas of Hertford in the County of Hartford, maulster & Edward Byllinge of Westminster of the county of Middlesex, gentleman to John Farrington of London, merchant. William Penn, Gaven Laury, Nicholas Lucas & Edward Byllinge for £350 granted to John Farrington a tract of land now in his actual possession, lying in the province of West New Jersey being one full equal 90th share of 90 parts of 100. Signed William Penn in the presence of Harbart Springett, Mark Swaner, Thomas Coxe & Isaac Swinton. Signed Gaven Laury in the presence of Robert Moett, Benj. Beacon, Harbart Springett & Mark Swaner. Signed Nicholas Lucas in the presence of Harbart Springett, Mark Swaner, Isaac Swinton & Thomas Coxe. Signed Edward Byllinge in the presence of Harbart Springett, Isaac Swinton & Thomas Coxe. (B:16).

Lease & Release. On 22 & 23 Jan 1676. William Penn, late of Bickmersworth in the County of Hertford now of Berminghurst in the county of Sussex, Esq., Gaven Laury of London, merchant, Nicholas Lucas of Hertford in the County of Hartford, maulster & Edward Byllinge of Westminster of the county of Middlesex, gentleman to Richard Mew of Ratcliffe in the parish of Stepney, Steben Heath in the County of Middlesex, merchant, Percivall Toule of the same place, baker, Peter Hailes of Lymehouse in the parish & county aforesaid, Distiler Thomas Martin of the same place, mealman, Nicholas Bell of Ratcliffe aforesaid, mariner & Richard Clayton of Bishopsgate Street London, linen draper. William Penn, Gaven Laury, Nicholas Lucas & Edward Byllinge for £58 6 shillings 8 pence paid to Edward Byllinge from each of the said men granted to Richard Mew, Steben Heath, Percivall Toule, Peter Hailes, Thomas Martin, Nicholas Bell & Richard Clayton one full equal 90th share of 90 parts of 100. Signed William Penn, Gaven Laury, Nicholas Lucas & Edward Byllinge. Delivered in the presence of Harbart Springett, Thomas Rudyard, Benj. Griffith, Thomas Poynett & John Burley. (B:22)

Lease & Release. On 27 & 28 Feb 1681. Gaven Laury of London, merchant, Nicholas Lucas of Hertford in the County of Hartford, maulster & Edward Byllinge of Westminster of the county of Middlesex, gentleman to Joseph Helby of Lymehouse in the county of Middlesex, carver. Edward Byllinge for £500 & Gaven Laury & Nicholas Lucas for 5 shillings each granted & conveyed to Joseph Helby one full equal 90th share of 90 parts of 100 parts of the westerly most part of the tract commonly called West New Jersey. Signed Edward Byllinge, Gaven Laury & Nicholas Lucas. Delivered in the presence of M.Gillolkson, M. Gillolkson, John Wheatley, John Booker & Samuel Collman. (B:28).

Lease & Release. On 1 & 2 Sep 1682. Joseph Helby of Lymehouse in the County of Middlesex, carver to Richard Sizer, Citizen & fletcher of London. Joseph Helby for £25 granted to Richard Sizer one full equal undivided 32nd part of a ninetieth part of 100 parts in the West New Jersey. Signed Joseph Helby. Delivered in the presence of M. Gillolkson, John Wheatley & John Booker. (B:37).

Lease & Release. On 12 & 13 Mar 1682. William Penn, late of Bickmersworth in the County of Hertford now of Berminghurst in the county of Sussex, Esq., Gaven Laury of London, merchant, Nicholas Lucas of Hertford in the County of Hartford, maulster & Edward Byllinge of Westminster of the county of Middlesex, gentleman to John Hinde of London, goldsmith. William Penn, Gaven Laury, Nicholas Lucas & Edward Byllinge for £350 granted to John Hinde one full equal 90th share of 90 parts of 100 parts of the westerly most part of the tract commonly called West New Jersey. Signed William Penn, Gaven Laury, Nicholas Lucas & Edward Byllinge. Delivered in the presence of John Cause, John Culliford, John White, George Bradbury, Samuel Rand, Harbart Springett & Mark Swanner. (B:46).

Lease & Release. On 27 & 28 Feb 1682. Gaven Laury of London, merchant, Nicholas Lucas of Hertford in the County of Hartford, maulster & Edward Byllinge of Westminster of the county of Middlesex, gentleman to John Hinde of London, goldsmith. William Penn, Gaven Laury, Nicholas Lucas & Edward Byllinge for £350 granted to John Hinde one full equal 90th share of 90 parts of 100 parts of the westerly most part of the tract commonly called West New Jersey. Signed Edward Byllinge, Gaven Laury & Nicholas Lucas. Delivered in the presence of Richard Eason, Nat. Symms & Mr Bartholomew Pickeringser. (B:54)

Lease & Release. On 7 & 8 July 1682. Thomas Martin of Lymehouse in the parish of Stepney at Stebun Heath in the county of Middlesex to Joseph Helby of Limehouse aforesaid, carver. Joseph Helby for £26 granted to Joseph Helby a 1/6 part of one full equal 90th share of 90 parts of 100 parts of the westerly most part of the tract commonly called West New Jersey. Signed Thomas Martin. Delivered in the presence of M. Gillolkson, M. Gillolkson & John Booker. (B:62).

NEW CASTLE COUNTY BOOK C.

Deed. On 1 Oct 1706. Andrew Peterson of Appoquinimink, yeoman to Thomas Hyatt of the County of West Chester in the province of New York, yeoman & Andrew VanDike of the same county, yeoman. Whereas Ralph Dawson of Talbot County in the province of Maryland, planter & Mary his wife & John Dawson of the said county & Mary his wife by deed dated 20 Dec 1704 granted to Andrew Peterson a tract of land on the north side of Appoquinimink Creek bounded by the first point of land in a small creek called Drawyers Creek & the swamp containing 400 acres, having formerly been seated & manured by Claers Kerson & Bernard Brand, the first settlers, who had patent for the same & by them sold to Bryant Onelle who made improvements & is certified in the records office in the province of New York Book of Patents begun 1666 No. 12 at the wrong end of the book page 88. Now Andrew Peterson for £90 granted to Isaac Gooding, Thomas Hyatt & Andrew VanDike the said tract of land. Isaac Gooding is to hold two full fifths parts of said tract, Thomas Hyatt to have two full fifths parts of said tract & Andrew VanDike to have one full fifth part. Signed Andrew Peterson. Delivered in the presence of John Heally, Hans Hanson & John Demaree. Acknowledged in open court 21 Feb 1707. (C3:1)

Bond. On 27 Feb 1702. I, John Jones of Philadelphia, gentleman, am firmly bound to Mathias Vanbeeber of the said place, merchant in the true sum of £120 to be paid to Mathias Vanbeeber. The condition of this obligation if the above John Jones shall pay to Mathias Vanbeeber the sum of £60 on 12 Dec 1704 with interest then this shall be void. Signed William Hinton, Jacob Isaac Vanbeeber & Francis Jones. (C3:6).

Bond. On 1 Mar 1702. I, John Jones of Philadelphia, gentleman, am firmly bound to Mathias Vanbeeber of the said place, merchant in the true sum of £5 10 shillings to be paid to Mathias Vanbeeber. Signed John Jones. (C3:6).

Bond. On 9 Mar 1702. I, John Jones of Philadelphia, gentleman, am firmly bound to Mathias Vanbeeber of the said place, merchant in the true sum of £600 to be paid to Mathias Vanbeeber. The condition of this obligation is that Mathias Vanbeeber at special request & for proper debt of the above bound John Jones, standeth bound to Joseph Woods of New Castle, gentleman for the sum of £200 by one obligation dated the same with the condition of payment of £100 on 29 Sep next & condition whereas also the said Mathias Vanbeeber at the request for the proper debt of John Jones standeth bound to Joseph Wood £106 conditioned on payment of £53 on 29 Sep 1704. Security of said bond is a tract of land called Melrum Island, situated in New Sale in West New Jersey, lately purchased by John Jones from Adam Baldridge of New Castle, inn holder containing 500 acres. Signed John Jones. Delivered in the presence of Joseph Wood, Adam Baldridge & William Tonge. (C3:7).

Deed. On 1 Sep 1707. Engelbert Lott of New York in the province of New York, cordwainer to Abraham Saulfoort of New York, cordwainer, John Harberdinck of the same place, cordwainer & Jane Tuttell, late wife of Jeremiah Tuttell, late of New York, dec., widow. Whereas Richard Nicholls, Governor by patent dated 6 Jan 1667 granted to Sergeant John Arskin, Thomas Brown & Martin Garrettson in common a tract of land lying on the south side of Christiana Creek, west of Swart Nutten Island, southwest by a little spring called Bessy & east of Fearn Hook containing 500 acres. Whereas Governor Lovelace by patent dated 1 Oct 1669 granted & confirmed to John Arskin, Martin Garrettson & Gysbert Dirckson, a piece of land on Christiana Creek bounded by the said creek containing 100 acres. Whereas Martin Garrettson having for many years improved the lower most part of the said land next to Fearn Hook by virtue of a patent dated Feb 1677 for valuable consideration granted to Hendrick Vanderburgh, late of New Castle, merchant, all his right & interest in the above said land. Whereas Hendrick Vanderburgh by deed dated 29 Nov 1687 did grant & confirm unto Engelbert Lott all that part of the land aforesaid mentioned belong to Martin Garrettson by 2 patents. Whereas William Markham, Thomas Ellis & John Goodson by virtue of a commission by patent dated 10 Feb 1687 did confirm unto the said Engelbert Lott all the 2 tracts of land situated on the north east end of the town of New Castle, one which being the same whereon the old fort stood both which lots are bounded on the SW with the highway or street which leads to the woods, NE with the town commons, SE with the street by the water side & NW with Land Street being 277 foot in length & 280 foot in breadth. Now Englebert Lott of £125 granted to Abraham Saulfoort, John Harberdick & Jane Tuttell, the lower part or share of 600 acres above mentioned next to Fearn Hook & the 2 lots in New Castle. Engelbert Lott does appoint John Bisk of New Castle, tailor as his attorney to deliver these presence in court. Signed Engelbert Lott. Delivered in the presence of Richard Halliwell, Robert French & William Tonge. Memorandum. Full & peaceful possession was delivered by the with named Engelbert Lott to Andrew Graveuraet, attorney of the with named Abraham Saulfoort, John Harberdink & Jane Tuttell of one of the within lots on 2 Sep 1707. Signed Sylvester Garland & Jan Bisck. New York. Memorandum. Cornelia Lott, wife of the said Engelbert Lott does relinquish all her right to said premises to Abraham Saulfoort, John Harberdink & Jane Tuttell. Signed Cornelia Lott. Delivered in the presence of Abraham Vanhorne & ? Broughton. New York, 18 Sep 1707. Cornelia Lott came before me, William Merrett, one of her majesties Justices of the Peace, & acknowledge the above writing to be hers & she consents to said endorsement. Signed William Merrett. Acknowledged in open court on 27 May 1708 by John Bisck, attorney for Englebert Lott. (C1:7)

On 18 May 1708. John Nanlcoyne of Appoquinimink, yeoman to Isaac Vigoreu of Appoquinimink, gentleman. John Nanlcoyne for £48 granted to Isaac Vigoreu a tract of land being on the north west side of Appoquinimink Creek called the Drummers Neck adjoining the land of Isaac Vigoreu containing 80 acres being part of a tract of 180 acres granted by patent from Edmund Andros, late Governor General. Signed John Nanlcoyne. Delivered in the presence of Nicholas Lockyer & Thomas Jauvier. Acknowledged in court 22 May 1708. (C1:15).

Deed. On 18 May 1708. Joseph Stoll of New Castle, gentleman to John Stout of the township of Freehold in the county of Monmouth in the province of New Jersey, yeoman. Joseph Stoll for £145 granted to John Stout a tract of land called Liberty being part of 1000 acres situated on the north side of Dragon Swamp, said tract called Liberty is bounded by Beaver Dam containing 200 acres. Signed Joseph Stoll. Delivered in the presence of Hendrick Picker, Peter King & Isaac Truax. Acknowledged in court 20 May 1708. (C:18).

Deed. On 12 May 1708. Robert French of the town of New Castle, merchant to John Thomas of the said county, yeoman. Robert French for £50 granted to John Thomas all that tract of land called Exeter situated on the north side of Drawyers Creek bounded by a marsh, Hoggs Branch, & Drawyers Creek containing 256 acres. Signed Robert French. Delivered in the presence of John Reece & Wessell Allrichs. Acknowledged in court 20 May 7108. (C1:21)

Deed. On 5 Mar 1706 Joseph MacGregory of White Clay Creek, yeoman to

Thomas Wolliston of White Clay Creek, cordwainer. Whereas there is a tract of land situated at White Clay Creek bounded by the creek & other land of Joseph MacGregory containing 67 acres which is part of a tract of 570 acres granted to Charles Rumsey & Walraven Johnson Defoe by patent dated 25 Mar 1676 & by the said Charles Rumsey by deed dated 10 Jan 1679 sold to John Cann, late of New Castle dec. & by John Cann by deed dated 5 Sep 1682 granted to Joseph Barnes, late of White Clay Creek, dec. Whereas there is another tract of land situated on the north side of White Clay Creek bounded by a line dividing this land from other land of Joseph Barnes, White Clay Creek containing 82 acres, which last mentioned tract is part of a tract of land formerly granted by Governor Andross by patent dated 25 Mar 1676 unto John Nommers & by John Nommers by deed dated 5 Sep 1682 recorded in Book B Page 263 & granted to Joseph Barnes. Which said tracts of land herein mentioned came to Thomas Mercer & Elizabeth his wife, the only daughter & heir of Joseph Barnes, who by their deed of Gift dated 22 Nov 1704 gave & granted to Joseph MacGregory. Now Joseph MacGregory for £75 granted to Thomas Wolliston the said 2 tracts of land. Signed Joseph MacGregory. Delivered in the presence of Edward Jenings & William Tonge. Acknowledged in court 20 May 1708. (C1:26).

Mortgage. On 14 July 1708. Joseph Wood of the County of New Castle, gentleman Whereas John Jones, late of Philadelphia, gentleman & Mathias Vanbeeber of Philadelphia, merchant did stand bound to me, Joseph Wood by 2 tracts of land by obligations dated 9 Mar 1702, the one of the penalty of £200 conditioned for payment of £100 the other of the penalty of £106 conditioned on payment of £53 being the proper debt of John Jones. Whereas Joseph Wood has obtained a judgment against Mathias Vanbeeber & do acknowledge to have received of Mathias Vanbeeber the sum of £153 with interest. Joseph Wood now releases & discharges Mathias Vanbeeber & John Jones of said debts. Signed Joseph Wood. Delivered in the presence of Joseph Hammerton, Anthony Houstowne & James Vanbeeber. (C1:30).

Deed. On 19 Apr 1707. John Cann of White Clay Creek, yeoman & William Cann of the same place, yeoman to Francis Land of the County of New Castle, yeoman. John Cann & William Cann for £155 granted to Francis Land all that lot of land in the town of New Castle bounded on the E with the lot of Peter _ddin, W with the lot of John Paris, S with the Susquehanna Street & N with Beaver Street containing in length 164 foot & in breadth 120 foot, which said lot of ground is part of a piece of land granted by William Markham, Robert ____ & John Goodson, commissioners of property by patent dated 13 Jan 1691 to John Cann, late of White Clay Creek, deceased father of the aforesaid John Cann & William Cann. Signed John Cann & William Cann. Delivered in the presence of Edward Jennings & William Tonge. Receipt. On 19 May 1707, received of Francis Land the sum of £155. Signed John Cann & William Cann. Delivered in the presence of James Bayley & Dorothy Empson. Acknowledged in court 20 May 1708. (C1:31)

Deed. On 20 Aug 1707. John Bisk of New Castle, tailor & Sarah Brett, wife of John Brett, late of New Castle, carpenter to Richard Clark of New Castle, merchant. Whereas John Bisk & John Brett & Sarah his wife stand lawfully seized in a tract of land in the town of New Castle bounded to the E with Water Street, W with [there is a section of this page missing], S with the lot of George Ha___ & N with the land of Thomas Jauvier, for as much as this is a water lot belonging to the same & where in they the said John Bisk, John Brett & Sarah his wife are not able to perform according ___ There for witness that John Bisk & Sarah Brett by virtue of a letter of attorney granted to her by her husband John Brett dated 20 Feb 1706, in consideration of the sum of £21 10 shillings granted to Richard Clark the above mentioned lot. Signed John Bisk & Sarah Brett. Delivered in the presence of ___ ___sk & John French. Acknowledged in court 20 __ 1707. (C1:35).

Deed. On __Aug 1707. John Brewster of the town of New Castle, yeoman to Roeloffe Dehaes, Sylvester Garland & Thomas Jauvier all of the town of New Castle, merchants & agents for the erecting or building of a Presbyterian Church or place of worship in the town of New Castle. John Brewster for £10 granted to Roeloffe Dehaes, Sylvester Garland & Thomas Jauvier, agents of the aforesaid to & for the use of the church or house of worship a lot in the town of New Castle bounded by a lot of Thomas Jauvier & the Market place being 50 foot in breadth & 23 foot 4 inches in length being part of the lot John Brewster purchased of Susannah Osterhaven by deed dated 17 June ___ recorded in page ___ & 250. Signed John Brewster. Delivered in the presence of Richard Empson & Edward Jennings. Acknowledged in court 22 May 1707. (C1:37).

Deed. On 15 Aug 1707. Thomas Jauvier of New Castle, merchant & Sarah his wife to Roeloffe Dehaes & Sylvester Garland both of New Castle, merchants & agents for the erecting or building a Presbyterian Church in the town of New Castle. Thomas Jauvier & Sarah his wife for £12 granted to Roeloffe Dehaes & Sylvester Garland a lot in the town of New Castle bounded by land lately of John Brewster & now for the use of the church, a lot of John Bisk, market place & the river being 50 foot in breadth & 27 foot. Signed Thomas Jauvier & Sarah Jauvier. Delivered in the presence of Charles Springer & Jacob ___. Acknowledged in court 24 Feb 1707. (C1:40).

Deed. On 16 ___ 1707. Joseph Wood of the town of New Castle, gentleman to Adam Huke of the county of New Castle, yeoman. Joseph Wood for £65 granted to Adam Huke a tract of land in the town of New Castle bounded by the Queen's Road & Swanwick Road containing 58 1/2 acres. Signed Joseph Wood. Delivered in the presence of Matthias Vanderhayden & Hypolitns Lefever. Acknowledge in court 21 Nov 1707. (C1:42).

Deed. On 15 May 1708. Samuel Bushell of St. George's Creek, husbandman to Samuel Bayard of Bohemia River in the County of Cecil in the province of Maryland, merchant. Whereas there is a tract of land on the north side of St. George's Creek commonly called Deacon Swamp being part of a tract formerly belonging to Joseph Hanson bounded by land of Henry Pikers, Dragon Swamp, land of John Boyers & land of Joseph Stolls containing 171 acres being part of 400 acres granted to Samuel Bushell by Henry _____ by a deed from Joseph dated 7 Feb 1701. Now Samuel Bushell for £_7 granted to Samuel Bayard the above mentioned 171 acres. Signed Samuel Bushell. Delivered in the presence of James Phillips & Thomas Pierson. Acknowledged 18 May 1708. (C2:43).

Deed. On 12 May 1708. John Garrettson of Christiana, yeoman to Samuel Silsby of New Castle, blacksmith. Now John Garrettson for £12 granted to Samuel Silsby a lot of land in the town of New Castle bounded by Richard Reynolds garden, other lots of John Garrettson & Beaver Street resurveyed & laid out by George Dakeyne, surveyor of said county dated 20 July 1701 unto John Garrettson by virtue of a warrant from James Logan, Esq. bearing the date 25 June in the same year. Abiah the wife of John Garrettson consents to said sale. Signed John Garrettson & Abiah Garrettson. Delivered in the presence of Elston Wallis & William Tonge. Acknowledged in court 20 May 1708. (C1:46)

Deed. On 16 Aug 1708. John Nanlcoyne of Appoquinimink Creek, yeoman to James Hayes of Duck Creek, administrator. Whereas there is a tract of land lying on Appoquinimink Creek bounded by the land of Andrew Peterson & Mill Branch containing 150 acres, which said tract was sold to Job Nanlcroyne & confirmed by deed dated 20 Mar 1693 acknowledged in court 23 of same month being recorded in New Castle Book B Page 250 by John Cox of Brandywine Creek. Now John Nanlcoyne for £28 granted to William Burrows, late of Appoquinimink Creek, aforesaid, smith in the lifetime whereof do acknowledge have granted to James Hayes of Duck Creek, miller, as administrator of the above mentioned William Burrows, dec. but for the use of the said William Burrows heirs forever. John Nanlcoyne appointed his trusty friend, John Taylor to deliver the above land to James Hayes. Signed John Nanlcoyne. Delivered in the presence of Absolam Cuff & John Taylor. Acknowledged in court 19 Aug 1708. (C1:49).

Deed. On 2 Sep 1707. Edward Williams of Appoquinimink Creek, yeoman to John Taylor & Samuel Griffin both of Duck Creek. Whereas there is a tract of land on the north side of the main branch of Duck Creek being the east end of a tract of 700 acres formerly belonging to Thomas Harris & William Osborne & called the Exchange & the east end containing 400 acres bounded by a the line that divides this from the other 300 acres being part of the 700 acres including all the land & marsh contained in the fork of the said main & smaller run of Duck Creek Mill falling to William Osborne, & sold by him to Edward Williams by deed dated 1 Feb 1706. Now Edward Williams for £45 granted to John Taylor & Samuel Griffin the aforesaid 400 acres. Edward Williams appoints his trusty friends James Hayes & Absalom Cuff to by my attorneys to deliver this in court. Singed Edward Williams. Delivered in the presence of Absalom Cuff, John ___, Joseph England & Caleb Offley. Acknowledged in court 19 Aug 1708. (C2:51).

Deed. On 1 Aug 1707. Mathias Erickson of St. George's Creek, yeoman to Harmanus Allrichs of New Castle, yeoman. Mathias Erickson for £30 granted to Harmanus Allrichs a tract of land lying on the south side of Scott's Run being part of a tract of land formerly surveyed for Amos Niccolls & by Amos Niccolls conveyed to Peter Oellson & by Peter Oellson conveyed to Conrade Constant & by Conrade Constant to Mathias Patker & Mathias Parker conveyed 100 acres to Mathias Erickson bounded by Scott's Run & land of Mathias Parker containing 100 acres. Signed Mathias Erickson. Delivered in the presence of Joshua Story & Elston Wallis. Acknowledged in court 20 Aug 1707. (C2:53).

Deed. On 1 June 1708. Henry Gibbs of White Clay Creek, son & heir of Edward Gibbs, late of St. George's Creek, gentleman, dec., yeoman to Robert Smith of St. George's Creek, yeoman. Henry Gibbs for £162 10 shillings granted to Robert Smith a tract of land called Barwicke lying on the south side of St. George's Creek bounded by St. George's Creek, Doctor's Swamp & a plantation formerly belonging to Jacob Young (but now in the tenure of John Cox) containing 210 acres. Henry Gibbs appoints Richard Empson of the County of New Castle to be his attorney to deliver this in open court. Signed Henry Gibbs. Delivered in the presence of John Blunston, James Crawford & Hans Hanson. Acknowledged in court 17 Aug 1708. (C1:56).

Mortgage. On 15 May 1707. Hypolitos Lefever of the town of New Castle, yeoman to Robert French & Richard Halliwell, surviving executors of the last will & testament of John Donaldson, late of New Castle, merchant, dec. on behalf of the heirs of John Donaldson. Hypolitos Lefever in consideration of £63 now due or owed to the estate of John Donaldson & for securing said debt granted to Robert French & Richard Halliwell all the lot in the town of New

Castle bounded by the river side, Land Street, land of Henry Williams & land of James Jones, Esq. containing 300 foot in length & 51 foot in breadth, provided always that Hypolitos Lefever shall truly pay the sum to Robert French & Richard Halliwell on behalf of the heirs of John Donaldson, dec. the sum of £63 on 20 May 1711, then this shall be void. Signed Hypo. Lefever. Delivered in the presence of Elston Wallis & William Tonge. Acknowledged in court 20 Aug 1707. (C1:59).

Deed. On 25 Apr 1707. Michael Moyers of the County of New Castle, yeoman to Hans Peterson of the county of New Castle, gentleman. Michael Moyers for £24 granted to Hans Peterson a tract of land situated on a creek called Dogg Creek bounded by the land of Peter Mounson containing 100 acres being part of a tract of land formerly granted by Francis Lovelace, Esq. Governor General by deed dated 7 Apr 1___ to Olle Franson, Peter Mounson & Neils Neilson, which said 100 acres by the said Olle Franson & Neils Neilson after the death of Peter Mounson granted to Martin Lawrenson & by Martin Lawrenson by his deed dated 21 Oct 1685 granted to Stoffell Moyers, late of the County of New Castle, (father of the aforesaid Michael Moyers). Also, one moiety or half part of a small piece of marsh situated on the Delaware River in a place called The Bought, adjoining the aforesaid 100 acres which said piece of marsh was by William Markham & John Goodson commissioners by patent dated 12 Apr 1689 granted to Stoffell Moyers & Wolla Franson. Signed Michael Moyers. Delivered in the presence of Humphrey Johnson & William Tonge. The within named Michael Moyers appoints William Tonge of New Castle to be his lawful attorney to deliver this in open court. Signed Michael Moyers. Delivered in the presence of John Brewster & Humphrey Johnson. Acknowledged in court 22 Aug 1707. (C1:62).

Deed. Samuel Underwood of Brandywine Creek in the county of New Castle, husbandman to John Griggs of Brandywine Creek, yeoman. Whereas there is a tract of land situated on Brandywine Creek bounded by land of John Griggs & land of Samuel Underwood containing 38 1/4 acres, (surveyed 7 Apr 1708) being a part of a tract of 200 acres which by virtue of a warrant from Thomas Holme, surveyor General dated 20 May 1685 laid out to John Grigg the 16 June 1685 & at the special request of John Grigg was by patent granted by William Markham, Robert Turner & John Goodson on 18 Feb 1692 confirmed to Samuel Underwood. Now Samuel Underwood for £7 13 shillings granted to John Griggs the above mentioned land. Signed Samuel Underwood. Delivered in the presence of John Bullah & Edward Jennings. Acknowledged in court 20 Aug 1708. (C1:68).

Deed. On 20 May 1708. Isaac Sheffer of St. George's Creek, yeoman to Jacob

Truax of the township of Middletown in the county of Monmouth in the province of New Jersey, yeoman. Whereas Griffith Owen, Thomas Story & James Logan, commissioners for William Penn by patent dated 16 Apr 1706 granted & confirmed to Isaac Sheffer a tract of land situated between Dragon Run & Red Lyon Run bounded by land of Joseph Stolls & a swamp containing 408 acres, recorded in Patent Records in Philadelphia Book A Vol. 4 Page 79. Now Isaac Sheffer for £250 granted to Jacob Truax the said 408 acres. Signed Isaac Sheffer. Delivered in the presence of Isaac Gooding, Edward Edwards & Peter Hance. Acknowledged in court 20 May 1708. (C1:69).

Deed. On 21 Aug 1706. Joseph Young of North East in the county of Cecil in the province of Maryland, planter to Charles Anderson of the same place, planter. Joseph Young for £50 granted to Charles Anderson, the 1/3 part of a tract of land containing 1280 acres laid out by survey for Jacob Young, father of the said Joseph Young, situated on the north side of St. George's Creek bounded by the uppermost part of the said tract granted to the said Jacob Young by patent dated at New York 5 Nov 1675. Signed Joseph Young. Delivered in the presence of Andrew Cock, Elton Wallis & John Cock. Acknowledged in court 20 Feb 1707. (C1:73).

Deed. On 20 July 1708. Charles Anderson of Northeast River in the province of Maryland, planter & John Cock of St. George's Creek, yeoman to Joseph Neal of Salem in the county of Essex in the province of Massachusetts Bay in New England, joiner. Charles Anderson & John Cock for £125 granted to Joseph Neal a tract of land situated between St. George's Creek & Dragon Run bounded by land called James Andersons, St. George's Road, Dragon Swamp containing 437 acres besides the cripple surveyed George Dakeyne surveyor, on 22 Feb 1707 being part of a tract of land formerly surveyed for Jacob Young, dec. by patent dated 5 Nov 1675 & by Jacob Young & Joseph Young, sons of the above named Jacob Young, dec. conveyed over to Charles Anderson & John Cock all their right or interest by 2 deeds, one dated 10 Nov 1700 & the other dated 21 Aug 1706 Signed Charles Anderson & John Cock. Delivered in the presence of William Owen & John Stanley. Acknowledged in court by Elston Wallis & John Grantham, attorneys legally appointed on 20 Aug 1708. (C1:76).

Letter of Attorney. On 10 Aug 1708. Charles Anderson of Cecil County in the province of Maryland, planter, do appoint by trusty & well beloved friends, John Grantham of the County of New Castle & Elston Wallis of the County of New Castle, my true & lawful attorneys to acknowledge a certain deed dated 20 July 1708 granted to Joseph Neal, late of Salem in the county of Sussex in the province of Massachusetts, joiner, in open court. Signed Charles Anderson. Delivered in the presence of William Owen & John Stanley. (C1:80).

Deed. On 15 June 1708. Urin Malson Screek of St. George's Creek, husbandman to Urin Anderson of St. George's Creek, yeoman. Urin Malson Screek for £19 granted to Urin Anderson all his share & part of 400 acres of land given & devised by John Malson Screek, Jr. by his last will & testament to his 4 sons, Urin Malson Screek, Thomas Malson Screek, Mathias Malson Screek & John Malson Screek, which said share of part of the said Urin Malson Screek of the said land is bounded by the lands of John Morgan, Dragon Run, land of Mathias Malson Screek & lands late of John Darby. Signed Urin Malson Screek. Delivered in the presence of Edward Edwards, Cle. Clemmetson & John Reece. Acknowledged in court 20 Aug 1708 by Mathias Malson Screek, attorney of the said Urin Malson Screek. (C:80).

Letter of Attorney. On 15 June 1708. Urin Malson Screek of St. George's Creek, husbandman, do appoint my dear & loving brother Mathias Malson Screek to be my attorney to acknowledge the deed granted to Urin Anderson in open court. Signed Urin Malson Screek. Delivered in the presence of Edward Edwards, Cle. Clemmetson & John Reece. (C1:83).

Deed. On 16 Aug 1708. John French, high sheriff of the county of New Castle to Howell James of the County of New Castle. Whereas James & Hercules Coutts of the town of New Castle, merchants in a court of common pleas recovered against William James, late of the county of New Castle, millwright, a debt of £60 6 shillings also £3 6 pence for damages, also one other debt of £24 16 shillings & also £3 6 pence for damages, whereas by a write dated 8 July 1707 I have seized the lands of William James, with mill & plantation situated on Christiana Creek bounded by land of David Thomas, land of Howell James containing 200 acres being part of a tract of 1300 acres surveyed to William James on 3 June 1702 by virtue of a warrant dated 25 Oct 1701. John French for £120 granted to Howell James the said tract of land & mill containing 200 acres. Signed John French. Delivered in the presence of Benjamin Charriere & Joseph Wood. Acknowledged in court 18 Aug 1708. (C1:84).

Deed. On 12 Jan 1707. Nicholas Lockyer of Swanwick, yeoman to Peter Jacquett, Jr. of Swanwick, yeoman. Nicholas Lockyer for £100 granted to Peter Jacquett a tract of land bounded by land of Robert French, land of Artman Hains, the River Delaware containing 86 acres, granted by the commissioners of property by patent dated 24 Dec 1701 to Nicholas Lockyer & also another tract of land with the marsh commonly called Fynne Hook near Swanwick bounded by the land late in the possession of Nicholas Lockyer & land of John Jacquett containing 600 perches in length & 25 perches in breadth. Signed Nicholas Lockyer. Delivered in the presence of George Dakeyne & William Tonge. Acknowledged in court 20 Feb 1707. (C1:87).

Deed. On 8 May 1708. Adam Hyke of the County of New Castle, yeoman to George Peterson of Swanwick, yeoman. Adam Hyke for £56 granted to George Peterson a tract of land situated on Swanwick heretofore the inheritance of Ambrose Baker, but now in the tenure of Adam Hyke by virtue of a deed by Edward Cole & Harmania his wife, daughter & heir of Ambrose Baker dated 19 Mar 1700, bounded by the land of Peter Jacquetts, the river & land of George Peterson containing 50 acres. Signed Adam Hyke. Delivered in the presence of John Wood & Joseph Wood. Acknowledged in court 20 May 1708. (C2:91).

Deed. On 7 Apr 1702. Cornelius Empson of the county of New Castle, yeoman to Richard Clark of the county of New Castle, merchant. Whereas Francis Lovelace, late Gov. by patent dated 28 May 1669 granted to Bernard Eken & Margaret his wife, a lot in the town of New Castle. Bernard Eken by deed dated 19 Sep 1693 granted the same to John Cann. Whereas John Cann by deed dated 20 Nov 1701, granted to Jacob Vangerel, merchant pat of the before mentioned lot containing 3 foot more than the ground whereon standeth an old kitchen & backwards the equal half of the whole lot of 60 foot. Whereas Jacob Vangerel by deed dated the day before the date of this made over his right & interest in the said lot to Cornelius Empson. Now Cornelius Empson for £85 granted to Richard Clark all the aforesaid lot bounded by Front Street. Signed Cornelius Empson. Delivered in the presence of John Prew & Richard Reynolds. Acknowledged in court 17 Aug 1703. (C1:95).

Deed. On 16 Feb 1707. Roeloffe Dehaes of the town of New Castle, merchant to Christopher Stanley of New Castle, yeoman. Roeloffe Dehaes for £15 granted to Christopher Stanley a lot of ground situated in the town of New Castle bounded on the east with Beaver Street, west by Otter Street, south with by a street leading from the river to the woods & north by ground lately belonging to Joseph Griffin containing 60 foot in breadth & 300 foot in length. Signed Roeloffe Dehaes. Delivered in the presence of Christopher Hussey & Edward Jeffries. Acknowledged in court 21 Feb 1707. (C1:100).

Deed. On 15 Feb 1702. Alexander McKenny of the county of New Castle & Katherine his wife to Nicholas Lockyer of the county of New Castle. Alexander McKenny & Katherine his wife for £34 granted to Nicholas Lockyer that tract of land which was formerly granted to Jan Sibrinson by patent from Governor Francis Lovelace, dated 26 mar 1669, the piece of land being over the horse neck commonly called Paerdt Hook containing in breadth by the river side 150 rod reaching the land of Arent Johnson in length to the woods having within the land much marshy & swampy land. Alexander McKenny & Katherine his wife appoint Robert Hutchinson to be their lawful attorney to deliver this in court. Signed Alexander McKenny & Katherine McKenny. Delivered in the presence of George Dakeyne & John Smith. Acknowledged in court 20 May 1707. (C1:103).

Deed. On 10 May 1707. Hans Marcusson of Cecill County in the province of Maryland, planter to George Dakeyne of the County of New Castle, surveyor. Hans Marcusson for £28 granted to George Dakeyne a tract of land situated on the south side of the main branch of St. George's Creek adjoining the land of John & Robert Darby containing 228 acres. Hans Marcusson appointed Richard Reynolds to be his attorney to deliver this in open court. Singed Hans Marcusson. Delivered in the presence of John Ogle & Joseph Clayton. Acknowledged in court 1 Nov 1707. (C1:104).

Deed. On 16 Aug 1707. Richard Cantwell of Appoquinimink, gentleman, son & heir of Edmund Cantwell, late of Appoquinimink, dec. & Henry Garrettson of Appoquinimink, gentleman & Elizabeth his wife, daughter of Edmund Cantwell, dec. to William Dyre of Appoquinimink, gentleman. Whereas Francis Lovelace, late Governor of New York by patent dated 17 June 1671 granted to William Sincleer a tract of land containing 400 acres with 50 acres of marsh on the south side of Drawyers Creek. Whereas William Sincleer by confirmed said land to Captain Edmund Cantwell by patent dated 1 Sep 1672. Whereas George Dakeyne did on 15 Nov 1706 resurveyed said tract of land from the land of Henry Garrettson according to the old dimensions formerly divided by Walter Wharton bounded by Appoquinimink Creek & land of John Heally containing 400 acres. Now Richard Cantwell, Henry Garrettson & Elizabeth his wife for £80 granted to William Dyre all the above mentioned tract & also the 50 acres of marsh. Richard Cantwell, Henry Garrettson & Elizabeth his wife appoint William Tonge to deliver this in open court. Signed Henry Garrettson & Elizabeth Garrettson in the presence of John Heally & Samuel Vance & Signed Richard Cantwell in the presence of John French & Sylvester Garland. Acknowledged in court 18 Nov 1707. (C1:107).

Deed. On 14 June 1708. Isaac Vigoreu of Appoquinimink Creek, yeoman & Heleitie his wife to Mathias Van Bebber of Cecil County in the province of Maryland, merchant & Hermintie his wife, daughter of Adam Peterson, late of Appoquinimink Creek, gentleman, dec. & Adam Peterson the younger of Appoquinimink Creek, son of Adam Peterson, dec. Whereas by one deed dated 19 Feb 11th year of King William III England, Hllitie by her then name Hillitie Anderson of Appquinimink Creek, widow to Adam Peterson of Appoquinimink Creek, gentleman. Hilitie for the consideration mentioned granted to Adam Peterson all that tract of land on the north side of Appoquinimink Creek late in the possession of Abell Dodd containing 380 acres & all that tract of land on the south side of Appoquinimink Creek late in the possession of John & Job

Nanlcoyne containing 400 acres & all that lot of land in New Castle purchased by Hilitie from James Read, late in the tenure & occupation of Samuel Vans with all buildings, waters, etc. to the said uses hereafter expressed concerning the tract of land lying north of Appoquinimink Creek late in the tenure of Abel Dodd to the use of Andrew Peterson, son of Adam Peterson the father & all that tract of land on the south side of Appoquinimink Creek late in the tenure of John & Job Nanlcoyne to the use of Garret Paterson, the other son of Adam Peterson the father, & the lot in the town of New Castle to the use of Hermintie Peterson, daughter of Adam Peterson the father. Which said deed it is provided that it shall be lawful for the said Hilitie at anytime during her life at her pleasure by writing her last Will & Testament to alter or change any uses conditioned in the said deed. Now Hilitie Vigoreu by virtue of the power to her reserved by the said deed does at this present time by deed sealed & delivered in the presence of witnesses, whole names are here after subscribed & by the consent of her husband, Isaac Vigoreu, hereof revoke & make void all uses in the said deed declared limited . Isaac Vigoreu & Hilitie his wife do declare & appoint that all persons seized in said tracts of land by the above recited deed, granted or mentioned to be granted shall from hence forth stand seized of every part thereof uses following. That is to say concerning the said tract of land on the north side of Appoquinimink Creek containing 380 acres in the possession of Abel Dodd & the lot of land in the town of New Castle the Hilitie purchased of James Read to the use of Hermintie Vanbebber And the said tract of land on the south side of Appoquinimink Creek containing 400 acres to the uses of Adam Peterson, the younger. Signed Isaac Vigoreu & Hilitie Vigoreu. Delivered in the presence of Jacob Williams & Patrick Bromfield. Acknowledged in court 20 Aug 1708. (C1:111).

Letter of Attorney. On 19 Aug 1708. Isaac Vigoreu & Hilitie his wife for good causes appoint Hans Hanson & William Tonge to be their lawful attorneys to deliver a deed of conveyance & acknowledge said deed in open court. Signed Isaac Vigoreu & Hilitie Vigoreu. Delivered in the presence of John Huwey & John Lawes. (C1:114).

Deed. On 19 Dec 1706. John Mundroe & John Russell both of the County of New Castle, planters to George Dakeyne of the County of New Castle, planter. John Mundroe & John Russell for £25 granted to George Dakeyne a tract of land situated near the branches of Blackbird Creek bounded by land of Nicholas Smith containing 308 acres formerly granted to John Mundroe by a warrant dated 25 June 1705 which said warrant was assigned over by said Mundroe to John Russell on 29 May 1706. Signed John Russell. Delivered in the presence of Elizabeth Bade, Nathaniel Russell, Thomas Dakeyne & Nicholas Smith. Acknowledged in court 20 Aug 1708 by William Tonge by letter of attorney lawfully followed, the said Richard Reynolds being dead. (C1:115).

Letter of Attorney. On 19 July 1708. John Russell of the County of New Castle, yeoman appointed my trusty friend William Tonge, gentleman of New Castle to acknowledge a deed made by me the said John Russell to George Dakeyne for 300 acres of land. Signed John Russell. Delivered in the presence of John Heally & Samuel Vance. Proved in court 20 Aug 1708. (C1:118).

Deed. On 18 May 1708. John Brewster of the town of New Castle, merchant to David Miles of the County of New Castle, yeoman. Whereas there is a tract of land situated on the south side of White Clay Creek bounded by land of John Nomerson [all this name is written as Nomer] containing 300 acres, surveyed & laid out on 19 June 1685 by virtue of a warrant from Thomas Holmes. Surveyor General to John Brewster. Now John Brewster for £60 granted to David Miles the said 300 acres with another piece of land purchased by John Brewster from John Nomers of the County of New Castle bounded by land of James Anderson, White Clay Creek & land of John Nomers containing 11 acres by deed dated 16 Feb 1696. Signed John Brewster. Delivered in the presence of Edward Long & Elston Wallis. Acknowledged in court 21 May 1708. (C1:119).

On 20 Mar 1706. Edward Viscount Cornbury, Captain General & Governor in Chief of the province of New York, New Jersey & territories in America & Vice Admiral of the same. To all whom the presents concerns, greetings. Know ye that at New York this 20 May, Catherine Donaldson, aged about 13 years & Mary Donaldson aged about 12 years, daughters of John Donaldson, dec. did elect & choose before me Peter Vanbrugh of Albany & Andrew Gravenaet of the City of New York as their guardians, who admitted by me accordingly. Signed Cornbury. Entered in the Secretaries office, George Clark. (C1:121).

Sheriff's Deed. On 5 June 1708. John French, High Sheriff of New Castle County to Maurice Liston of the County of New Castle, yeoman, in the court of common pleas on 15 Aug 1699 did recover against Joseph Wheelden & William Robinson, executors of the testament of Isaac Wheelden, late of the County of New Castle, dec. a debt of £14 13 shillings 2 pence & also court costs as by the records by a writ by John Donaldson, (one of his Majesties Justices of the Peace) on 19 Sep 1699 to the Sheriff of the county of New Castle, directing him to seized the goods & chattels of Isaac Wheelden, dec. in the hands of Joseph Wheelden & William Robinson, executors of the last will & testament of Isaac Wheelden, dec. The then sheriff of New Castle county, Wessell Allrichs, Esq. did seized a tract of land which was the land of Isaac Wheelden at the time of his death & then in the hands of Joseph Wheelden & William Robinson. Said tract of land bounded by the east side of a branch called Herring Run, the main branch of Blackbird Creek, land of Snelling, Walnut Neck by Blackbirds Creek containing 282 acre, which said land was sold for £30 to Maurice Liston according to law. Now John French, Sheriff of the county according to the judgment, made full satisfaction of the judgment the remainder thereof being paid to Joseph Wheelden & William Robinson as executors of Isaac Wheelden, dec. John French has granted to Maurice Liston all the said tract of land. Signed John French, Sheriff. Delivered in the presence of Peter MacFarland & William Tonge. Acknowledge in court 17 Feb 1708. (C1:122).

Deed. On 9 June 1708. Marurice Liston of the County of New Castle, yeoman to Samuel Vance of Appoquinimink Creek,. Whereas John French, sheriff of New Castle County by deed dated 5 June 1708 for satisfaction of a judgment obtained by Maurice Liston in the Court of Common Pleas 15 Aug 1699 against Joseph Wheelden & William Robinson, executors of the testament of Isaac Wheelden, late of the County of New Castle, dec. for a debt of £14 13 shillings 2 pence & costs sustained, confirmed to Maurice Liston a tract of land bounded by Herring Run, the main branch of Blackbird Creek, Snelling's line & Walnut Neck by Blackbirds Creek containing 282 acres. Now Maurice Liston for £50 granted to Samuel Vance all the said 282 acres. Signed Maurice Liston. Delivered in the presence of Ann Richardson & Thomas ___ hams. [the rest of this page is missing]. (C1:125).

Deed. On 29 Nov 1705. Casparus Smith of Bohemia River in the county of Cecil in the province of Maryland, planter to Richard Davies of the County of New Castle, husbandman. Whereas there is a tract of land being on the south side of ___ Branch, near Reeden Island bounded by the King's Road, other land of Casparus Smith [a section in the middle of this page is missing] containing 204 acres surveyed 1684 by Thomas ___, by virtue of a warrant from William Penn dated 1 July 1684 to Daniel Smith, late of the County of New Castle, dec. the father of Casparus Smith. Now Casparus Smith for £5 10 shillings granted to Richard Davies the aforesaid 204 acres. Signed Casparus Smith. Delivered in the presence of John Brewster, Alex. Finley & Thomas Pierson. Acknowledged in court 20 Nov 1705. (C1:128).

Deed. On 26 Mar 1707. George Dakeyne of the County of New Castle, surveyor to Thomas Dakeyne, son & heir of George Dakeyne. George Dakeyne for the fatherly love he bears his son Thomas Dakeyne granted & confirmed to Thomas Dakeyne all that tract of land on the north side of Red Lyon Creek bounded by Pigeons Run, other land of George Dakeyne, Red Lyon Creek, land of Peter Anderson, the King's Road, Poplar Neck, the main branch of Red Lyon Creek, Red Lyon Creek Bridge & land of Christopher Shegell containing near 600 acres, also 1 acre on the south side of Red Lyon Creek where Thomas

Dakeyne shall take occasion to build a mill. Thomas Dakeyne shall reserve a maintenance for George Dakeyne, shall find for his father sufficient meat, drink, washing & lodging during his natural life & 1 small lodging room & his office for the afore said terms & liberty to keep 1 horse or more in the pasture & shall yearly pay to his said father 10 bushels of oats or Indian corn & 8 bushels of wheat for Nowells plantation, but if George Dakeyne shall have occasion to leave his son, then the said Thomas Dakeyne shall yearly pay to his said father only £10 with 8 bushels of wheat for Edward Thomas Nowells plantation & for want of Thomas Dakeyne not performing & paying his said father as per agreement, that it shall be lawful for George Dakeyne to reenter the aforesaid premises by distress until sufficient satisfaction be had. Signed George Dakeyne. Delivered in the presence of Edward Thomas Nowell & Obidiah Houll. Recorded 3 Dec 1709. (C1:130).

Lease & Release. On 18 & 19 Sep 1705. Richard Reynolds of the town of New Castle, yeoman to Richard Halliwell & Robert French of both of New Castle, merchants. Richard Reynolds for £160 granted to Richard Halliwell & Robert French a lot in the town of New Castle bounded on the market place or Wood Street, Susquehanna Street, a lot laid out for Giles Barret & Beaver Street containing 162 foot in length & 60 foot in breadth granted by order of the Court of New Castle dated 5 Sep 1684 & laid out by the surveyor on 18 Sep 1682 to James Walliam & by William Penn, Esq. by patent dated 20 Feb 1683 confirmed to James Walliams. James Walliam by deed dated 24 Feb 1691 granted to Richard Reynolds. Signed Richard Reynolds. Delivered in the presence of Joseph Griffen & William Tonge. (C1:132).

Lease & Release. On 20 & 21Apr 1709. Richard Halliwell & Robert French of the town of New Castle, merchants to Peter Vanbrugh of the City of Albany in the province of New York, merchant & Andrew Gravenraet of the City of New York, as guardians of Catherine & Mary Donaldson, daughters of John Donaldson, dec. Richard Halliwell & Robert French for £160 granted to Peter Vanbrugh & Andrew Gravenraet a lot in the town of New Castle bounded by the market place or Wood Street, Susquehanna Street, the lot laid out to Giles Barret & Beaver Street being 162 foot in length & 60 foot in breadth. granted by order of the Court of New Castle dated 5 Sep 1684 & laid out by the surveyor on 18 Sep 1682 to James Walliam & by William Penn, Esq. by patent dated 20 Feb 1683 confirmed to James Walliams & sold by James Walliams by lease & release dated 18 & 19 Sep 1705 to Richard Halliwell & Robert French. Signed by Richard Halliwell in the presence of Abraham Gouverneur & Richard Clark. Signed by Robert French in the presence of G. Bonde & Abraham Gouverneur. (C1:141).

Deed. On 17 Nov 1709. Cornelius Williamson of the County of New Castle, laborer & John Gorsett of Appoquinimink Creek & Jane his wife to Francis King of Appoquinimink Creek. Whereas Francis Lovelace, late Governor by patent dated in New York 26 Feb 1671 confirmed to Derrick Williamson & Derrick Lawrenson a tract of land containing 250 acres situated on the north west side of Appoquinimink Creek bounded a swamp land called Knowl Bush Haven, also the marsh lying on the creek. The said land equal moiety whereof both woodland & marsh nearest the mouth of the creek after the decease of Derrick Lawrenson, by a decree of the provincial Judges at a court held 24 Sep 1686 was adjudged to be the proper right & estate of Hybert Lawrenson & as the only heirs of said Derrick Lawrenson & the said Hybert Lawrenson in his lifetime sold the said moiety to John Heally of Appoquinimink Creek, yeoman. Which said moiety was sold to Marinns DeWitt & Anne King & whereas Cornelius Williamson aforesaid & Jane the wife of John Gosset, son & daughter of Derrick Williamson have a right & interest in said land. Now Cornelius Williamson, John Gossett & Jane his wife for consideration already paid granted to Francis King of Appoquinimink, son & heir of Anne King all right of the above said tract. Cornelius Williamson, John Gossett & Jane his wife appoint John Gossett their lawful attorney to deliver this in court. Signed Cornelius Williamson, John Gossett & Jane Gossett. Delivered in the presence of Isaac Gooding, Alexander Adams & Hans Hanson. (C1:150).

Deed. On 28 Feb 1709. John Brewster of the town of New Castle, innholder & Elizabeth his wife to Richard Halliwell of New Castle, merchant. John Brewster for the consideration of love & affection which he has for his wife, has granted to Richard Halliwell a lot in the town of New Castle containing 50 foot in breadth & 250 foot in length bounded by land of Thomas Jauviers, the burying ground, the Presbyterian Meeting house & the street, for the intent & purpose to the use of Elizabeth his wife & their assignees for & during the terms of their natural life & the life of the longer liver of them & after the determination of that estate then to the use of Richard Halliwell during the natural lives of Brewster & Elizabeth his wife. John Brewster & Elizabeth his wife to take rents & profits from said lot for their natural life. Also John Brewster for the consideration has given to Richard Halliwell one silver quart tankard & 7 silver spoons all marked with the letters IBE. Signed John Brewster, Elizabeth Brewster & Richard Halliwell. Delivered in the presence of Benjamin Swett, R. Dehaes & Isaac Gooding. (C1:154).

Deed. On 18 May 1703. Whereas Edward Braning for the sum of £40 paid by Sampson Atkinson of the County of New Castle, whereas he does acknowledge, granted & sold to Andries Anderson of the County of New Castle, one half of a tract of land situated on the north side of Augustine Creek known by the name

Canoe Branch, the said moiety containing 108 1/2 acres. Said land to be held between both their heirs in common. Signed Edward Braning. Delivered in the presence of John Bolton & John Smith. Acknowledged in court 20 may 1703. (C1:158).

Deed. On 15 Nov 1709. Joseph Neal of St. George's Creek, joiner to James Anderson of St. George's Creek, yeoman. Joseph Neals for £30 granted to James Anderson a tract of land lying between St. George's Creek & Dragon Swamp bounded by the King's Road & Dragon Swamp containing 100 acres, surveyed by George Dakeyne on 21 May 1709 being part of a tract formerly surveyed to Jacob Young, Sr., dec. as by patent dated 5 Nov 1675 & by Jacob Young & Joseph Young, sons of Jacob Young, dec. granted to Charles Anderson & John Cocks by 2 deeds, one dated 10 Nov 1703 & one dated 21 Aug 1706 & by another deed dated 20 July 1708 437 acres of land besides the cripple by the said Charles Anderson & John Cocks granted to Joseph Neals. Signed Joseph Neal. Delivered in the presence of J. Ashton, John Cocks & Elston Wallis. Acknowledged in court 23 Feb 1709. (C1:159).

Lease & Release. On 27 & 28 May 1709. Richard Halliwell of the town of New Castle, merchant, one of the surviving executors of the last will & testament of Henry Williams, late of New Castle, dec. to Peter Mouns of the County of New Castle, yeoman. Richard Halliwell for £32 10 shillings granted to Peter Mouns a tract of land on the Second Drawyers Creek bounded by the creek, land of John Walke called Green Spring containing 200 acres formerly beloning to Richard Huddon, late of Drawyers Creek, dec. & by Richard Huddon granted to Henry Vanderburgh & by Henry Vanderburgh granted to Henry Williams, late of New Castle by deed dated 19 Sep 1694 & by Henry Williams be his last will & testament dated 13 Nov 1694, bequeathed & full power given to his executors therein named to dispose of, should they think fit to the use & benefit of his children which said tract of land was by a division of the estate of Henry Williams, dec. allotted to Henry Williams, son of the aforesaid (now deceased) & by Henry Williams, the son, sold to John Mundroe of the County of New Castle, yeoman, but not conveyed, where upon Richard Halliwell for the performance of the agreement between the said Henry Williams & the said John Mundroe by virtue of the power given to him by the last will & testament, has thought fit to convey & confirm the said land to Peter Mouns, the assignee of John Mundroe. Signed Richard Halliwell & Anne Williams. Delivered in the presence of John Mundroe & William Tonge. (C1:162).

Deed. On 1 May 1709. John Huey of Drawyers Creek, yeoman to George Williams of Drawyers Creek, husbandman. John Huey for £10 granted to

George Williams a tract of land situated at the head of Second Drawyers Creek bounded by the creek & other land of John Huey containing 100 acres. Signed John Huey. Delivered in the presence of Samuel Bushell, Andrew Anderson, Thomas Rodwell & James Crawford. (C1:170).

Deed. ON 15 Jan 1708. William Grant of Appoquinimink Hundred, son & heir of William Grant, late of Appoquinimink, yeoman, dec. to John Demareer of St. George's Hundred, yeoman. William Grant for £95 granted to John Demareer all that 318 acres of land situated on the south side of St. George's Creek bounded by the creek, by lands late in the tenure of Edmund Lindsey, lands now in the tenure of John Bolton & lands now or late in the tenure of William Grant. Signed William Grant. Delivered in the presence of John Ashton, Thomas Adams, J. Anderson & John Reece. Acknowledged in court 17 Feb 1708. (C1:172).

Deed. On 30 Apr 1709. Barne Tooste of Flatbush in Kings County on the island of Nassau in the colony of New York to Isaac Gooding of the County of New Castle. Whereas there is a tract of land situated on the Delaware River commonly called St. Augustine bounded by Appoquinimink Creek, the Delaware River, St. Augustine Creek, land formerly sold to William Pattison, the Queens Road, land of Edward Green & a branch of Appoquinimink Creek called Stond Kill containing 2809 acres, the eighth part of said tract belongs to Barne Toostie by patent. Now Barne Tooste for £150 granted to Isaac Gooding all the just one eighth part of the said 2809 acres. Barne Toostie appoints his loving friend, Hans Hanson of the County of New Castle to delivered the above premises to Isaac Gooding. Signed Barnes Toostie. Delivered in the presence of Henry Filkin, Peter Stryker & Peter Mevyno. Acknowledged in court 17 May 1709. (C1:177).

Letter of Attorney. On 30 Apr 1709. Barne Toostie of Flatbush in Kings County on the island of Nassau in the colony of New York have appointed my loving friend, Hans Hanson of the County of New Castle my lawful attorney deliver unto Isaac Gooding a tract of land as in aforesaid deed. Signed Barne Toostie. Delivered in the presence of Henry Filkin, Peter Stryker & Peter Nevyno. City of New York. Ebenezer Wilson, Esq. mayor of the City of New York send greetings, that Peter Stryker & Peter Nevyno of Flatbush on the Island of Nassau, gentleman, being person well know & worthy of good faith & credit, who being sworn before mighty god, that they saw the within named Barne Toostie deliver the Letter of Attorney as his voluntary act. Signed on 3 May1709, Ebenezer Willson. Acknowledged 17 May 1709. (C1:180).

Deed. On 1 Apr 1710. John Wood of Duck Creek, yeoman to Richard Enos of the County of New Castle, laborer. John Wood for £45 granted to Richard Enos a tract of land situated on one of the branches of Duck Creek called Dentor bounded by land of James Crawford, Thomas Boll & James Boswick containing 200 acres, granted by patent dated 12 Apr 1686 to Robert Marsh & granted by Robert Marsh to John Wood by deed dated 25 Oct 1709. Signed John Wood. Delivered in the presence of Harbort Corrie & Joseph Wood. Acknowledged in court 18 May 1710. (C1:182).

Deed. On 3 Apr 1710. John Wood of Duck Creek to Paul Paulson & Elizabeth his wife of Crane Hook. John Wood for £105 granted to Paul Paulson & Elizabeth his wife a tract of land situated on the north west branch of Duck Creek bounded by the creek, land of Morris Liston, land of Michael Offley & land of Andrew Lous containing 200 acres. Signed John Wood. Delivered in the presence of Harbort Corrie & Joseph Wood. Acknowledged in court 18 May 1710. (C1:184).

Mortgage. On 1 Oct 1709. Jonas Arskin of the County of New Castle, yeoman to Sylvester Garland of the town of New Castle, merchant. Jonas Arskin for £100 granted to Sylvester Garland a tract of land situated on White Clay Creek bounded by the creek & land now or late of Andrew Tilly containing 200 acres, which said tract is commonly known by the name of Oakbeirns, provided that Jonas Arskin pay to Sylvester Garland 220 1/4 ounces plate on 1 Oct 1710 in one entire payment, then this deed be void. Signed Jonas Arskin. Delivered in the presence of Joseph Wood & John Stooll. Recorded 15 Apr 1710. (C1:187).

Deed. On 1 Oct 1709. John Heally of Appoquinimnk Creek, gentleman to Sylvester Garland of the town of New Castle, merchant. John Heally for £186 granted to Sylvester Garland a tract of land called The Change situated on Sassafras Creek being bounded by land formerly belonging to David Jones & the said creek containing 500 acres, as by certificate from the surveyor, which said tract of land was granted by patent from Francis Lovelace, Governor, dated 20 Feb 1672 to Timothy Low & Edward Sapp & late in open court on 8 Feb 1676 confirmed to John Walker, late of the County of New Castle, dec. but before his death by his last will & testament among other bequests gave & devised the said tract of land unto Dorothy his wife, who intermarried with Walter Smith, which Walter Smith & Dorothy his wife by deed dated 20 Sep 1692 granted the said land to Mary Mayle & Mary Mayle by deed dated 31 Oct 1695 granted to John Heally. Provided that if John Heally shall truly pay the said Sylvester Garland the just quantity of 26 1/2 ounces of Spanish plate on 1 Oct 1710 & the same on 1 Oct 1711 & 356 2/3 ounces of good Spanish plate of 1 Oct 1712, then this shall be void. John Heally shall cause to pay the value of plate according to the rate of 9 shillings & a penny the ounce in good merchantable wheat, tobacco or other produce at the market price on the days mentioned. Signed John Heally. Delivered in the presence of Wessell Allrichs & Joseph Wood. Recorded 3 Apr 1710. (C1:191).

Deed. On 22 July 1708. John Pitt of Talbot County in Maryland, yeoman to Peter Hanson of the County of New Castle, yeoman. John Pitt for £150 granted to Peter Hanson a tract of land situated on the swamps of Red Lyon Creek bounded by land late of Quan Salisbury now in the possession of Isaac Sheffer, land of Peter Hanson & the swamp containing 528 acres, the same tract being formerly granted by patent from Edmund Andros, late of Governor of New York & since by patent from William Penn, Governor dated 18 June 1706 confirmed to John Pitt. Signed John Pitt. Delivered in the presence of Samuel Lowman & William Tonge. Recorded 8 May 1710. (C1:196).

Deed. On 2 July 1709. Sigfriedus Allrichs of the County of New Castle, yeoman, son & heir of Peter Allrichs, late of the county, gentleman, dec. to Jasper Yeates of Chester in the County of Chester, merchant. Whereas Sigfriedus Allrichs stands fully seized in a tract of land bounded by the Queens Road, land of Wessell Allrichs which is also land late of John Donaldson, dec., a swamp the Delaware River & Mill Creek containing 785 acres being part of a greater quantity granted to the said Peter Allrichs by a grant from William Penn dated 5 Aug 1684, & since subdivided by the consent of the said Peter Allrichs to the direction of his last will & testament. Now Sigfriedus Allrichs for £500 granted to Jasper Yeates all the tract of 785 acres. Sigfriedus Allrichs appointed Robert French to be his lawful attorney to deliver said deed in open court. Signed Sigfriedus Allrichs. Delivered in the presence of Robert French, Richard Clarke, Mary French & Isabella Trent.. Acknowledged 23 Feb 1709. (C1:199).

Deed. On 9 Nov 1709. Jacob Bonsall of Darby in the county of Chester, yeoman, being son & heir of Richard Bonsall of the same place to George Cummins, late of Staton Island in the province of New York but now of Duck Creek, yeoman. Jacob Bonsall, for £106 granted to George Cummins, 3 tracts of land being between Blackbird's Creek & the Thoroughfare bounded by land of Thomas Ward & the cypress swamp containing 192 acres, the other tract bounded by land of John Cocks, land of Matthew Walton & Thomas Ward & land of Joseph England containing 131 acres & the third tract of land bounded by a branch of Duck Creek, land of Widow Owens & the cypress swamp containing 163 acres. Which said 3 tracts are part of a greater tract purchased by Richard Bonsall of John Donaldson. Jacob Bonsall shall protect against any claim from his brother & sisters & their heirs & against the heirs of Casparus Augustine Herman. Signed Jacob Bonsall. Delivered in the presence of John Heally & Thomas Dakeyne. Recorded 10 May 1710. (C1:203).

Deed. On 9 Nov 1709. Jacob Bonsall of Darby in the county of Chester, yeoman, being son & heir of Richard Bonsall of the same place to Thomas Ward, late of Staton Island in the province of New York, yeoman. Jacob Bonsall for £106 granted to Thomas Ward 2 tracts of land situated between Blackbirds Creek & the Thoroughfare bounded by land of George Cummins, the swamp & land of Matthew Walton containing 325 acres & the other tract bounded by the bridge, land of Matthew Walton, land of George Cummins & land of the Widow Owens containing 163 acres. Which said 2 tracts are part of a greater tract purchased by Richard Bonsall of John Donaldson. [the last of this deed is missing]

[this is the last page & is the last part of a deed.
Deed. On 9 May 1715. Thomas Rothwell & Margaret his wife granted to Robert Wetherspoon a tract of land. [the description is missing]. Signed Thomas Rothwell & Margaret Rothwell. Delivered in the presence of Alexander Adams, Hans Hanson, Garrett Duchesne. [there is no page number on this deed but it is the last deed in this book].

INDEX

...ACKEWEN, H., 26
...DDIN, Peter, 141
...HAMS, Thomas, 152
..OTTERHAVEN, Leond., 90

-A-

ABRAHAM, Andries, 127; John, 53
ABRAHAMS DELIGHT, 26
ABRINK, Peter, 30
ACQUITTANCE, THE, 84
ADAMS, Alexander, 97, 110, 154, 159; John, 21, 22, 96; Thomas, 156
ALBERTSON, Dirick, 2
ALLEN, Francis, 122, 132; Thomas, 47, 63
ALLMAN, ---, 62; John, 64; Joseph, 62, 64, 65; Margret, 62, 64
ALLOWAY, William, 52, 81
ALLRICH, Peter, 84
ALLRICHS, Harman, 86, 130; Harmanus, 96, 113, 144; Herman, 101, 109; Hermanus, 105; Jacob, 4, 22, 76; Jacobus, 82, 84, 85, 89, 102, 105, 113; M. Peter, 13; Peter, 2, 4, 15, 17, 23, 25, 26, 29, 32, 33, 40, 42, 46, 51, 52, 53, 55, 58, 60, 61, 62, 69, 70, 71, 78, 85, 86, 87, 96, 98, 113, 158; Sigfridus, 113; Sigfriedus, 105, 113, 158; Wessell, 92, 105, 113, 117, 140, 151, 158
ALLRIDGE, Peter, 31
ALMAN, Joseph, 64, 94
AMES LAND, 11
ANDERSEN, Jan, 15
ANDERSON, Andrew, 156; Andries, 154; Anries, 66; Charles, 146, 155; Elke, 26; Erick, 88; Euron, 128; Gustavus, 12; Helletye, 79;

Hillitie, 149; J., 156; Jacob, 9, 15, 16; James, 105, 124, 151, 155; John, 5, 43; Justa, 15, 26, 52, 53, 54, 66, 69, 71, 72, 73; Justus, 13, 38, 39, 54, 67, 68; Paul, 106; Peter, 88, 105, 106, 133, 152; Roalofe, 52; Roaloffe, 28; Roeloffe, 8, 9; Rowlif, 95; Rowliff, 95; Urian, 88, 132, 147; Urin, 107, 147
ANDERSONS, James, 146
ANDRESEN, Jan, 15
ANDRESON, Roeloff, 24
ANDRESSON, Governor, 71
ANDREW, Edmomd, 3; Edmund, 13
ANDRIES, Alicte, 15; Jacobus, 48; Jurion, 59; Justa, 12, 15, 75, 120; Justus, 41; Margrieta, 11; Roalofe, 48; Roaloffe, 55
ANDRIESON, Jurion, 59
ANDRISON, James, 14
ANDROS, E., 23, 40, 41; Edmond, 3, 5, 6, 7, 9, 10, 40, 86, 91; Edmund, 2, 6, 7, 9, 10, 12, 13, 16, 17, 18, 19, 21, 23, 24, 27, 29, 32, 35, 55, 62, 63, 71, 79, 84, 91, 92, 93, 106, 107, 113, 114, 118, 120, 123, 130, 134, 140, 158; Governor, 34, 41, 42, 46, 48, 49, 52, 53, 88
ANDROSS, Governor, 58, 59, 141
APIN ISLAND, 38
ARENSON, Jam, 14; John, 9, 55
ARINSON, John, 24
ARONSON, John, 5, 15, 16
ARSKIN, Jane, 98; John, 74, 98, 139; Jonas, 26, 74, 75, 98, 122, 157
ARSKINS, Jonas, 26, 84, 85, 122, 133
ARTSON, Jacob, 52, 95

ASHELBORNE, 20, 21
ASHTON, J., 155; John, 156; Robert, 52, 73, 74, 95, 124
ASKEW, James, 104, 111, 123; John, 125; Jonas, 123
ASKHAM, Jonas, 66
ASKIN, Jonas, 74
ASTONS, George, 57
ATKINSON, Sampson, 154; Timothy, 132
AUGUSTINA, 96
AVANT, Alexander, 97
AXTON, George, 18, 27

-B-
BABB, Thomas, 132
BABBS, Thomas, 132
BACKMAN, William, 35, 36
BACON, Machiel, 18
BADE, Elizabeth, 150
BAINTON, ---, 58, 59; Peter, 58, 59, 63, 68
BAKER, Allicia, 99; Ambrose, 25, 91, 99, 107, 130, 133, 148; Harmania, 148; Harmina, 133; Hermana, 99; John, 32
BAKERS DELIGHT, 5
BALDRIDGE, Adam, 101, 139
BALDWIN, Cicily, 121; Cirily, 101
BALL, John, 102; William, 87, 102
BALLINGS, Joshua, 133
BALLS, William, 87
BANSSENS, Hans, 13
BARKER, Ann, 117; John, 13, 31, 84; Mary, 31; Samuel, 35, 117, 123
BARNES, Elizabeth, 141; Joseph, 102, 118, 121, 141; Paul, 117, 128; Penelope, 128; Powell, 117
BARNS, ---, 26; Branch, 26, 27; Engelly, 26, 27; Jan, 26, 27; Joseph, 35, 36; Samuel, 36

BARNS DALE, 118
BARNS LAND, 26, 27
BARON, John, 109; Margell, 28; Michael, 79
BARREN POINT, 26
BARRENTSON, Jan, 11
BARRET, Giles, 33, 55, 153
BARRETSON, Jan, 3; John, 107
BARRETT, Giles, 153; Gils, 25
BARRETTSON, Jan, 25
BARWICKE, 144
BAWDEN, Hugh, 101, 132
BAYARD, N., 23; Samuel, 143
BAYLEY, James, 142
BAYNTON, ---, 49, 93; Peter, 49, 92, 93
BEACHAM, Richard, 104
BEACON, Benjamin, 136
BEERS, John, 74
BEESON, Edward, 100, 121
BELDIYDGE, Adam, 97
BELL, Nicholas, 136, 137; Thomas, 29, 80, 113
BENNETT, William, 130
BERKLEY, John Lord, 134
BEST, Humphrey, 46, 53, 82; Humphry, 31, 32
BESTERLY, Adam Bardrige, 120
BESWICKE, James, 29
BESWICKS, James, 113
BEZER, Edward, 67
BICKBY, Abraham, 97
BICKS, Jan, 38
BILSON, Miles, 63
BINGFIELD, 21
BIRD CREEK HOOK, 71
BISCH, James, 88
BISCK, Jan, 102, 103, 140; John, 93, 140
BISCUS, Jan, 28; John, 28
BISCUSS, Jean, 18
BISH, Elizabeth, 76; John, 76

BISHK, Jan, 66
BISHOPS CASTLE, 94
BISHYE, 44
BISK, Elizabeth, 75, 76; John, 75, 76, 82, 89, 140, 142; Sarah, 76
BISKE, John, 131
BLACK, Hans, 27
BLACKLEACH, Benjamin, 48, 49, 50; Richard, 34
BLACKLIDGE, Benjamin, 74
BLACQS, Hans, 11
BLAKE, Edward, 44, 58, 60, 61, 64, 75, 85, 86, 87, 88, 95, 108
BLANCHARD, John, 81
BLAY, Anne, 130; Edward, 130
BLOCK, H., 11; Mary, 33, 96, 97, 122
BLOCQS, Hans, 11
BLUNSTON, John, 144
BOEWICK, James, 80
BOHEMIA, 54
BOLL, Joseph, 60; Thomas, 157
BOLTON, John, 93, 155, 156
BOMBEYS HOOK, 21
BOMPIES HOOK, 21
BONDE, G., 153
BONES, Hans, 124
BONIOT, Lewis, 45
BONSALL, Jacob, 158, 159; Richard, 113, 114, 158, 159
BONSELL, Richard, 79, 80
BONYART, Lewis, 47
BONYAT, Lewis, 45
BOOKER, John, 137, 138
BOON, Hans, 10
BOSWICK, James, 62, 157
BOUDE, Grimstone, 125
BOUGHT, 7
BOUGHT, THE, 41, 145
BOULTON, Edward, 25; John, 116
BOWDEN, Hugh, 121
BOWEN, James, 49, 50

BOWERLY, 95
BOWYER, Elizabeth, 120; Hylike, 96; John, 96, 120, 133, 134
BOYER, John, 95
BOYERS, John, 143
BOYNTON, Peter, 71, 72
BRADBARNE, John, 2
BRADBORNE, John, 10
BRADBURN, John, 85
BRADBURY, George, 137
BRADSHAW, James, 67, 68
BRAMING, Edward, 86
BRAND, Bernard, 49, 138
BRANING, Edward, 154, 155
BRASHER, Abraham, 127
BRASON, Thomas, 91
BREAD & CHEESE ISLAND, 5
BRETT, John, 103, 142; Sarah, 142
BREWER, Senica, 12
BREWSTER, ---, 154; Abraham, 101, 129; Elizabeth, 154; John, 99, 101, 102, 103, 116, 142, 145, 151, 152, 154
BRIDGE NECK, 48
BRIDGEMAN, Richard, 62
BRIDGMAN, Capt., 62
BRISTOL, 37
BRISTOW, Anne, 109; John, 109
BROMFIELD, Patrick, 150
BROOKE, Henry, 125
BROUGHTON, ---, 140
BROWN, Thomas, 70, 74, 139
BROWNE, Thomas, 115
BROWNING, John, 2
BROXEN, Elizabeth, 132; William, 132
BRUSSELLS, 25
BRUYN, Harmon Reynderson, 22
BRYANT, Anthony, 56, 98; Robert, 117; Rovert, 117
BUCKLEY, John, 85; Richard, 104; Samuel, 37, 38

BUD-WICK, 34
BUDD, John, 101; Sara, 34
BULLAH, John, 145
BUMLEY, Benjamin, 63
BURCH, Hendrick Vander, 24; Henry Vander, 24
BURGH, Hend., 70, 73; Henry, 53
BURGRAVE, John, 73
BURLEY, John, 135, 137
BURNHAM, Joseph, 67, 69, 72
BURROWS, William, 54, 89, 90, 143
BURSGRAVE, James, 91
BURWICK, 30
BUSHEL, William, 107
BUSHELL, Samuel, 143, 156
BUYO, Cornilius, 1
BYARD, Peter, 21, 43, 44
BYARD'S PLANTATION, 43
BYLLINGE, Edward, 134, 135, 136, 137, 138, 137

-C-

C..., Claus, 2
CALTON, 13
CANAAN, 19
CANANN, 20
CANMILL, Margret, 20
CANN, John, 24, 30, 31, 32, 33, 35, 36, 43, 44, 45, 53, 55, 58, 60, 61, 62, 63, 71, 77, 86, 88, 102, 108, 109, 117, 121, 122, 123, 130, 141, 142, 148; William, 130, 141, 142
CANTWELL, ---, 6; E., 24, 32; Edmond, 3, 6, 25, 86, 90; Edmund, 2, 3, 5, 6, 7, 13, 14, 15, 20, 32, 38, 39, 40, 54, 55, 62, 97, 100, 107, 121, 131, 149; Elizabeth, 131, 149; Richard, 78, 79, 86, 89, 113, 120, 126, 131, 132, 149
CARDEN, William, 111

CAROLSON, John, 80
CARR, Anne, 109; Capt., 41, 98; John, 14, 23, 41, 78, 90, 109; Patrick, 58; Peternella, 109; Petroeleas, 78; Richard, 78, 90, 109; Robert, 98
CARSON, Claus, 49, 50
CARTERET, George, 135
CARTERETT, George, 134, 135
CATT, Robert, 98
CAUSE, John, 137
CEESSELLS, A. Geranrdry, 58
CHAMBERS, William, 54
CHAMPION, John, 87
CHANGE, THE, 157
CHARRIER, Benjamin, 111
CHARRIERE, Benjamin, 147
CHELSEY, 4, 95
CHELSY, 52
CHESTERFIELD, 93
CHESTNUT HILL, 34
CHESTNUT WOOD, 40
CHEUIGE, THE, 78
CHEW, Joseph, 1, 22
CHILD, Thomas, 94
CHILDE, John, 123
CLARK, George, 151; John, 3; Kenhelm, 89, 111, 133; Kenhelme, 133; Kenholm, 111; Richard, 142, 148, 153; Thomas, 128
CLARKE, Kenhelme, 124; R., 113; Richard, 158; T., 105; Thomas, 118
CLASON, Jacob, 52
CLASSEN, Jan, 70
CLASSON, Peter, 26
CLAUSON, Jacob, 83; Peter, 66
CLAWSON, Jacob, 54, 126, 129
CLAWSONS, Jacob, 45
CLAYPOOLE, James, 30, 36, 42, 43, 45, 46, 47, 48, 50, 60, 62, 65, 68,

71, 73, 76, 77, 80, 81, 82, 85, 87, 88, 92, 93, 107, 108, 124, 127, 131; John, 88, 108; Mary, 131; Nath., 79
CLAYSBURGH, 55
CLAYTON, Joseph, 84, 104, 107, 149; Richard, 137
CLEMENS, Elizabeth, 103; Jacob, 100
CLEMENT, Jacob, 80
CLEMENTS, Jacob, 121
CLEMENTSON, John, 94
CLEMISON, Elizabeth, 103
CLEMMETSON, Cle., 147
CLIFTON, Thomas, 41, 49, 72
COATTS, James, 101
COCK, Andrew, 146; John, 146; Lawrence, 113, 114
COCKER, William, 128
COCKS, John, 134, 155, 158; Peter, 130
CODERUS, Hans, 32
COFFIN, ---, 22; Abraham, 2, 6, 22, 85
COFFINA, Abraham, 22
COLBY, Robert, 129
COLE, Edward, 99, 133, 148; Harmania, 148; Harmina, 133; Herman, 99; Hermana, 99; Hermann, 99
COLESBURY, Swan, 128
COLLET, Jer., 35
COLLETT, Jer., 32; John, 135
COLLIER, John, 2
COLLMAN, Samuel, 137
COLVE, A., 23; Anthony, 23
COLVERT, John, 128
COLWART, John, 107
CONSTNAT, Conrade, 144
CONTENT, 61
CONWEN, Peter, 6
COOK, Neal, 90, 128

COOKE, Arthur, 93
COOKS, Neal, 127, 128
COOKSON, Joseph, 3, 31, 36, 63, 121
COOLEN, Reneer Vander, 45
COOLY, Reyner Vande, 22, 23
COOPER, Cornelius Claus, 124; William, 124
CORDERUS, Hans, 25, 28, 32; John, 33
CORK, Alchee, 89; Andrew, 89, 112, 115
CORNBURY, ---, 151; Edward Viscount, 151
CORNELIUS, Andries, 69; Jan, 11; Lassy, 66, 67
CORRIE, Harbort, 157
COSEYNS, John, 14
COURTRIE, Elisabeth, 62
COUTT, Hercules, 103; James, 103
COUTTS, Hercules, 103, 128, 147; Ja., 132; James, 103, 104, 105, 120, 128, 147
COWENHOVEN, Peter, 23
COX, Benjamin, 94; John, 93, 94, 113, 116, 143, 144
COXE, Thomas, 136
CRABER, Alexander, 88
CRACKSEE, William, 90
CRAFFORD, James, 2
CRAFORD, James, 10
CRANE HOOK, 57, 73, 81, 82, 128, 129, 157
CRANE HOOKE, 56, 57
CRANFORD, James, 70, 71
CRANSFORD, James, 70
CRAWFORD, James, 29, 64, 69, 79, 80, 91, 113, 114, 124, 125, 144, 156, 157; John, 79, 85, 125; Judith, 29; Mary, 91, 125
CROOKER, Alexander, 71
CROSSE, Mary, 75; William, 35, 75

CROWE, Charles, 93
CRUSE, William, 25
CUFF, Absalom, 144; Absolam, 143
CULLIFORD, John, 137
CUMMINS, George, 158, 159
CURRIER, William, 3
CURTIS, Samuel, 51, 52

-D-

D' BADOS, Manuell, 47
D:HAES, R., 101
DAKEYNE, George, 98, 106, 110, 112, 116, 125, 126, 133, 134, 143, 146, 147, 149, 150, 151, 152, 153, 155; Thomas, 134, 150, 152, 153, 158
DALTON, 84
DANIEL, Marris, 85; Nicholas, 108
DANIELS, Claus, 14; Maurice, 111; Morris, 1, 2
DARBY, ---, 28, 109; Elizabeth, 44; John, 4, 15, 44, 71, 86, 95, 120, 147, 149; Robert, 133, 149
DARBY'S ISLAND, 44
DARKEN, Richard, 52
DARKIN, Richard, 95
DAVENPORT, Humphry, 33
DAVIES, Joseph, 100; Richard, 152
DAVIS, Joseph, 102, 103, 116; Lucretia, 102, 103; Thomas, 134, 135
DAWSON, John, 138; Mary, 138; Ralph, 138
DAY, John, 76
DAYKIN, George, 98
DE BURGH, Henry, 37
DE FOX, Wallraven Johnson, 123
DE HAES, Johanes, 2; Johannes, 1, 2, 3, 6, 14, 22, 98; Johannus, 2
DE HINYOSA, Alexander, 8
DE LAGRANGE, ---, 60, 61; Arnoldus, 60, 61, 68

DE LEGRANGE, Arnoldus, 59
DE RING, Emelius, 46, 118; Emelus, 66; Mathias, 118; Mathyas, 46; Mathys, 46
DE RINGE, Emilius, 51
DE RINGH, Emelius, 69, 75, 102, 103; Lucretia, 103; Mathias, 69, 75
DE VOES, Gisbert Jansen, 60; Gisbert Janson, 59; Jonas, 59; Wallraven Janson, 59
DE WIT, Peter, 34
DE WITT, Elinor, 107; Marinna, 110; Marinns, 154; Peter, 82, 107, 126
DEACON SWAMP, 143
DECON, Isaac, 52; Jacob, 52
DECONINK, Pieter, 54
DECOW, Abraham, 95, 103; Hannah, 95; Isaac, 95; Jacob, 95
DEERING, Cornelius, 42; Mathias, 42
DEFFOES, Mathias, 66, 67; Mathyas, 66
DEFFOX, Walraven Johnson, 5
DEFOE, Wallraven Johnson, 130; Walraven Johnson, 141
DEFOSS, Mathias, 88
DEFOX, Walraven Johnson, 35
DEHAES, Johannes, 58, 90, 97, 108, 118, 131; John, 98; R., 104, 107, 120, 154; Roeloffe, 105, 111, 116, 119, 120, 122, 142, 148; Roliff, 101; Sara, 107; Sarah, 119, 120
DELAGRANGE, ---, 54, 59, 60; Arnold, 38; Arnoldus, 24, 28, 35, 36, 38, 54, 59, 77
DELEGRANGE, Arnoldus, 35
DEMAREE, John, 138
DEMAREER, John, 156
DENNIS, John, 134, 135; Samuel,

134, 135
DENNIS POINT, 64
DENTOR, 157
DERIKSON, Gisbert, 70
DERING, Emelius, 116; Mathias, 115, 116; Nicholas, 115, 116
DERKSON, Girbert, 35
DERRICK, Robert, 2
DERRICKSON, Cornelius, 91, 130; Gisbert, 75
DERRITT, Peter, 11
DEVOS, Walraven Janson, 16
DEWITT, Peter, 2, 3
DHINIOSA, Alexander, 115
D'HINOYOSSA, Alexander, 113
DIMPY, John, 106; Thomson, 106
DIRCKSON, Gysbert, 139
DIRING, Mathias, 25
DIRKSEN, Gisbert, 11
DIVOS, Mathyas, 28, 30; Mathyasan, 28; Matthyas, 28
DIXON, 48; Augustine, 16
DIXSON, William, 113
DOCTORS COMMONS, 17, 57, 73
DODD, Abel, 150; Abell, 149
DOMINY, ---, 56
DONALDSON, Catherine, 151, 153; Elizabeth, 79, 80, 108, 113, 114; John, 71, 72, 74, 78, 79, 80, 83, 84, 86, 87, 90, 93, 94, 96, 105, 108, 109, 113, 114, 144, 145, 151, 153, 158, 159; Mary, 151, 153
DOUGLAS, Ann, 117; George, 117; William, 117, 131
DOWLE, Richard, 128
DOWSE, Richard, 127
DRAGON SWAMP, 143
DRAYER, Jane Hendrichson, 15
DRUETT, Mary, 134; William, 132
DRUMMER'S NECK, 111, 140
DUNN, John, 21, 83

DUTHY, ---, 24; Daniel, 24
DUVILL, Peter, 25
DYASON, 49, 50
DYER, Major, 51; Robert, 44, 85; William, 49, 51, 52, 112
DYRE, James, 102, 112, 126; Robert, 125; William, 102, 111, 112, 125, 126, 149

-E-

EASON, Richard, 138
EASTERN, 66
EBERTSON, Matthi., 130
ECKELSON, Mathias, 8; Mathy, 8
EDMONDSON, John, 5
EDMUNDS, John, 3, 35; Sarah, 3
EDMUNDSON, John, 3, 10, 20, 21, 33, 123; Sarah, 3
EDRIDGE, John, 136
EDWARDS, Edward, 109, 146, 147
EGBERTS, Bernard, 130
EGBERTSON, Eldred, 28
EGBURTS, Bernard, 16
EGGE, Barrent, 2, 3
EGLINTON, Edward, 67
EKEN, Bernard, 148; Margaret, 148
EKINS, Bernard, 22
ELLET, Christopher, 26
ELLETT, Christopher, 20
ELLIS, Hannah, 125; John, 85, 91, 125, 130; Thomas, 66, 67, 100, 139
ELLIT, Christopher, 80
ELLITS, ---, 47; Christopher, 64
ELLITT, Christopher, 80
EMMETT, James, 31
EMPSON, Benony, 94; Cornelius, 32, 33, 34, 35, 74, 78, 80, 84, 86, 87, 90, 93, 94, 95, 97, 104, 121, 122, 124, 148; Cornett, 45; Dorothy, 142; Richard, 121, 122, 124, 142, 144

ENGLAND, Hannah, 95; Job, 78;
  Joseph, 112, 118, 144, 158;
  Rebecca, 118; Thomas, 95
ENLOFF, Abraham, 57
ENOS, Richard, 156, 157
ERICKSON, Erick, 128, 132; Erik,
  82; Mathias, 73, 83, 84, 86, 92,
  128, 144
ERSKIN, Jane, 61; John, 61, 70, 115;
  Jonas, 61; Sergeant, 69
ERSKING, Serjant, 44
ESCHELSEN, Mattys, 115
EUCHELSON, Bartle, 11
EVANS, Robert, 70, 71, 125
EVERSON, Hendrich, 56; Hendrick,
  57; Henry, 56
EVERTSON, Evert, 109; Henry, 80,
  81, 92
EWISTER, Edward, 51, 52
EWSTER, Edward, 49
EXCHANGE, THE, 24, 47, 90, 95,
  123, 144
EXETER, 116, 140
EXPECTED, 84

-F-
FARRINGTON, John, 136
FAUCET, John, 1
FAUVIER, Thomas, 81, 103
FEARN HOOK, 70, 115, 139, 140
FENWICKE, John, 20
FERN HOOK, 52
FERNE HOOK, 54
FIAEN, Jacob, 111
FIAENS, Jacob, 111
FIANA, Jacob, 85
FIANNA, Jacob, 2
FIENA, Jacob, 22
FILKIN, Henry, 156
FINLEY, Alexander, 152
FIRHELD, John, 54
FISHER, George, 67, 68, 72; John, 3

FISHING PLACE, 36, 90
FLACKE, Robberd, 1
FOLK, John, 61
FORATT, John, 82
FORD, Reuben, 132; William, 19
FOREMAN, George, 67
FORKINS KILL, 34
FORRATT, John, 85
FORREST, Hendrick, 4
FOSTER, John, 31
FOUR BROTHERS, 29
FRAMPTON, Elizabeth, 97; William,
  29, 97
FRANSEN, Olle, 7
FRANSON, Alias, 92; Hendrick, 25;
  Henrick, 25; Oalla, 59; Olla, 41,
  49; Olle, 7, 145; Wolla, 71, 72,
  145; Woola, 58, 59, 92, 93
FRENCH, John, 84, 97, 104, 109,
  120, 125, 128, 129, 132, 142,
  147, 149, 151, 152; Mary, 158;
  Ro., 66, 73; Robert, 61, 72, 76,
  77, 78, 94, 104, 105, 108, 109,
  115, 129, 140, 144, 145, 147,
  153, 158
FRIEND, Andries, 50
FYNNE HOOK, 147

-G-
GANNEN, Arent, 30
GARDINER, Elizabeth, 97; Thomas,
  97
GARLAND, Sylvester, 81, 85, 89,
  95, 96, 97, 101, 113, 116, 122,
  140, 142, 149, 157
GARNERALL, John, 87
GARRET, Martin, 69, 74
GARRETS, Martin, 70, 125
GARRETSON, Elizabeth, 122, 123,
  131, 132; Henry, 131, 132; John,
  64; Martin, 70; Paul, 122, 123;
  Powell, 122

GARRETTSON, Abiah, 143;
　Elizabeth, 149; Garret, 98;
　Henry, 149; John, 40, 143;
　Martin, 28, 139
GARRITSON, Martin, 18
GARROT, Richard, 133
GARROTSON, Henry, 97
GARROTTSON, Martin, 98
GEADY, George, 132
GEORGE, Cornelius, 22
GERRITS, Martin, 115
GERVAIZE, Isaac, 106
GERWICK, 79
GEVIN, Martin, 47
GIBBEN, Edward, 31
GIBBENS, Edward, 31
GIBBS, Edward, 57, 70, 71, 77, 79,
　82, 83, 84, 86, 87, 91, 108, 128,
　144; Henry, 144; Judah, 70, 71;
　Judith, 79
GILBERT, Phillip, 105
GILLET, Thomas, 60
GILLOLKSON, M., 137, 138
GODDIN, Peter, 76
GODIN, Peter, 85, 94
GOLDSMTH, William, 3
GOOD LAND, 64, 80, 113, 114
GOOD NEIGHBORHOOD, 18, 27
GOODING, Isaac, 127, 133, 138,
　146, 154, 156; Isaih, 96
GOODOUNE, Abraham, 134, 135
GOODSON, John, 65, 66, 67, 100,
　139, 141, 145
GOODSPRING, 67
GOODWIN, Gatrick, 127; Geartroy,
　127; Isaac, 127
GORDON, Ch., 31
GORSETT, Jane, 154; John, 154
GOSSET, Jane, 154; John, 154
GOSSETT, Jane, 154; John, 154
GOUVENEUR, Abraham, 153
GOUVERNEUR, Abraham, 153

GRAHAM, James, 51; Thomas, 94
GRAMPTON, John, 53
GRAMTON, John, 56, 57, 60
GRANT, Alexander, 74; William, 37,
　39, 84, 93, 118, 156
GRANTAM, John, 73
GRANTHAM, John, 91, 94, 117,
　134, 146
GRANTHOM, Henry, 81; John, 81
GRAVENAET, Andrew, 151, 153
GRAVENRAET, Andrew, 108, 153
GRAVEURAET, Andrew, 140
GREAT RUN, 53
GREEN, ---, 37; Anthony, 67, 72, 88;
　Charles, 37; Edmond, 65;
　Edward, 31, 32, 36, 37, 41, 46,
　68, 77, 87, 95, 96, 97, 156
GREEN SPRING, 93, 155
GREENE, Edward, 48, 49, 50, 52, 53
GREENWATER, John, 128
GREGG, John, 112
GREY, Thomas, 112, 118, 125
GRIFFEN, Joseph, 133, 153
GRIFFIN, Joseph, 84, 89, 102, 111,
　112, 120, 133, 148; Samuel, 144;
　Sarah, 111, 112
GRIFFING, Samuel, 111
GRIFFITH, Bemam, 135; Benjamin,
　135, 137; Joseph, 37
GRIGG, John, 145
GRIGGS, John, 145
GROG, John, 130
GRONODICKE, Pot., 51
GRUB, Justis, 93
GRUBB, John, 92; Thomas, 97
GUEST, John, 104, 124, 127, 128,
　129, 130; Susannah, 104, 129,
　130; Will, 36; William, 32, 33,
　60, 67, 68, 71, 94, 97, 116, 117,
　126
GUMBY, Benjamin, 14, 15, 16
GUMLEY, Benjamin, 78, 80, 92

GYERBERTSON, John, 96
GYESBERTSON, John, 96

-H-
HA..., George, 142
HAES, J., 21; Jo., 38; Richard, 86
HAGEN, William, 32
HAGG, Hugh, 109
HAGUE, William, 34
HAIG, William, 32
HAILES, Peter, 136, 137
HAINS, Artman, 147
HAIS, J. D., 17
HALL, Nicholas, 117; William, 101
HALLAWELL, ---, 32
HALLIDAY, James, 27
HALLIWELL, Richard, 81, 86, 89, 94, 97, 99, 102, 109, 112, 113, 114, 120, 123, 125, 126, 130, 140, 144, 145, 153, 154, 155
HALLMAN, ---, 62; Joseph, 62, 65; Peter Andries, 32
HALLYDAY, James, 46, 61, 126
HALLYWELL, Richard, 78
HAMBLEY, Richard, 111
HAMBLY, Richard, 110, 111
HAMILTON, John, 75, 76, 87; Josiah, 76; Margaret, 76
HAMMERTON, Joseph, 141
HAMPTON, 16
HANCE, Peter, 146
HANCOCK, Richard, 62
HANGMANS HOOK, 12
HANLY, John, 10
HANSON, Hans, 9, 14, 15, 16, 90, 93, 95, 119, 127, 138, 144, 150, 154, 156, 159; hans, 119; Johannes, 127; John, 127; Joseph, 95, 120, 133, 143, 120; Peter, 113, 158; William, 127
HARBERDICK, John, 140
HARBERDIN, John, 140

HARBERDINCK, John, 139
HARBERDINK, John, 140
HARLAN, George, 112, 117
HARMAN, Elizabeth, 113; Eph., 12; Ephraim, 35, 113, 114
HARMANSON, Anna, 99, 100; Dorcas, 99; John, 99
HARMON, ---, 35; Casparus, 6, 13; Casperus, 13; Ephraim, 13, 14, 15; John, 30
HARMONSON, ---, 53; Jan, 4, 57; John, 53, 57
HARMS, Jan, 96; John, 87
HARRIS, Elizabeth, 123; Hannah, 123; Rachel, 122, 123; Thomas, 123, 144
HARTOP, Henry, 12; John, 12, 13; Robert, 89
HARTUUP, Robert, 84
HASTINGS, Joshua, 81
HATTON, John, 117; Mary, 117
HAVE, Thomas, 3
HAWK, Reynold, 73
HAY, Adam, 46, 52, 53, 54, 131
HAYES, James, 143, 144
HAYLES, John, 10
HAYLS, John, 95
HAYM, Artman, 27, 34, 54; Matty, 27
HAYNE, Arman, 126; Artman, 115; Isaac, 15; Matty, 115
HAYNES, Artman, 52
HEADY, Jan, 13
HEALEY, John, 107
HEALLY, John, 78, 79, 81, 82, 83, 84, 89, 90, 117, 118, 119, 122, 124, 126, 132, 133, 138, 149, 151, 154, 157, 158
HEALY, John, 45, 47
HEARNE, William, 93
HEATH, Margaret, 117; Steben, 136, 137

HEDGE, Samuel, 101
HELBY, Joseph, 137, 138
HENDRICK, John, 124; William, 23
HENDRICKS, Huybert, 88; John, 10
HENDRICKSON, Barnard, 111;
    Barnett, 85; Barrent, 10;
    Hendrick, 88; Hupbert, 23;
    Hybert, 93; Jacob, 30, 88; Jan,
    38; John, 73, 118, 131; Laurans,
    52, 53; Lawrence, 39
HENRICKS, Evert, 131
HENRICKSON, Barrent, 1; John, 54,
    64; Susanna, 80
HENYOSSIA, Alexander, 1;
    Alexander D., 1
HERMAN, ---, 35; Augustine, 1, 13,
    108; C. August, 108; Casp., 26;
    Casparas, 92; Casparus, 18, 23,
    24, 27, 28, 37, 55, 108, 127;
    Casparus Augustine, 127, 158;
    Casperus, 18, 23; E., 38;
    Elizabeth, 108; Ephraim, 1, 2, 3,
    4, 5, 15, 16, 18, 20, 21, 22, 23,
    24, 25, 28, 29, 31, 32, 35, 36, 41,
    43, 45, 46, 47, 48, 54, 58, 60, 62,
    64, 65, 67, 70, 77, 84, 98, 106,
    108, 121, 133; Katherine, 127;
    M. Augustine, 12
HERMANSON, John, 28, 108
HEWITT, Joseph, 59
HICKEY, Barbara, 96
HICKY, Barbara, 96
HIG, William, 32
HIGH HOOK, 24, 48, 55
HIKE, Adam, 96
HILLINGTON, Edward, 91
HILYARD, John, 37
HINDE, John, 137, 138
HINDERSON, John, 19, 100
HINDRICKSON, John, 18
HINIOSA, Alexander, 109
HINTON, William, 138

HOBART, Joseph, 119; Josiah, 119
HOGG, George, 72, 94, 102, 103,
    107, 111, 112
HOLDEN, Joseph, 94, 129
HOLDING, Joseph, 62
HOLDINGS, Joseph, 64
HOLISWORTH, Henry, 50
HOLLIDAY, James, 83
HOLLINGSWORTH, Henry, 93;
    Valantine, 105
HOLME, Thomas, 145
HOLMES, Thomas, 151
HOLT, THE, 110
HOME LOT, 127
HOP YARD, THE, 129
HOPE, 63
HOPYARD, 26
HORSE NECK, 82
HOSUR, William, 20
HOUH, Martin, 67
HOULL, Obidiah, 153
HOUSTON, William, 77, 104, 105
HOUSTOWNE, Anthony, 141
HOWE, Thomas, 10
HUCKIN, Francis, 54
HUDDEN, Richard, 93
HUDDON, Richard, 155
HUDDOW, Richard, 9
HUEY, John, 155, 156
HUGHLIS, Walter, 106
HUKE, Adam, 142, 143
HULK, Jans, 11
HULKES, John, 11
HULKS, John, 26, 27
HUMPHREY, Ellis, 130
HUMPHREYS, Ellis, 130
HUNT, William, 76
HUSSEY, Chris., 106; Christopher,
    85, 124, 148; Frederick, 106;
    Jedediah, 116; Jedidah, 131;
    John, 74, 104, 106, 111, 116,
    124, 131

HUTCHINSON, Francis, 62; Robert, 33, 60, 82, 94, 129, 148
HUTCHISON, Ralph, 15; Robberd, 4; Robert, 14, 20, 37, 40, 50, 90
HUWEY, John, 150
HYATT, Thomas, 138
HYBERTS, Mary, 38
HYKE, Adam, 96, 133, 148; Solomon, 133
HYKES, Adam, 96
HYKEY, Adam, 122
HYNE, Earthman, 83

-I-

IKA, Adam, 99
IKE, Adam, 99; Garratte, 99
INDIANS, THE, 11
INGELLOES, Richard, 89, 111
INGLOS, Abraham, 26
ISAKE, Edward, 43

-J-

JACKSON, George, 105; Stephen, 103
JACOBS, Peter, 127; Thomas, 17
JACOB'S LAND, 88
JACOBSON, Thomas, 5, 43
JACQUATT, Mary, 106; Peter, 106
JACQUET, Jan, 29; Jean Paul, 6; John, 34
JACQUETT, John, 147; Mary, 106; Peter, 75, 106, 133, 147
JACQUETTS, Peter, 148
JACQUITT, Jean Paul, 14
JAFFREY, George, 74; John, 74
JAFFRY, George, 74
JAMES, Howell, 147; William, 129, 147
JANES, Nathaniel, 94
JANSEN, Arent, 8, 11, 17; Cornelius, 3; Garret, 88; Gisbert, 59, 60; Hendrick, 4, 11; Jurian, 8, 39; Walraven, 12
JANSENS, Arent, 27
JANSON, Belica, 16; Cornelius, 3; Garret, 88, 98; Gisbert, 59; Harmon, 16; Janvier, 2; Jurian, 52; Mathias, 56, 57
JANSONS, Jurian, 115
JANUARY, Thomas, 102
JANVIER, Thomas, 102, 106, 116
JASPERS, Jamethia, 14
JAUVIER, Sarah, 75, 142; Thomas, 75, 140, 142
JAUVIERS, Thomas, 154
JAWERT, John, 111
JAYNE, Isaac, 22
JEFFRIES, Edward, 148
JENINGS, Edward, 141
JENNINGS, Edward, 141, 142, 145
JENSEN, Hendrick, 4
JEOFFREYS, Edward, 132
JERVISES, John, 132
JOHN, Lewis, 22
JOHNSOGOE, Peter, 132
JOHNSON, Adam, 94; Arent, 148; Belchy, 34; Bilchy, 83, 126; Bilchye, 46; Catherine, 34; Durian, 82; Elizabeth, 120; Elizabeth Gill, 120; Gerherd, 83; Gisbert, 59; Harman, 10, 124; Herman, 34, 61; Humphrey, 145; John, 16; Lewis, 1, 22, 119; Sybran, 61; Sybrance, 46; Thomas Gill, 120; Wallraven, 118
JOHNSONS, Aron, 27
JOHNSTON, Mary, 128
JONE, Charles, 32
JONES, Charles, 29, 32; David, 78, 157; Francis, 138; Grif, 100; Griffith, 37, 43, 44, 45, 47, 48, 84; Grift, 75; Henry, 45, 47, 48; James, 145; John, 138, 139, 141; John Henry, 98; Robert, 28, 129; Thomas, 67, 121; William, 38

JOOSTEN, Baroner, 127
JORRIGISON, Cornelius, 4; Gurtie, 4
JOURDAIN, John, 75; Mary, 75
JUAVIER, Sarah, 75; Thomas, 75
JULOES, Peter, 117
JURIANS, Sophia, 20
JURIANSEN, Andries, 31; Christian, 31
JURIANSON, Andrew, 20, 21; Andries, 20, 31; Christian, 31, 90; Sophia, 20, 21
JURIONSON, Andries, 59

-K-
KANYON, Thomas, 109
KELLIS, Mat., 50
KERSON, Claers, 138; Clais, 49
KERSTON, Clawes, 55
KETTLE, Cornelius, 89, 96, 97, 107, 112, 117
KILLINGTON, Edward, 108
KING, Anne, 154; Cornelius, 110; Francis, 154; Francois, 110; Jacob, 110; Peter, 110, 140
KINGS, John, 127, 128
KINGSLAND, Isaac, 30, 31; Nathaniel, 30, 31
KIPP, Hendrick, 22
KIRTON, Claus, 12
KNIGHT, John, 63
KNOLBUSHAUER, 16
KNOTSENBURGH, 57
KNOWL BUSH HAVEN, 154
KRISTON, Claus, 24

-L-
LACKFORD HALL, 41, 42
LAMB, George, 88, 90, 128
LAND, Edward, 33; Francis, 107, 121, 122, 141, 142; Henry, 131; Jan, 27; John, 120; Sam, 98; Samuel, 10, 15, 16, 17, 25, 29, 34, 35, 36, 39, 44, 47, 48, 49, 51, 52, 71, 131, 132; Thomas, 96, 117
LAND OF SMOTHERS, 116
LANDDOS, Charles, 77
LANDERY, 78
LANDERY, THE, 109
LANDRIKEN, John, 54
LANDS, Samuel, 73
LANNEGAN, John, 65
LARKFORD HALL, 97
LARKSFORD HALL, 110
LARSE, Pawell, 54
LARSEN, Neils, 15
LARSON, Mary, 38, 39; Paul, 38, 39
LARUENSON, Marcus, 41
LATHAM, John, 69
LAURANSON, Marcus, 41, 58, 59
LAURENSON, Hibert, 28; Marcus, 41; Paul, 52; Payl, 53
LAURY, ---, 136; Gaven, 134, 135, 136, 137, 138; Gven, 135
LAWERNCESON, Marchus, 7
LAWES, John, 150
LAWRENCE, Marcus, 92; Thomas, 106
LAWRENCESON, Marchus, 7
LAWRENSEN, Marcus, 71, 72; Marius, 63
LAWRENSON, Derrick, 12, 154; Hybert, 154; Marchus, 7; Marcus, 49, 92, 93; Martin, 145
LAWSON, Hendrick, 59; Mathias, 73
LAX, Nicholas, 135
LAYMAKERS HOOK, 2, 126
LAYMAN'S HOOK, 83
LEACH, Ebenezer, 119
LEBAHY, Isaiah, 87
LEECH, John, 128; Toby, 128
LEFEVER, Hip., 117; Hyop., 87; Hypo., 81, 145; Hypolitns, 143; Hypolitos, 144, 145; Hypolitus,

81
LEMMENS, Hend., 49; Henry, 46; Hind., 44
LEMMON, Hendrick, 84, 106; Henry, 29, 129
LEMMONS, Elizabeth, 106; Hendrick, 84, 106
LEMONS, Elisabeth, 74; Henry, 74
LEO, John, 14
LEVIS, Samuel, 94
LEWDEN, John, 88, 90
LEWIS, Henry, 130
LIBERTY, 140
LILLINGTON, Edward, 93
LIMMON, Hendrick, 25
LIMMONS, Hendrick, 24, 25
LINDSEY, Daniel, 30; Edmund, 156
LISTON, Maurice, 104, 151, 152; Morris, 26, 62, 157
LITTLE, Maurice, 127
LITTLE EGG HARBOR, 135
LLOYD, ---, 51; David, 74, 79, 104; Thomas, 30, 36, 42, 43, 45, 47, 51, 65, 80
LOAMS, Robert, 28
LOCKYER, Elizabeth, 82, 83, 126; Nicholas, 75, 82, 83, 96, 104, 118, 126, 140, 147, 148; Nichols, 82; Nicolas, 109
LOGAN, James, 99, 110, 112, 143, 146
LOMAN, Samuel, 109
LONG, Edward, 151
LONG NECK, 127
LOT, ---, 24; Angle Bratt, 34; Engelbirt, 24; Englebert, 70
LOTS, Englebrit, 30
LOTT, Cornelia, 140; Engelbert, 139, 140
LOUIS, Thomas, 50
LOUS, Andrew, 157
LOVE, Andrew, 62; Mary, 1; Timonthy, 1; Timothy, 1, 2, 78
LOVELACE, ---, 12; Francis, 2, 3, 5, 6, 7, 8, 9, 10, 11, 12, 13, 14, 15, 16, 18, 19, 21, 22, 23, 46, 54, 55, 65, 66, 69, 70, 78, 82, 93, 98, 100, 116, 125, 145, 148, 149, 154, 157; Governor, 22, 34, 38, 39, 41, 44, 48, 52, 59, 66, 71, 76, 119, 139
LOVELAND, Francis, 16
LOW, Timothy, 157
LOWDER, George, 101
LOWMAN, Samuel, 122, 158
LOWTHER, George, 127, 128, 129
LUCAS, Ncholas, 137; Nicholas, 134, 135, 136, 137, 138
LUCKINS, Francis, 83
LUCOSY, Elye, 45
LUMBY, John, 103
LYNCH, Francis, 107

-M-
MAANKIN, Richard, 87
MC DONALD, Brian, 122
MAC FARLAND, Peter, 152
MAC GREGORY, Hugh, 68, 71, 72; Joseph, 140, 141
MC GREGORY, Joseph, 120, 121
MC KEAN, Thomas, 56
MC KENNY, Alexander, 148; Katherine, 148
MACARTY, Elinor, 86; Ellinor, 86; John, 86
MACKARTY, Daniel, 65
MACKENZY, John, 104
MACLAND, Barbara, 83; Peter, 83
MAIDSTONE, 92, 107
MAINARDO, Peter, 109; Peternella, 109
MAISAPPLNACKIN, 21
MAKER, William, 20, 21
MAN, Abraham, 17, 43, 45, 49, 68

MANDY, John, 26, 30, 34, 47, 58, 64, 131; Mary, 64
MANKIN, Richard, 54, 68
MANN, Abraham, 122; William, 72, 73
MANOR OF RACKSLAND, 105
MANOR OF ROCKLAND, 100, 132
MANOR OF ROCKLANDS, 121
MANOR OF STAINING, 112
MANSON, Hans, 37
MARCUSON, Hans, 133
MARCUSSON, Hans, 149
MARKHAM, Capt., 67; Col., 77; William, 65, 66, 67, 70, 72, 77, 78, 80, 88, 100, 139, 141, 145
MARKHAM'S HOPE, 77
MARLEY, Robert, 125
MARSELLOTTHE, Lymon, 86
MARSH, Hugh, 113; Robert, 113, 114, 157
MARSH CRIPPLE, 10
MARSLAND, Hugh, 53
MARSLANDER, Barbara, 26, 27, 30, 33; Peter, 30
MARTIN, John, 127, 128; Thomas, 136, 137, 138
MARTINSON, Martin, 11, 130, 131
MASLANDER, ---, 122; Barbara, 126; Cornelius, 96; Peter, 126; William, 96, 122
MATEYSEN, Andries, 11
MATHEWS, John, 14
MATHISON, Mathias, 18
MATHYAS, ---, 51
MATHYSON, Matty, 115; Peter, 115
MATSON, Andries, 34; Care, 44; John, 44
MATTSEN, Andries, 11
MATTSON, John, 57, 81; Mattys, 11
MAURITTS, Johannes, 4; William, 4
MAYLE, Mary, 78, 157
MECHACKSITT, 21

MECHACKSITT, CHIEF SACHAMA, 21
MELRUM ISLAND, 139
MERCER, Elizabeth, 141; Thomas, 141
MERRETT, William, 140
MEVYNO, Peter, 156
MEW, Richard, 136, 137
MICOLLS, Mathias, 22
MIDDLE WAY, 60
MILES, David, 151
MILL, Reyer, 120; Reyes, 40
MILL FORK, 89, 111
MILL LAND, 111
MILL POINT, 40
MILLER, David, 105; Hans, 9, 14, 15, 16, 37; Hans Hanson, 55; James, 125
MINEQUES PLANTATION, 16
MINVEIL, Capt., 33
MOETT, Robert, 136
MOLISTEYNES, Alexander, 3
MOLL, Christian, 35, 62; Christina, 88; John, 2, 3, 14, 15, 17, 24, 29, 33, 35, 36, 43, 44, 45, 46, 47, 54, 58, 62, 70, 71, 73, 84, 85, 88, 90, 91, 92, 98, 118, 123
MONEY, Robert, 119
MONNEY, Robberd, 1; Robert, 1
MONY, John, 85; Robert, 86
MOORE, ---, 37; Anna Maria, 99, 100; George, 2, 3, 4, 14, 16, 17, 24, 25, 33, 38, 56, 91, 99; John, 81, 93; Joseph, 37, 99, 100, 118, 129; Thomas, 69
MORELY, John, 33
MORGAN, Gwen, 106; John, 147
MORREY, John, 93
MORRIS, Anthony, 101; Appollo, 134, 135
MORTON, Bobbin, 16; Rob., 12; Robart, 69; Roberd, 12; Robert,

79, 90
MOUNCE, John, 100, 121; Peter, 80, 100, 105, 121
MOUNS, Peter, 155
MOUNSEN, Paul, 11, 63; Peter, 63
MOUNSON, Peter, 7, 71, 145
MOUSE, Paul, 11
MOUSON, Peter, 59
MOYERS, Michael, 145; Stoffell, 145
MR. TOM'S PLANTATION, 38, 132
MT. THOM., 69
MUNDROE, ---, 150; John, 150, 155
MUSSELL CRIPP, 3
MUSSELL CRIPPLE, 10
MYARA, ---, 72; Hofell, 71, 72
MYERS, Stoffell, 41, 49

-N-
NANCOIM, Job, 116; John, 110, 111
NANLCOYNE, Job, 150; John, 140, 143, 149, 150
NANLCROYNE, Job, 143
NANSCOIM, Job, 116
NANSCOYRE, Job, 85; John, 85
NARINGLY, William, 21
NEAL, Joseph, 146, 155
NEALS, Joseph, 155
NEARING, John Williams, 36
NEERING, James William, 25; John Williams, 24, 41, 57, 120; Lunder William, 25; Sarah, 120; William, 70, 74
NEEVE, John, 102
NEILS, Neil, 100
NEILSON, ---, 92; Hendrich, 18; Hendrick, 19, 100; Mathias, 100; Matty, 18, 19; Neil, 7, 18, 19, 71; Neils, 7, 18, 19, 41, 49, 58, 59, 63, 71, 72, 92, 93, 100, 145
NELLISSHIP, Benjamin, 20
NELSON, John, 94

NEST, John, 74
NETTERSHIP, Job, 73
NETTLESHIP, Benjamin, 20; Job, 25; Vissimus, 20, 21
NEVELL, Thomas, 102
NEVYNO, Peter, 156
NEW CESARIA, 134
NEW DELIGUE, 102
NEW ENGLAND MANS LAND, 124
NEW JERSEY, 134
NEW NYBREGHT, 28
NEW SAXONY, 33, 111
NEW ULRICK, 9
NEW VIEN, 40
NEWILL, James, 68
NEWSINK, 21
NEWTON, 50
NEWTOWN, 54
NICCOLLS, Amos, 144
NICHOLLS, Amos, 86; Mathias, 4, 5, 6, 7, 8, 9, 10, 11, 12, 13; Richard, 4, 8, 10, 79, 139
NICHOLS, Amos, 83, 106; Governor, 125; Mathias, 11, 12; Richard, 16, 78
NICOLLS, Amons, 50; Amos, 48, 49, 50, 54; Governor, 40, 44, 70; Mathias, 18, 19, 21, 22, 23, 24, 27, 35, 41, 46, 55, 62, 69, 70, 98, 107, 115; Matthew, 2; Richard, 18, 19, 22, 61, 69, 70, 114, 115, 124
NICOLS, Governor, 17; Mathias, 15, 16, 17, 18; Richard, 17
NIELSON, Hendrick, 18; Matthys, 18; Mattys, 18; Niel, 18; Niels, 18
NIN A TRACT, 44
NIXSON, Grace, 93; Thomas, 92, 93
NOBBER, John, 78
NOBLE, Richard, 37, 43, 45, 47, 48,

50, 54, 72, 73, 81
NOMER, John, 151
NOMERS, John, 29, 56, 118, 151
NOMERSON, John, 151
NOMMER, John, 32
NOMMERS, ---, 53; John, 23, 46, 53, 141
NONSUCH, 37, 61
NORNER, John, 5
NORRIS, Samuel, 134, 135
NORTH PARTITION, 135
NOWELL, Edward Thomas, 153; Thomas, 125
NOWELLS, ---, 153; Edward Thomas, 153
NUSTIEL, 30

-O-
O' NEAL, Bryan, 85
OAKBEIRNS, 157
OAKBURNE, 122
OAKE HOLEYIN, 37
OALSON, Lasse, 32; Peter, 32, 46, 53; Suker, 32
ODE, Clocka, 15
OEKLY, Thomas, 115
OELLSON, Peter, 144
OFFLEY, Caleb, 116, 144; Michael, 26, 157
OFFLY, Micall, 62; Michael, 29
OGLE, ---, 14; Elizabet, 37; Elizabeth, 4, 5, 14, 16, 33, 37, 56, 60, 64, 123; John, 3, 4, 5, 10, 14, 16, 26, 33, 36, 37, 39, 56, 64, 79, 84, 85, 98, 123, 124, 129, 133, 149; Mary, 91, 125; Thomas, 39, 85, 87, 91, 125; William, 135
OILSON, Peter, 23
OLDFIELD, George, 1, 14, 78, 90; Paternella, 14; Peternella, 90; Petroeleas, 78

OLLASON, Oele, 18, 19; Olla, 100; Olle, 19
OLLESON, Henry, 67; Olle, 67
OLLSON, Olla, 92
OMELLA, Bryan, 48, 49
OMMELAND, 29
ONELLE, Bryant, 138
ORTON, John, 83
OSBORNE, Bazaliell, 119; Bazeliell, 124; Bezeliell, 119; Jonathan, 119; Joseph, 118, 119; William, 123, 144
OSBOURN, William, 60
OSBURNE, William, 122, 123
OSTERHAVEN, Lendorr, 76; Leonard, 102, 103; Susannah, 102, 103, 142
OTTA, Garret, 1
OTTO, Garret, 14; Garrett, 8, 9; Gerret, 4; Gerrett, 4; Gurteen, 4; Gurtie, 4
OWEN, Griffith, 146; Hugh, 101, 121; William, 146
OWENS, Widow, 158, 159
OXFORD, 39
OXMELTER, 116

-P-
PAERDT HOOK, 148
PARET HOOK, 104
PARIS, John, 141
PARKER, ---, 28; Henry, 3, 20, 21, 133; Mathias, 144
PARRIS, John, 82
PARSON, Mary, 90
PARSONS, John, 26
PARTNERS ADVENTURE, 67
PATENT, Hannah, 123; Morgan, 123
PATERSON, Garret, 150
PATKER, Mathias, 144
PATRICK, Henry, 50
PATTISON, William, 92, 96, 156

PATTON, Hannah, 122, 123; Morgan, 122, 123
PAULSON, Elisabeth, 74; Elizabeth, 75, 106, 129, 157; Henry, 1; Justa, 48; Mounse, 11; Oalla, 112; Oele, 106, 125; Paul, 74, 75, 105, 106, 129, 157; Powell, 128; Wolla, 132
PAWELLS, Olla, 54
PEARDEHOOK, 82, 83
PEARL, Jane, 128, 129
PEARSON, John, 4, 26, 73
PEARSON'S LODGE, 26
PECCO, Peter, 32
PEERDE HOOK, 126
PEERDEHOOK, 126
PEERED HOOK, 126
PEIRSON, John, 68; Thomas, 60, 73, 81, 84, 95
PENN, Governor, 26, 33, 41, 63, 68, 89, 111, 132; Letitia, 112; William, 25, 26, 28, 29, 30, 31, 35, 36, 37, 39, 40, 42, 43, 45, 47, 55, 57, 63, 64, 65, 66, 67, 77, 80, 85, 87, 97, 101, 104, 110, 112, 114, 118, 125, 127, 134, 135, 136, 137, 138, 146, 152, 153, 158
PENNINGTON, Edward, 112; James, 72
PERCUS, Edmund, 50
PERDRAIN, P., 87
PERES, Samuel, 78
PERKINS, Ebenezer, 93; Edmund, 83; Joseph, 92, 93, 132; Mathew, 106
PERKUS, Edmund, 54; Edward, 54
PERRY, Samuel, 91
PERT HOOK, 54
PETERS, Hans, 38
PETERSON, Adam, 8, 10, 30, 78, 84, 91, 126, 149, 150; Andrew, 33, 116, 126, 138, 143, 150; Charles, 7, 41, 100, 121; George, 148; Hans, 11, 12, 24, 32, 34, 35, 48, 56, 57, 73, 80, 81, 145; Has, 105; Herminitie, 150; Hermintie, 149; Hillitie, 149; Jan, 16; John, 14, 49, 50, 115; Justa, 48; Lucas, 25, 30; Peter, 80; Samuel, 40, 48, 66, 77; Thomas, 40; William, 115
PETIT, Abraham Clement, 2
PHIANA, Ann, 81; Anna, 82
PHILLIPS, ---, 42; James, 143; William, 33, 42
PHILLIPS POIT, 42
PHOKER, John, 20
PICKER, Hendrick, 140
PICKERING, Charles, 37, 41, 66, 67, 77
PICKERINGSER, Bartholomew, 138
PIDGEON, Joseph, 81
PIERSON, Thomas, 50, 52, 53, 87, 88, 106, 114, 124, 127, 128, 143, 152
PIKERS, Henry, 143
PIPE STAVE NECK, 127
PITT, John, 158
POMPIES HOOK, 43
POMTREL, 39
POOLE, Nathaniel, 133; William, 93
POPLAR HILL, 79, 90
POPLAR NECK, 28, 29, 106, 112, 125, 132, 152
PORT HOOKE, 61
PORTER HOOK, 52
POST, Cornelius, 91, 125
POULSEN, Oele, 15
POULSON, Oele, 17; Olla, 25; Olle, 25, 28, 29, 30
POUTTS, James, 102
POWELL, John, 130
POWELLSON, Olah, 84
POYNETT, Thomas, 137

PRESTNER, John, 46
PREW, John, 148
PRICE, Margaret, 90; Nicolass Daniel, 47; William, 90
PRIESTNER, John, 53, 54, 61
PRISCOT, E., 31
PROVOAST, D., 127; David, 127
PROW, John, 84
PUCKLE, Nathaniel, 105
PURO, Peter, 46
PURT, Cornelius, 32
PUTNEY, 25

-Q-
QUARTERMAN, John, 38

-R-
RAINBOE, William, 59
RAINBOES, William, 59, 61
RAKESTRAW, William, 35, 36, 123, 130
RAMBO, William, 16
RAMSEY, Charles, 5
RAND, Samuel, 137
RANELS, John, 82
RAPP, ---, 45
RAPPE, ---, 44, 45, 47; Capt., 45; G., 24; Gabriel, 24, 44, 45, 47
RAUAU, Ferninand, 47
RAWSON, Oele, 15
READ, Ann, 81; Anna, 82; George, 102; James, 72, 79, 81, 82, 83, 88, 91, 150
REALL, Jacob, 111
RED MEADOW, 94
REECE, John, 140, 147, 156
REED, Charles, 78; Elizabeth, 59; George, 59; James, 73
REEDIN POINT, 9
REEDY HOOK, 105
RENALDS, Richard, 119
RENDALL, Marmaduke, 4

REYNERS, Harman, 14; Harmen, 13; Harmon, 13, 14; Jamethia, 14
REYNERSON, Harmon, 6
REYNOLDS, Richard, 75, 76, 99, 104, 109, 122, 124, 126, 130, 143, 148, 149, 151, 153
RICE, Evan, 56, 104; John, 110
RICHARDS, John, 133; Philip, 78; Susannah, 133
RICHARDSON, Ann, 152; Francis, 47; John, 43, 52, 60, 61, 74, 83, 87, 88, 95, 111, 117, 124
RIDE HOOK, 8
RILE, Thomas, 2
RING, E. D., 44; F. D., 18
ROARSON, John, 121
ROBERTSONS, Robert, 38
ROBINS, Andries, 32; George, 54; John, 51; Robert, 24, 54
ROBINSON, George, 105, 112; John, 94, 105; Patrick, 78; Robert, 24, 58; William, 84, 151, 152
ROCKLAND, 30
RODWELL, Thomas, 156
ROE, John, 57, 109, 110
ROMAN, Martin, 3; Philip, 132
RONNALD, Robert, 132
ROSAMOND, ---, 98; Martin, 33, 98
ROSEMOND, Marten, 58
ROTHWELL, Margaret, 159; Thomas, 68, 73, 92, 159; thomas, 73
ROTIER, Jacob, 81
ROWELL, Thomas, 98
ROWELS, Susanna, 63
ROWLAND, James, 29; Samuel, 29
ROWLES, Susanna, 63; Walter, 42
ROWLES SEPUCKRE, 42
ROWLS GRATS, 29
ROYDEN, William, 135
RUDYARD, Thomas, 137
RUMLEY, Charles, 115, 118

RUMSEY, Ch., 108; Charles, 20, 24, 30, 34, 35, 37, 38, 39, 48, 61, 74, 120, 121, 123, 130, 141
RUSSELL, George, 129; Jacob, 129; John, 129, 150, 151; Nathaniel, 128, 129, 150
RUSSENBURGH, Hendrick Peterson, 80
RYNDERSON, Herman, 22

-S-

SADLER, Thomas, 89, 111
SADLERS, Thomas, 9
ST. AUGUSTINE, 12, 156
SALISBURY, Quan, 158
SAMPTONS, William, 78
SANDERS, Garret, 15; Garrett, 8
SANDERSON, Garret, 11
SAP, Edward, 78
SAPP, Edward, 1, 157
SAULFOORT, Abraham, 139, 140
SAVAGE, Jonathan, 99, 133; Jonathon, 133
SAWER, ---, 117; Thomas, 117
SAWTELL, John, 101
SAWYER, Thomas, 94
SCHARGIN, Jonas, 25
SCHELLINKS, William, 119
SCOTT, J. Walter, 92; Jarvis, 107; John, 92, 95, 107; Joseph, 95; Mary, 99; Walter, 92, 107
SCREEK, John Malson, 147; Mathias Malson, 147; Thomas Malson, 147; Urin Malson, 147
SCREEKES, Mathias, 109
SECOND DENNIS POINT, 64
SENICA, Brewer, 12
SENICKA, Brewer, 12
SENNEXEN, Brewer, 31, 32, 46, 53
SENNEXSON, ---, 53; Andries, 55; Brewer, 32, 46, 53, 55
SEWELL, Richard, 119

SHARKE, William, 29
SHARP, Richard, 76
SHARPE, Elizabit, 20; William, 19, 20
SHARPLES, William, 105
SHEFFER, Isaac, 145, 146, 158
SHEGELL, Christopher, 152
SHERRICKS, John, 8, 9
SHERRY, Moses, 82
SHIPPEN, Edward, 102; Rebekah, 102
SHUTE, William, 34
SHYKERS, Peter, 127
SIBRANSEN, Jan, 7, 8
SIBRINSON, Jan, 148
SILSBEE, Samuel, 99
SILSBY, Samuel, 143
SIMES, John, 86
SIMMONS, Hendrick, 12, 56, 57
SIMMS, John, 83
SIMPILL, Will, 17, 18
SINCLAR, William, 6
SINCLEER, William, 149
SINNEXEN, Brewer, 59, 60, 61, 87; Dorcas, 99, 100; James, 99, 100
SINNEXENS, Brewer, 60
SINNEXSEN, Brewer, 94
SIREEK, John, 57
SIZER, Richard, 137
SKILL POTES KILL, 11
SKILLPOT KILL, 34
SLOOBY, Olah, 80
SMART, Johannes, 127
SMITH, Casparus, 152; Claes Peterson, 120; Claise Peterson, 40; Claus Peterson, 15; Daniel, 31, 32, 37, 46, 152; Dick, 4; Dorothy, 78, 157; Garret, 88; Garrett, 47; Gerherd, 83; Hendrich Anderson, 73; Hendrick Anderson, 73; John, 10, 20, 29, 31, 36, 54, 67, 68, 72,

73, 75, 76, 82, 83, 84, 85, 86, 89, 90, 91, 92, 94, 96, 101, 102, 103, 105, 107, 111, 116, 117, 121, 130, 131, 134, 149, 155; Mary, 67, 72; Mathias Mattysen, 12; Nicholas, 150; Richard, 36, 121; Robert, 144; Sarah, 102; Walter, 78, 157
SMOTHERS, James, 105
SNELL, Thomas, 1
SNELLING, ---, 152; Thomas, 17, 63, 84
SOUTHERN LAND, 5
SOUTHERN PARTITION, 135
SPARK, Margaret, 76; William, 76
SPARKS, William, 76
SPRINGER, Charles, 80, 107, 120, 122, 124, 142
SPRINGETT, Harbart, 135, 136, 137; Harvert, 135
SPRY, Doctor, 29; Thomas, 4, 14, 17, 52, 73, 108; thomas, 57
STALCOP, ---, 77; Andrew, 40; Christian, 33; Christiana, 77; John, 5, 24, 40, 43, 66, 77; Peter, 77
STALCOPS, John, 61
STANDBOROUGH, Elizabeth, 119; Josiah, 119
STANDBURROUGH, Elizabeth, 119; Josiah, 119
STANDLY, John, 3
STANLEY, Christopher, 148; John, 33, 146
STEDHAM, Adam, 88; Erasmus, 65, 66; Lucas, 40, 61, 65, 66, 80, 88; Simon, 66
STEELE, John, 129; William, 134, 135
STEIN BAKERS, 36
STEVENS, Anthony, 104
STEWART, John, 127

STIDHAM, Adam, 50; Arman, 48; Benedictus, 50; Christian, 50; Erasmus, 50; Lucas, 24; Simon, 38; Timothy, 50; Tymen, 15; Tynam, 7
STILLMAN, Christian, 130
STOCDALL, Will, 44
STOCKDALE, William, 72, 74
STOLL, Joseph, 140
STOLLS, Joseph, 143, 146
STOND KILL, 156
STONE, William, 76, 111
STONE HOOK, 100
STOOBY, Olla, 97
STOOLL, John, 157
STORY, Joshua, 144; Thomas, 127, 146
STOUT, John, 140
STOVER, Isaac, 28
STRATE, John, 12
STRAUGHAN, David, 106
STREET, Joan, 69; John, 69
STRYKER, Peter, 156
SVERSONS, Olle, 11
SWAART NUTTON ISLAND, 88
SWAMWICK, 147
SWANDER, Mark, 136
SWANER, Mark, 136
SWANHOOK, 96
SWANNER, Mark, 137
SWANWICK, 46, 52, 53, 54, 96, 99, 107, 122, 126, 148
SWARTE NEWTON ISLAND, 4
SWARTEN NULLEN ISLAND, 44
SWARTON NUTTEN ISLAND, 44
SWEATNAM, William, 68
SWEET, Benjamin, 76
SWEETTIN, ---, 107
SWENSON, Derrick, 5
SWERINGEN, Garrett, 14
SWETT, Benjamin, 76, 82, 85, 89, 103, 106, 111, 116, 124, 131,

132, 154; Sarah, 131
SWIN, Isam, 79
SWINTON, Isaac, 136
SWITZERLAND, 120
SYBRANCE, John, 46, 61
SYBRANS, John, 126
SYBRANSON, John, 83, 126
SYBRANT, John, 83
SYERICKS, Jan, 48
SYMMS, Nat., 138

-T-
TALLANT, Robert, 119
TATE, William, 34
TAVEHAMNAKER, Peter, 42
TAYLOR, Ebenezer, 14, 15, 16; George, 62; Jacob, 112; Jane, 41, 97; John, 38, 41, 42, 47, 62, 80, 97, 143, 144; Thomas, 29, 32; William, 9, 20
TAYLORS CHANCE, 47
TAYNE, Isaac, 38; Mary, 38
TECCO, Peter, 23
TEMPLE, William, 25
TEST, John, 4, 14, 88
THACKENS, Hendrick, 11
THAXSTONE, Thomas, 130
THEE, Adam, 54
THEO, Adam, 52, 53
THOMAS, Alderman, 107; Benjamin, 102; David, 147; Hylike, 96, 97; John, 140; Ollah, 80; Paul, 96, 97; Reec, 129; Widow, 102
THOMASON, Oele, 23, 24; Olla, 46, 53; Peter, 23, 32, 46, 53
THOMASSON, Peter, 46
THOMPSON, John, 91, 107
THOROLD, Robert, 111
THOROUGH FARE, 62
TILLE, Andrew, 84
TILLIES, Andrew, 122

TILLY, Andrew, 105, 157
TIMES, John, 54
TINE, Isaac, 75, 76
TOARSON, Else, 30; Henry, 100, 101, 121; John, 100, 101, 121; Margaret, 100, 101, 121; Mathias, 100, 101, 121; Oalla, 57, 58; Ola, 30; Olla, 30, 101, 121; Olle, 27; Stephen, 100, 101, 121
TOLLIER, Casparus, 65
TOM, ---, 19; Will, 38; William, 3, 17, 19, 20, 38, 40, 55
TOMKINS, Anthony, 37, 39
TONGE, William, 109, 113, 120, 122, 124, 125, 126, 128, 130, 139, 140, 141, 143, 145, 147, 149, 150, 151, 152, 153, 155, 158, 110
TONSOGOE, Peter, 38
TOOLSON, Woola, 52
TOOSTE, Barne, 156
TOOSTIE, Barne, 156; Barnes, 156
TOOTSIE, Barne, 156
TOUGE, William, 104
TOULE, Percivall, 136, 137
TOULES, Henry, 1
TOWSON, Olle, 8
TRANSON, Olla, 41; Wolla, 63
TRENT, Isabella, 158; William, 105
TRESSE, Thomas, 104
TREWOLLA, Samuel, 102
TROY, Joseph, 47
TRUAX, Isaac, 140; Jacob, 146; Phillip, 133
TUDER, Abell, 128
TUIL, Van, 15
TURKS ISLAND, 129
TURNER, Robert, 30, 36, 42, 43, 45, 46, 47, 58, 65, 80, 145; Susannah, 58
TUTTELL, Jane, 139, 140; Jeremiah,

139
TWO BROTHERS, 39, 85
TYBRANTS, Belica, 16; Harmon Janson, 16

-U-

UNDERWOOD, Samuel, 145
URIANSEN, Andries, 12
URIANSON, Christian, 87
URINSON, Christian, 92, 107

-V-

VALSK, Sybrant, 22
VAN BEBBER, Hermintie, 149; Mathias, 149
VAN DIKE, Andrew, 138
VAN EKELEN, Johannes, 127
VAN SWERIGEN, Gerrit, 1
VANBEBBER, Hermintie, 150
VANBEEBER, Jacob Isaac, 138; James, 141; Mathias, 138, 139, 141
VANBRUGH, Peter, 151, 153
VANCE, John, 101; Samuel, 149, 151, 152
VANDEBURGH, Hendrick, 51
VANDENBURGH, ---, 125; Anna, 52, 74, 112, 125; Derrick, 54, 72, 73; Hannah, 74; Hendrich, 49, 56; Hendrick, 28, 30, 35, 39, 44, 49, 56, 57, 70, 74, 112, 125, 70; Henry, 28, 34, 39, 52, 73, 74, 80, 81, 86, 87, 91, 92, 125, 130
VANDENHAYDEN, Mathias, 81
VANDER COILEN, Reynir, 2, 3
VANDER COOLSEN, Reynier, 57
VANDERBURGH, Derrick, 126, 127; Hendrick, 139; Henry, 93, 155; Rymereth, 127
VANDERCOOLEN, Margaret, 47; Reyner, 46, 47, 48; Zachariah, 66
VANDERCOOLIN, Reynier, 70, 72

VANDERCOULIN, Alchee, 90; Alehe, 75; Margaret, 91; Mary, 82; Reyneir, 67, 81, 82, 89, 98; Reynier, 67, 76, 87, 89, 91, 97, 128; Zachariah, 75; Zacharias, 89, 90, 111, 112; Zachary, 89
VANDERHAYDEN, Mathias, 87; Matthias, 143
VANDERHDEN, Mathyas, 31
VANDERHEYDEN, Mathias, 82, 90
VANDERVEER, ---, 65; Jacob, 62, 65, 66
VANDERVERE, Jacob, 2
VANDEVERE, Jacob, 3
VANDRICHTS HOOK, 17
VANGEREL, Jacob, 148
VANHORNE, Abraham, 140
VANLAERE, John, 135, 136
VANMER, Eglsbert, 118
VANS, Samuel, 120, 150
VANSNEERING, Garret, 109
VEDDETTE, Jamethia, 14
VENDENBURGH, Hendrick, 44
VENDERBURGH, Hendrick, 44
VENTURE, 113
VERDERBYS HOOK, 58
VERDERYBYS HOOK, 59
VERDITIGE HOOK, 121
VERDRETIGH HOOK, 94
VERDRITIGE HOOK, 100
VERTIGE HOOK, 121
VESSELL, Phillip, 128
VIGOREU, Heleitie, 149; Hilitie, 150; Isaac, 140, 149, 150
VIGOREUX, Isaac, 86
VIGUREE, Isaac, 119
VINN, Andries, 12

-W-

WALE, George, 46
WALKE, John, 155
WALKER, Dorothy, 78, 157; John,

1, 32, 33, 48, 52, 76, 78, 89, 91, 93, 116, 117, 118, 157; Wiborough, 33; Wybergh, 48; Wybrough, 89
WALLEMS, James, 24
WALLEN, James, 17, 18
WALLIAM, James, 62, 68, 71, 86, 153
WALLIAMS, James, 153
WALLIS, Elston, 86, 118, 120, 122, 123, 128, 129, 130, 133, 143, 144, 145, 146, 151, 155; Elton, 146
WALLRAVEN, Gilbert, 80; Gisbert, 59, 60, 61; Jonas, 80
WALRAVEN, Hendrick, 5
WALTON, Matthew, 158, 159
WARD, ---, 91; Henry, 9, 91; John Edmundson, 10; Thomas, 158, 159
WARFORD, John, 134
WARNER, Edmond, 136; Isaac, 67; William, 16
WATERLAND, 87
WATKINS, John, 35, 36, 37, 38, 61, 74, 123
WATSON, Luke, 3
WATTKINS, John, 61
WATTS, Hester, 81; John, 79, 80, 81, 83, 95
WEAVER, Samuel, 115, 133
WEBBER, John, 23, 88, 109
WEDGEBERRY, 68
WEDNESBURY, 71
WELDEN, Isaac, 31
WELSH, ---, 34; Sarah, 34, 46, 58; Susanna, 34; Susannah, 34, 58, 104; William, 24, 27, 58, 104, 135, 136; Wim, 40
WELSH TRACT, 122
WERDESTIES HOOK, 63
WESSELL, Gerardus, 44; Gerhardus,
88
WESSELLS, Gerardus, 46, 52; Gerrardus, 72
WEST, John, 40
WEST NEW JERSEY, 135, 136, 137, 138
WEST STONE, 38
WESTERNDALE, Ann, 63
WESTMINSTER, 26
WETHERSPOON, Robert, 159
WHALE, Ann, 73; Anna, 3; Anne, 4, 14, 17; George, 16
WHALES, ---, 57, 58; Ann, 57
WHARTON, Walt., 55; Walter, 1, 5, 9, 12, 20, 21, 24, 85, 131, 149; Walts, 55
WHATE, Anne, 3
WHEATLEY, John, 137
WHEELDEN, Isaac, 151, 152; Joseph, 151, 152
WHEELDON, Isaac, 84, 94, 95; Joseph, 84
WHEELER, John, 119
WHITE, Alice, 90; Christopher, 95, 120, 121; James, 90; Jan, 27; John, 24, 26, 27, 28, 29, 30, 32, 33, 34, 35, 36, 37, 38, 39, 41, 44, 46, 49, 51, 52, 53, 54, 56, 57, 58, 61, 63, 64, 67, 68, 69, 71, 72, 73, 81, 90, 115, 137; Magnus, 26; Mary, 33, 57, 63; Robert, 38; William, 84, 92
WHITE CLAY HALLS, 5
WHITEWILL, Lyman, 31
WHITPINS, John, 78
WIGAND, William, 63
WILDE HOOK, 11, 34
WILKISON, Gabriel, 62
WILLIAM, Henry, 101; James, 27, 33; John, 25
WILLIAMS, ---, 41; Anne, 155; Edward, 13, 122, 123, 144;

Elinor, 107; George, 155, 156; Hemicus, 86; Hendrich, 16; Hendrick, 2, 3, 16; Henry, 81, 93, 120, 121, 145, 155; Jacob, 150; James, 13, 38, 44, 63; John, 15, 25, 30, 38, 40, 76, 84, 106, 107, 132; William, 111, 118, 129
WILLIAMSON, Cornelius, 154; Derrick, 5, 12, 154
WILLOCKS, George, 31
WILLSON, Ebenezer, 156; John, 89
WILSON, Ebenezer, 156; John, 89, 90, 91, 116
WINDSOR, 91
WOLFERSON, Peter, 23
WOLLASTON, Thomas, 10, 37, 38, 48, 49, 52, 79, 83, 94
WOLLASTONE, Thomas, 121
WOLLESTON, Martha, 124; Richard, 124; Thomas, 118, 124
WOLLESTONS, Thomas, 124
WOLLISTON, Thomas, 141
WOOD, John, 80, 113, 114, 133, 148, 156, 157; Joseph, 80, 83, 86, 87, 96, 97, 99, 100, 110, 113, 114, 120, 122, 123, 133, 139, 141, 142, 143, 147, 148, 157, 158
WOODROOFFE, Jo., 101
WOODS, ...anl, 80; Joseph, 139
WOOLLASTON, Thomas, 5
WOOS, Joseph, 120
WOSTERDELL, Persifill, 13
WOTTEN, Robert, 95, 111; Roger, 93
WRIGHT, Henry, 76
WYNHARTS, Cornelius, 22

-Y-

YEATES, Jasper, 77, 78, 81, 109, 158
YEATS, Jasper, 158
YEO, John, 3, 4, 10, 15
YOCOMBE, Peter, 64
YOE, John, 10
YORAS, Anna Maria, 99; Cornelius, 99, 100
YOUNG, Jacob, 2, 17, 57, 73, 134, 144, 146, 155; Joseph, 146, 155

www.ingramcontent.com/pod-product-compliance
Lightning Source LLC
Chambersburg PA
CBHW051057160426
43193CB00010B/1216